Mike Palmer from Greater Manchester, Andy Airey from Cumbria and Tim Owen, from Norfolk, known as 3 Dads Walking, all lost their daughters to suicide. They walked 300 miles in 2021, and 600 miles in 2022, to raise awareness of suicide, and raise funds (over £1M) for Papyrus. They won a Pride of Britain 'Special Recognition' award in 2022, have garnered nationwide media coverage and have the support of celebrities such as Daniel Craig, Nicole Kidman, Lou Macari, Dan Walker and George Ezra. In 2024 they were awarded MBEs in the King's Birthday Honours List for their fundraising work. They continue to campaign for suicide prevention to be included in the school curriculum.

https://www.3dadswalking.uk

Three Dads Walking

300 MILES OF HOPE

ROBINSON

ROBINSON

First published in Great Britain in 2024 by Robinson
This paperback edition published in 2025 by Robinson

3 5 7 9 10 8 6 4 2

A CIP catalogue record for this book
is available from the British Library.

ISBN: 978-1-47214-845-2

Typeset in Adobe Garamond by Hewer Text UK Ltd, Edinburgh
Printed and bound in Great Britain by Clays Ltd, Elcograf S.p.A.

Papers used by Robinson are from well-managed
forests and other responsible sources.

Robinson
An imprint of
Little, Brown Book Group
Carmelite House
50 Victoria Embankment
London EC4Y 0DZ

The authorised representative
in the EEA is
Hachette Ireland
8 Castlecourt Centre, Dublin
15, D15 XTP3, Ireland
(email: info@hbgi.ie)

An Hachette UK Company
www.hachette.co.uk

www.littlebrown.co.uk

For Sophie, Emily and Beth, and our families.

Along with George and all the other
suicide bereaved we've met along our way.

Download the OS Maps app and scan the
QR code so you can see the route digitally.

Contents

Foreword

I have interviewed thousands of people, but I will never forget speaking to Andy, Mike and Tim. They are three incredible men who are doing their best to change the world around them. Over the last few years, it has been a real privilege to talk to them, write about them, spend time with them, support them and get to know them.

These three dads, united by grief, have a fascinating relationship. A deep and meaningful friendship has emerged from a situation that all of them would give everything to avoid. From just a few minutes in their presence you realise that their bond is a strong one, cemented by the love of a father for a daughter and soaked in tears.

They have the utmost respect for each other, and they truly do want to make a difference. They cannot understand why they've lost their girls, but the driving force behind all that they do is the desire that other families would be able to avoid the paths they have had to walk down. Friendship has helped them rebuild their lives.

I remember Mike saying that he wouldn't know where he would be without the support of Tim and Andy but I find all three of them a huge source of inspiration and I know I am not alone in that.

Their love for Sophie, Beth and Emily led them to set out on their 300-mile trek across the country and, with each hill they climbed, each person they met and each story they shared, they were putting themselves back together. They have been to some of the darkest places it is possible for us to go and yet they are constantly searching for the light. There is so much to learn from each one of them.

I am not going to lie to you and tell you that this book is easy to read. I am not going to promise you that your tears won't fall onto the pages as you turn them. However, I can assure you that there is hope in here – hope that grows in the strangest of places, hope that can bring you back from the brink.

I get the feeling there is much more to come from the three dads. Each time I speak to them they tell me about their next challenge, their next idea, their next adventure. I can't wait to see what the next chapter holds for them but, for the moment, I'll enjoy reading this one.

Keep changing the world, my friends . . . one step at a time.

Dan Walker

Prologue

'I told you there were hills in Norfolk!' exclaimed Tim.

'Hmph, call those hills? Our back garden is more of a hill than that.'

Tim's comment prompted me to check the Ordnance Survey app on my phone; the 'hills' Tim had been pointing at reached a peak at 20 metres above sea level. We were walking along the Nar Valley Way, just to the south of King's Lynn; a beautiful and tranquil place to enjoy another autumn sunrise – but a long way south, and very flat for a Cumbrian like me.

I was with Tim and Mike, recently found friends; men whom I'd met only a few months before but men I now knew as well – if not better – than anyone. Our shared experiences had brought us together, creating a bond so strong that we would help, support and encourage one another whatever the situation. It was a bond forged in the crucible of extreme emotion and suffering; a bond that had inspired us to walk over 300 miles across the country.

We were (and are) three ordinary dads who found ourselves in a desperate place we never expected to be, engulfed by pain and suffering beyond imagination, but who chose to push back, not to allow the pain to overwhelm us, to build something positive from the shattered pieces of our lives. We wanted to do something . . . and this is what it became: 3 Dads Walking.

It was 7.30 a.m. and we had already been walking for over an hour. We were on a strict schedule as we had to be in Shouldham, Tim's home village, by 9.30 a.m. so that our arrival at the end of our walk could be broadcast live on *BBC Breakfast*. We'd been joined by a disparate group of people who wanted to support us on the last leg of our journey so we now resembled an ultra-enthusiastic rambling group, enjoying the dawn chorus.

The whole situation seemed unreal; the preceding few months had become increasingly busy as we developed the idea, which had taken on a life of its own. The fifteen days we'd been walking had flashed by in a blur. We'd relied on our network of family and friends for support, many of whom were with us that morning.

We all take our lives and families for granted. We expect everything to stay the same, or at least to be recognisable from one day to the next – but we had discovered that lives can change in an instant. You can be thrown onto a completely different trajectory, one you don't want to be on – and one you can't comprehend.

As we walked alongside the River Nar, I reflected on how I'd met Mike and Tim, the way our lives had changed beyond recognition and the inspirational people I'd met over the last three years. Our unconnected attempts to make sense of lives lost and lives changed for ever had brought us together. Three dads from three different families in three different parts of the country; separated geographically but living through the same torment and trying to hold everything together for the sake of ourselves and our families.

The trials we were enduring had given unexpected meaning to our grief. We discovered that by sharing our experiences and being open and honest about our emotions we were able to help others avoid going through the same thing, or show that there were practical ways to keep living. By a quirk of fate, we had stumbled on a message of hope that we were able to share.

On that October morning, the people walking with us wanted to help spread that message of hope. They were there because they wanted to support us with our mission and show that walking and talking was a powerful way to help us and help others.

Talking was at the heart of everything the 3 Dads were doing. When our lives exploded, we discovered that it was the only way to help ourselves. When your life is shattered it is very easy to hunker down, close the doors, curl up and shut up. But somehow, Mike, Tim and I started to talk, to speak about our experiences, our feelings and why we wanted to be heard.

I was now thirty-four months along this road; Mike and Tim were fourteen months behind me. When we first met, we spoke a lot about how I had managed to keep moving forward, to keep living. Now we were talking to others who had joined the club no one wants to join; we spoke about how we'd got to where we were, and what kept us going. Reaching out in this way clearly gave comfort to many; it had a positive impact on everyone we spoke to and we found that helping others sustained and encouraged us to tackle the unexpected paths our lives were now on.

Throughout the walk, our daughters Sophie, Beth and Emily were at the forefront of our minds, our daughters who had died by suicide. We spoke about them every day; we told stories filled with laughter. Sophie was a bit older than Beth and Emily, so I talked about the work she'd been doing; the places, pubs and holidays we'd enjoyed together; her wedding day. We smiled and laughed every day of our walk; we also cried a lot.

Losing a child is devastating; losing a child to suicide shatters your world into a million pieces. It is almost impossible to breathe, never mind anything else. At one point your life is happily trundling along in a direction that makes sense, the next the world around you has become unrecognisable, alien, not yours. You are living someone else's life . . . but you're not. This is YOUR life . . . and you've just got to deal with it.

As with so many things after we came together, the intrinsic kindness and love of our fellow humans came to the fore when we needed assistance. We had learned that being open about a problem and asking for help gave permission to those who could to step forward and help. It was a lesson we wished our daughters had understood, and one we wanted others to learn.

Looking around the people walking with us, I could feel the outpouring of love from everyone; it was something we saw and felt on every day of our walk. Living through these volatile, uncertain times we all rediscovered just how special people can be. Our faith in the general goodness of people had well and truly been restored.

'OK, Tim. I agree this is going up . . . but that's not a hill.'

The approach to Shouldham Warren was very gently uphill. We stopped at the edge of the Warren to record our last video diary of the walk – these diaries had been a critical part of us sharing our message of hope with the broadest audience. Three middle-aged dads going for a walk were unlikely social-media influencers, but the responses we received from our posts had come from all over the world. We knew we were reaching far and wide and our open discussion about suicide had prompted other conversations that had saved lives.

We got our selfie stick out for the last time and had a couple of abortive attempts to shoot a video. After too much chatter and laughing, we finally got it:

'Last day. One-and-a-half miles to go.'

'Shame that no one has turned up to follow us in . . .'

As we turned to walk our final mile, the 3 Dads support crew appeared, cheering in the background. Lots more smiles and laughter followed.

Every day of the walk we'd had situations that had forced our feelings to swing from joy and laughter to crushing grief and despair; our last day was to be no different. We felt buoyant striding into the last mile of our 324-mile walk, but just before we entered the village we met yet another family who had lost their child to suicide two weeks before. Another family who'd only found PAPYRUS Prevention of Young Suicide *after* the loss of their child; another family who'd discovered, too late, that suicide is the biggest killer of young people in the UK; another family who'd asked, 'Why did nobody tell us?'

We knew our walk was about to end – but we also knew that our work was only just beginning.

Andy Airey, Norfolk, October 2021

PART ONE

Andy and Sophie

Sophie died on 19 December 2018 at the age of twenty-nine. She killed herself.

Our beautiful daughter was living in Edinburgh and working as an oncology nurse. She was going through a turbulent time: that September she'd split from her husband. We were worried about her, as we wanted her to be happy – that's all parents really want for their children – but the thought that she might be suicidal hadn't even entered our heads.

On the afternoon of 19 December, my wife Fiona and I were in a pharmacy in Carlisle getting our yellow fever inoculations; we'd planned to travel to Africa to visit my brother-in-law early in 2019.

My phone rang – it was Sophie, laughing: 'You pocket-dialled me! You still need training on how to drive your phone.' We had a brief chat about my inability to control my device.

I told her where we were. She signed off the call with a cheerful, 'Happy jabs!'

It was the last time I would ever speak to her.

Sophie was due to travel back to see her mum George at her house in Kendal the following day and spend time with us all over Christmas. She had a new flat and new job organised for the new year. She was getting a grip on her life and was looking forward to a fresh start.

Just after 7 p.m. that evening Sophie messaged us in the family WhatsApp group: '*I love you all so much.*'

I was at home with Fiona. We looked at each other; we were both concerned. It wasn't unusual for us to express love for each other, but these words in this setting didn't sound right.

'Do you think she's alright?' Fi asked.

I called Sophie, but her phone immediately went to voicemail.

Before I could do anything else our house phone rang. It was George in absolute hysterics. It took me a while to take in what she was saying . . .

'She's going to kill herself! She's going to kill herself!'

'What? Slow down . . . What?!'

'She's going to kill herself!'

In a state of high agitation, George explained that she had received a message saying that Sophie was planning to take her own life, signed off with, '*Please don't bury me.*'

What could we do? What would *you* do?

We grabbed a load of clothes and headed for the car – we were going to Edinburgh.

As we left the village, we collected Gregor, our son, Sophie's brother – he was working in the local pub while back at home from university. We bundled him into the car, telling landlord Anton, 'We've got a family crisis, we'll call you tomorrow.'

The drive north was excruciating – we had no idea what to expect when we arrived, we had no idea what we could do to help. We had no idea where Sophie was.

* * *

Our family gathered at the flat Sophie had shared with her husband and waited. We spent two days in Edinburgh while the police and coastguards searched for her. On the third day, we returned to our home in the Lake District, as it was clear that we could not do anything in Scotland other than upset ourselves.

On Saturday 22 December, I received a call from the police: 'Mr Airey, I'm afraid I've got some bad news for you.'

Sophie's body had been found.

The police told us that a member of the public had found her. He immediately called the police and had then stayed with Sophie until the emergency services arrived.

Time stood still; our world shattered. The initial anguish, shock and horror was so acute that it felt like physical pain. Every atom of your body cries out, 'THIS ISN'T HAPPENING. THIS ISN'T TRUE.' But it is. We simply held onto each other and cried.

Until that moment, suicide was something that happened to other people. It was very sad, of course, but it had nothing to do with us . . . until it did. Then it became excruciatingly real. It was a destructive force that shattered our lives, fried our brains. Our world was nothing but pain and anguish. 'Why didn't we see this coming?' we asked ourselves, over and over.

Somewhere amongst the tears, Fiona, Gregor and I began to talk to each other. We spoke about Sophie, our love for her, the things we'd done together, and we questioned what had happened. Why? Why hadn't she told us how she was feeling? Was there something we'd missed? Was there anything we should have spotted? Was there anything we could have said? Why did she do it?

Sophie had been a lovely little girl with blonde hair and a ready smile; she loved to be with people, and people loved her. In her preschool years my mam and dad looked after her, taking her on bus trips around the Lake District and showing her off to their friends. She grew to be a very sociable teenager and a beautiful young woman. She was great fun to be around, always teasing me, always very loud. We spent loads of time outdoors walking, biking and skiing. Just a lovely person.

Sophie's split from her husband had been her decision, not his, so it was clear that she was going through a fairly difficult time in her life. We had been worried about her; worried about her being happy – NOT worried that she might be feeling suicidal. It just hadn't crossed our minds.

The doorbell rang – it was Stewart, the local vicar. He'd been told that Sophie was missing and wanted to offer support and comfort. He wasn't to know that we had just received the worst possible news. It was good to have someone else to talk to, someone who might understand what was happening to us.

We drank tea and talked. Stewart spoke about love, loss and grief. We told him about Sophie. We cried. We laughed. We cried a lot more.

After some time with us, Stewart offered a few words of hope: 'Some people will tell you that time is a great healer. That's rubbish. You'll always have a Sophie-shaped hole in your lives that can never be filled. At the moment, all you can see is that gaping void. As time goes by, you will begin to find and do things that slowly start to insulate you from the hole. It won't go away, but you won't fall in as often as you will over the next few weeks.'

This struck a chord with me. It gave me a glimmer of hope that the crushing pain of intense grief would be alleviated ... not now, but sometime in the future. If only we could keep going.

Looking back on it – and knowing what I now know about suicide, bereavement by suicide and the destruction wreaked by losing a child to suicide – the conversation we had that afternoon was peculiarly insightful. The first thing we decided was that we couldn't cancel Christmas. It would have been easy to take down the decorations and go into hiding for the festive period, but somehow we realised that doing so would indicate that we were giving in to grief. We couldn't allow it to crush us – we HAD to have Christmas.

Through more tears, I said, 'We have to create something positive out of this mess.'

I had no idea how we could even begin to do anything other than wallow in grief, but realised that the first step had to be some kind of statement of intent. We had to find something, anything, that would give some hope.

Fiona had an idea. 'We have to go out and face the village,' she said. 'We can't sit in here. We need to go out and tell people what's happened.'

She was right. We had so many family and friends who knew us, knew Sophie, that there was no use in trying to hide what she had done. We needed to get outside, we needed fresh air. Going out meant that we would bump into our friends and neighbours – and as we walked around the village we would have to tell the people we met what had happened.

Coats on, we headed for the door. Another idea, this time mine: 'We need to be aware what this news will do. We will act like emotional lightning conductors.'

I'm not sure where that thought came from, but it certainly proved to be true. Opening up about suicide gives others a safe space to share their stories; something we were about to learn. We would also learn that suicide is everywhere. Once you scratch the surface by mentioning the S-word, you begin to see it wherever you look.

Before losing Soph, suicide was a very sad thing, something that happened to other people. You could see that it was an awful loss, but lives went on. What we didn't realise was that those bereaved by suicide were suffering unbearable grief, anger, doubt, guilt and deep, deep sadness generally hidden from view by taboo and stigma. This complex grief is unseen by most in society; it's only when suicide explodes in your family that you realise how destructive and overwhelming it is – and also how prevalent.

The process of telling people about Sophie opened conversations which showed us that suicide had already touched many of the people we knew. The more we talked, the more we realised that suicide was everywhere around us.

Christmas came and we struggled through it. We talked about Sophie. We cried. Somewhere over the festive period we managed to smile, even to laugh.

As others worried about how long to cook the turkey or whether they had enough sprouts, we had to think about Sophie's funeral. It had to be a celebration of her life, and it had to do some good – we needed to find a relevant charity, one that focused on suicide prevention. I asked a friend with experience of working with mental-health charities, and she pointed us to PAPYRUS Prevention of Young Suicide. They looked to be a perfect fit.

As well as offering suicide prevention training and suicide first aid courses PAPYRUS also runs HOPELINE247, a telephone helpline staffed by mental-health professionals who offer help, support and advice for both people in crisis and concerned others. The work done by these quietly determined people at PAPYRUS helps save lives every day of the week. Raising money for this charity would directly help them prevent other families following us into this shattered post-suicide world.

Sophie's funeral was held in early January 2019, with hundreds attending the service and wake. It was a true celebration of a young life unnecessarily cut short, with plenty of tears, but loads of smiles and laughter too. Sophie would have loved it.

At the wake, I spoke to many of Sophie's friends from school, university, work and her life in Edinburgh. Not one of them had seen this coming. How could a lively, quick-witted, intelligent, funny girl get into a situation where she thought that the only way out was to take her own life? It just didn't make sense. If she had been feeling so low all she needed to do was ask for some help; there were so many people around her who loved her – so many of them, so many of us, would have reacted immediately. All she needed to do was reach out . . .

As the afternoon wore on, I found myself talking to some of Sophie's friends from university. Mid conversation, Fiona butted in: 'Andy, there's someone here you need to meet.'

'Hang on, Fi, I'm just talking to Soph's mates.'

More firmly this time, Fi said, 'There's someone here *you need to meet.*'

Taking my arm, Fiona led me towards a slim, dark-haired man I didn't recognise. He was standing with George. Fiona stopped in front of him. 'Andy, this is Sandy. He found Sophie's body.'

What? Who? We knew that the person who found Sophie had stayed with her until the emergency services arrived . . . but what was he doing here?

'Thank you. Thank you for what you did for Sophie, and thank you for coming,' I said.

Sandy explained that finding Sophie had been a massive shock, one he was still trying to process. He told us that since that moment he couldn't stop thinking about a young woman feeling so sad and alone that she'd taken her own life. Through social media he'd discovered who she was and when her funeral would be. He'd decided to attend to reassure himself that she was loved.

Sandy told us how relieved he'd been to see so many people at the crematorium. He'd come along to the wake not knowing whether he would come in or not. In the end he'd had no choice. My friend Nigel had got talking to him and once he'd realised who he was, he wasn't going to let Sandy escape. We all cried together: Sophie's family and the person who sat with her waiting for the police to arrive.

Before Sandy returned home, we exchanged contact details. We have been in touch regularly since and have enjoyed each other's company several times, always raising a glass of whisky to Sophie. We are firm friends. Sophie would have loved him.

Being introduced to PAPYRUS for Sophie's funeral was just the start of our ongoing relationship with the charity. Fiona, Gregor, George and I remained determined to do something that could make a positive difference for others. Although it was too late for Sophie, and we could never bring her back, perhaps we could do something that would prevent another family suffering this pain and torment. Everything I found out about PAPYRUS reinforced my initial impressions about the charity. I discovered that suicide is the biggest killer of under-thirty-fives in the UK, yet almost no one is talking about it. I began to think about how I could help PAPYRUS in their life-saving work.

Sophie had signed up to run the Northumberland Half Marathon in late February with her friend Laura. During the Christmas break I spoke to Laura about the run – she was still going to do it. Initially, I'd suggested to Fiona that we should go and support Laura, but I quickly realised that rather than cheering Laura on, I should run it myself.

I knew I could do 13 miles with next to no training. When I was younger and fitter, I'd entered many mountain marathons: two-day, long-distance orienteering events where you carry your food, tent and overnight kit. In my mind this run would be easily achievable – but when I pressed the '*enter*' button on the website I found that the race was full! I called the organisers, and once they had satisfied themselves that I really was who I said I was, they arranged to transfer Sophie's entry to me. I was literally going to be running in Sophie's place! And to motivate me even more, I planned to fundraise for PAPYRUS.

As soon as I put the phone down, it occurred to me that we had a fantastic human-interest story that would raise awareness for the charity: a heart-broken father running an event his daughter had entered before taking her own life, the father running on his daughter's entry . . . I knew that the media would pick it up.

I started posting a video training diary using the hashtag #RunforSophie on social media and shared it with the local press, many of whom ran features. I also called a contact at the BBC, Alison Freeman, a journalist based in Newcastle. My career had been in sales and marketing so I had always gone out of my way to get to know the local TV, radio and press journalists; I'd got to know Alison shortly after she began to cover Cumbria for *BBC Look North*. Little did I realise that the links I'd made for commercial purposes would be exactly what was needed when I wanted to help PAPYRUS save lives.

I phoned Alison. As soon as she realised who it was, she said, 'Thank God you've called me. I've been thinking about you ever since Sophie died.'

She told me that she was actually reading the *BBC Look North* news the night we put out the appeal to find Sophie and was also there to announce that her body had been found. Once she spotted the #RunforSophie content I was starting to put out she knew that there was a powerful story there . . . but she couldn't bring herself to call me. 'I thought that you would think that I was just another media vulture, only interested in the story, not you and your family,' she explained.

We spoke for a while about Sophie, about how our family was managing to live through her loss and how I was supporting PAPYRUS. In hindsight I didn't give Fiona and Gregor much choice in broadcasting our situation. I was laser-focused on raising funds for this lifesaving charity because I knew I could do something positive.

Gregor managed to avoid being dragged into my newfound passion as he returned to university where his friends did a good job of picking him up and looking after him. Fiona, on the other hand, was right at the epicentre of everything I was doing; she completely supported me and did what she could to help me with what became the #RunforSophie campaign. She understood my desire to make a difference; to save even one life would drive me on, and maybe start to help me to manage the waves of grief. Doing something is always better than doing nothing.

Alison was pleased to be asked to tell our story and we arranged a day to film a piece that would go out on regional *BBC News*.

After I appeared on local TV, the #RunforSophie campaign gathered great momentum and the cash flowing into my JustGiving page soon reached £20,000. People began to recognise me in the street, many pushing cash into my hand and telling me I was doing a great job.

By being open about Sophie, our loss and PAPYRUS, it encouraged others to tell me about their experience of suicide. Some shared their stories about losing friends or loved ones; others spoke about the time they had contemplated or even attempted suicide and how they were coping now. Hearing these stories from suicide survivors gave me extra impetus. This was direct proof that suicide wasn't inevitable; with support people could have a second (or third or fourth . . .) chance.

I began to realise that fundraising wasn't the most important part of what I was doing. Of course, it was a great, tangible measure of people's love, concern and support, and it helped PAPYRUS deliver their services, but the real outcome was getting people to talk about suicide and suicide prevention, raising the profile of PAPYRUS and encouraging those who were struggling or worried about someone else to pick up the phone and call HOPELINE247.

During the couple of months of my campaign I raised over £40,000 for PAPYRUS and after completing the half-marathon, I knew that my relationship with the charity would go on. I could use my communication skills and willingness to stand in front of audiences to keep spreading the word about their fantastic work.

On the day we were told that Sophie's body had been found, I knew that we couldn't put our lives on hold or be dragged down by the crushing pain we'd had thrust upon us. I had also said, 'We cannot let Sophie's suicide define the rest of our lives.' Yet here I was, less than three months later, dedicating a huge part of my life to suicide prevention. However, I was going in with a positive outlook. I knew I could make a difference and I got a boost out of helping others. It had to be done.

On 11 December 2020 (the day before what would have been Sophie's thirty-first birthday), Gregor, our son, attended a PAPYRUS Champions course at their head office in Warrington.

He wondered if he could channel his experience of losing his sister into something positive for himself and others.

At the meeting he sat next to a chap from Manchester called Mike. After they'd introduced themselves, Mike asked, 'Are you anything to do with this #RunforSophie bloke?'

'Yes, he's my dad.'

'Do you think he'd be up for another challenge?'

'I dunno . . . Probably . . . Here's his phone number – ask him yourself. The worst he can do is say no.'

After the event, Gregor mentioned that he had spoken to a bloke who seemed interested in talking to me, but what with it being Sophie's birthday, and the anniversary of her death and Christmas coming up, I put the conversation to the back of my mind.

At the beginning of April, the following year, I got a call – it was Mike, family man and firefighter based at Manchester Airport. He had lost his daughter Beth right at the start of the Covid-19 lockdown in 2020. We talked about our girls, how suicide had exploded our lives, how our families were coping, how *we* were coping . . . It was a conversation we've since had with dozens and dozens of suicide-bereaved people.

Talking to someone who completely understands how your life has been shattered and the awful state you collapse into really gives you the support you need. Knowing that you're not the only one feeling like this gives you strength to carry on.

During the call we talked about going for a walk together, and before I knew it we had a date in the diary: 30 April. We met in the car park at Kirkby Stephen and Mike greeted me with a firm handshake and a booming, 'Hello, Andy.' This was to be the first of many, many days I would spend walking with this inspirational Mancunian.

I had picked one of my favourite walks in the limestone country to the west of the town; we were going to walk up onto Smardale Fell before returning through Smardale Gill Nature Reserve. It was a six-mile route, starting along the old railway line heading back towards Kirkby Stephen before picking up lanes that led us out onto Smardale Fell.

Compared to the Lake District mountains Smardale Fell is rather diminutive, but it's in a special spot in the upper Eden Valley and boasts spectacular views of the surrounding uplands, from the Pennines round to Mallerstang and Wild Boar Fell then the northern flanks of the Howgill Fells and, in the distance to the west, the fells of the Lakes. It's a lovely place.

As we wandered up onto the fell we talked about what had brought us together: our daughters, their suicides and the impact on us and our families. It was clear that Mike carried his grief very heavily, almost as if he had a physical weight crushing his body and spirit. We shared our thoughts, feelings and emotions – what a difference it made to talk to someone who understood exactly how I was feeling.

As we stood on the tussocky grass at the fell's summit, Mike told me about Tim, another suicide-bereaved father.

'Without Tim, I wouldn't be here. Talking to him saved my life,' he said.

Mike explained how they'd come together after their surviving daughters had contacted each other over social media; Tim's eldest daughter had reached out to Mike's family after she saw a story online about a family who seemed to be going through the same situation as them. The link made between the suicide-bereaved siblings soon led to Mike and Tim talking on the phone. They began speaking only a few weeks after losing Beth and Emily when they were both living through the same nightmare. Mike told me that they were able to offer each other understanding and support during the darkest times in their lives. Tim sounded like a thoroughly nice bloke.

Our walk took us down into Smardale, a beautiful valley that gets thousands of visitors every year as they cross its upper reaches when following Wainwright's Coast to Coast Walk. But they miss the best bit: their route crosses the old railway before heading out of the valley towards Kirkby Stephen, whereas our route followed the old track bed back to our start point.

The railway ran from the West Coast Main Line at Tebay through Smardale to Kirkby Stephen before climbing over the Pennines at Stainmore and on to the industrial North East; it was built to carry coke to the iron and steel furnaces at Barrow and in West Cumberland – all gone now, of course. The line was closed in 1962 and is now managed as a nature reserve by Cumbria Wildlife Trust. At the heart of Smardale stands Smardale Gill Viaduct: fourteen stone arches soaring 90 feet above the beck, and a classic example of Victorian railway engineering.

As we walked over the viaduct, Mike said, 'I've had an idea. We could walk between our houses to show that suicide is a nationwide problem and could happen to any family, anywhere.'

Like me, he'd only discovered that suicide is the biggest killer of young people *after* Beth died; like me, he was shocked to find that suicide is happening across the country, and like me, he wanted to do something about it.

'Nice idea, Mike. Remind me where Tim lives?'

'Norfolk . . .'

'Hmm . . . you realise how far away that is?'

'I've got a plan. I'll show you when we get back to my van.'

Mike explained that he and Tim had begun to talk about 'doing something', maybe a walk, but they hadn't developed the idea. Then, after he'd met Gregor and seen what I'd been doing, he thought I might be up for a long walk with the two of them. He was right.

The idea of three ordinary dads from 'normal' families walking between our homes to show that suicide is a nationwide problem and can happen in any family seemed a simple yet effective concept that had potential to deliver a powerful suicide prevention message. I couldn't really say no.

Back at the van, Mike produced his masterplan . . . a 2010 *Road Atlas of Great Britain*! On the page showing the whole country, Mike had placed a dot on Penrith, a dot on Sale, a dot on Derby and a dot on King's Lynn. Three lines joined the dots, and each line was marked in 20-mile intervals.

Once I had stopped laughing, I suggested that the plan might need a little more finessing. 'How far is it?!' I asked.

'About 280 miles.'

'OK. That's doable. But why a dot on Derby?'

Mike explained that he had already sorted accommodation there with the Bishop of Derby. It turned out that one of the people who had helped Mike begin to put his life back together was George Lane, Manchester Airport chaplain; George's wife Libby, the first female bishop in the Church of England, was now Bishop of Derby. Mike had mentioned his idea of a cross-country walk to George, who had immediately offered their house as potential accommodation. Effectively, George knew about the walk before Tim and I did.

Before going our separate ways, Mike and I hugged. We had shared an emotionally charged walk and it felt as though we were on the verge of taking a significant step forward.

'It could be quite big,' Mike said as we parted.

The following day, I made my first call to my network, one built during a career in outdoor retail and tourism, when I contacted Ordnance Survey. I wasn't sure about the other two dads, but if I was going to plan a long-distance walk, I needed paper maps – I couldn't do route planning on a computer. Ordnance Survey immediately said yes and before we knew it, we each received a box of eighteen OS Explorer 1: 25 000 maps covering the full distance of our intended route. Let the planning begin!

We finally all got together (digitally) on 24 May. It was the first time I'd spoken to Tim. Like the many suicide-bereaved parents we subsequently met, we spoke about our girls, how we hadn't seen suicide coming, the effect it was having on us and our families . . . how hard life was.

We talked about Sophie and Emily, what they were like, how they behaved, how much we loved them . . . how much we missed them. Yet again there was a relief in talking to someone who completely understands your feelings – to be in a safe place where you feel able to be completely open allows an exploration of your emotions and develops a better understanding of how grief is affecting you. We were learning that by sharing our stories we were helping each other begin to move forward, to build some kind of resilience to the crushing pain and slowly, very slowly, begin to insulate ourselves from the gaping holes in our lives that had been left by the suicides of our girls.

After a while we moved on to Mike's plan and began to discuss dates. While we could wait for spring 2022, we were so excited about the idea of doing something positive that dates in September and October 2021 were also considered.

Over the next six weeks, there were many more Zoom meetings, refining the route, trying to work out where we could stay and how our overnight kit would be moved around (we intended to travel light with daysacks). This would rely on a network of friends, family and strangers upon whom we would be totally dependent.

We met for the first time face-to-face on 2 July at Mike's house in Sale. We talked and talked, sharing stories, emotions, hopes ... Mike's wife Helen cooked a great meal, and Mike supplied beer ... plenty of beer. Sometime during the evening we settled on doing the walk as soon as possible – October 2021.

In the morning, we pored over the maps in Mike's dining room. We had all looked at different parts of the route: me the northern section, Mike the middle bit and Tim the last third heading towards his home. We began refining the route, considering various options, trying to create a single line across the maps that led from my front door, through Manchester to East Anglia. The plan was coming together. We also took the opportunity to take some photos in the garden, each grabbing a different-coloured PAPYRUS T-shirt. Helen took the photos, little knowing that these images would define our brand: Mike

= Mr Teal, Tim = Mr Purple, me = Mr White. (I would later regret this non-colour choice as I have a real knack of finding any muck out there.)

'We need a name.'

'How about 3 Dads Walking? It does what it says on the tin,' said Tim.

3 Dads Walking was born.

Before we wrapped up our first planning meeting, I told the guys about Alison Freeman. 'I have a tame BBC reporter,' I said.

By this time I counted Alison as a friend as well as a professional contact. Mike and Tim agreed that, since I trusted Alison, they would be happy if I approached her with our plans.

I called Alison the following day. After I explained who I'd got involved with and what we were discussing, the line went quiet. I could almost hear her thinking.

'I think I can get you onto *BBC Breakfast* with this,' she said.

I checked with Mike and Tim – both were happy with the possibility, with one proviso: that their families would be kept out of the coverage. This was to be a story of dads and daughters – they didn't want to put any unnecessary pressure on their loved ones. They had the full support of their wives and families, but decided that it would be the best if the focus remained on the 3 Dads.

BBC Breakfast liked the idea, and commissioned Alison to make a film about 3 Dads Walking that would go out before our walk. The idea was to get one of us on the sofa to talk about our plans.

I also suggested we needed a 3 Dads Walking website, because it would make it easier for us to signpost potential supporters to our message. We could talk about our girls, why we were walking and the route. Most importantly, it would include a big '*DONATE*' button.

Again, I fell back on my network. I met with Cat Rumney, MD at The Creative Branch, local digital marketing specialists who'd been introduced to me by a mutual friend. I spoke to Cat about Beth, Emily and Sophie, how Mike, Tim and I got together, the fact that suicide is the biggest killer of young people in the UK, our plans to raise funds for PAPYRUS and to get people talking about suicide prevention. She listened intently, but admitted that they didn't have any spare capacity. We were in the midst of the turmoil of the Covid pandemic and their clients all wanted their websites updating – and they all wanted the work done immediately.

'What's your budget?' asked Cat.

'We don't have a budget.'

'Hmm . . . Let me talk to my colleagues and I'll get back to you.'

She called me the next morning: 'We have to do it. We will build you a website. I'm a mum and many of my colleagues have children in their teens and early twenties. We just have to help you.'

We are immensely grateful to Cat and her team – www.3dads walking.uk has become an incredibly powerful tool in helping us broadcast our message of hope and enabled us to help PAPYRUS save lives.

Whilst I was talking to Cat about the website, Mike got our JustGiving page up and running. After quite a bit of discussion we set a fundraising target of £3,000 each; 3 Dads, 3 homes, 300 miles, £3,000 – it had a nice ring to it.

Local media took notice of the JustGiving site and our fantastic website, and some interviews were requested through Dutch (Peter Holland – Media Manager at PAPYRUS), with Tim doing some local newspaper interviews in his neck of the woods. As a result, our initial fundraising target was already in sight, with each of us already at £2,200, so we had another Zoom meeting. After much sucking of teeth, we decided that we should try and raise £10,000 each. We amended our JustGiving page, feeling apprehensive about such an incredible target, and worried that we might fail.

Our virtual planning meetings continued; the logistics began to fall into place. We were building a chain of friends, friends of friends and people who just stepped forward to accommodate us and move our kitbags along the route. In one of these meetings Mike said, 'We need flags.'

'Why? What good would they be?' I asked.

'It'll look good and make a statement as we walk down the country,' Mike replied. 'I'll ask the team at PAPYRUS to find us some.'

At another meeting I suggested we carry a donation bucket to encourage people to donate as we walked by, but Mike and Tim disagreed. 'No one carries cash nowadays.' I happened to have a PAPYRUS collection bucket in our garage, so decided that to prove a point I'd attach it to my rucksack when we walked.

On 16 September, Alison came across to Morland with Adam Nolan (the same cameraman who had filmed me for #RunforSophie). They spent the morning filming me near Shap Summit before heading down to see Mike in Sale, then on to

Tim at Shouldham the following day. The BBC were clearly committed to 3 Dads Walking – they had invested in sending the pair out for two days to follow our story. The piece was due to be broadcast shortly before we started our walk in October.

The next big milestone came on Sunday 26 September, a launch event arranged by Mike at the Seven Bro7hers Brewery & Taproom adjacent to Media City in Manchester. This was only the second time the 3 Dads had met face-to-face. The event was filled with family, friends of Mike's from Manchester, plus Fi and Gregor and Tim's friend Rich from Shouldham. There were stories, tears and laughter – a theme that would characterise our walk. There was also the hottest curry ever, which resulted in tears of a different nature!

On the Monday, while Tim was returning to Norfolk and I was on my way home to Cumbria, Mike was called by the BBC. They wanted him to be on the Red Sofa along with Ged Flynn, PAPYRUS CEO, the following day. The BBC were really getting behind us. That night our JustGiving total was at £10,243.

Alison and Adam's finished film was superb. They had followed my journey of loss from a few weeks after Sophie's death; they had learnt a lot about suicide, suicide prevention as well as bereavement by suicide. Alison had become skilled at interviewing about this challenging subject, and her empathetic style, combined with Adam's creative videography and editing, had resulted in an engaging, informative and very emotional piece.

The week before we started, on Tuesday 28 September, the 3 Dads Walking video aired twice – once at 6.10 a.m. and then a second time at 8.10 a.m. – and Mike was on the sofa with Ged to talk about us, our girls and the walk. He came across extremely well – #3dadswalking was now in the public eye!

Visits to the website increased, donations started to roll in and within forty-eight hours our JustGiving total was at £48,313, our revised target smashed. We were blown away – all we'd done so far was plan a bit of a walk, drink some beer and have Mike sit on the *BBC Breakfast* Red Sofa. It felt like we had unleashed something that already had a life of its own – and none of us knew just how big it was going to get.

That journey from the shattering loss of Sophie to the verge of an adventure seemed bizarre. When you lose a child to suicide, your life instantaneously takes a new, unexpected trajectory. You have no idea how to survive – let alone how to come up with a plan about what to do to get out of the mess.

But here we were – we had a plan, and we knew what we wanted to achieve. Now all we had to do was get together – and start walking.

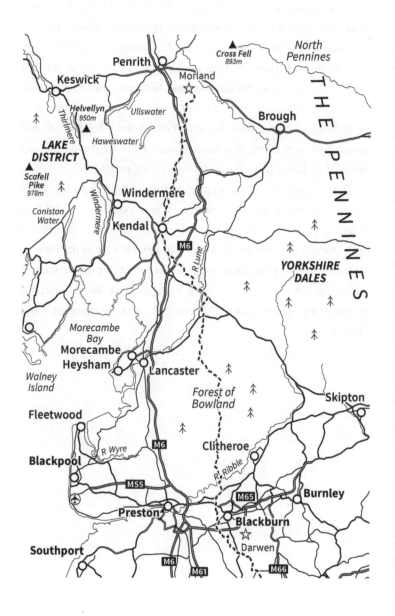

DAY 0

Meeting at Morland

It felt like it had been an awfully long time since we first talked about 3 Dads Walking, but suddenly start day minus one arrived. Tim was travelling from Shouldham to the Lake District by train and Mike had got a lift from his mate Russ. I'd arranged to meet Mike in Shap.

The morning was filled with faffing: several checks and rechecks of equipment, repacking the kitbag, taking another look at the route, reminding myself that we'd done everything we could to put support together and trying to feel reassured that our logistics would work.

Just before I headed to Shap, we got an email from PAPYRUS saying that Daniel Craig (James Bond!) had donated £10,000 and they were trying to get permission to publicise his generous gift.

'Fi, look at this.'

'What? *The* Daniel Craig? James Bond?' she asked incredulously.

How the heck did an A-list celebrity spot what we were planning to do – and why had he chosen to support *us*?

By the time I reached Shap, PAPYRUS had received permission from Daniel Craig's people to attach his name to his donation and our walk. I opened the 3 Dads Twitter and Instagram accounts to find that we had been tagged in a post picturing

James Bond captioned, '*From PAPYRUS with love*'. Our social media exploded!

At the time, Daniel Craig was the most high-profile actor in the world; *No Time To Die* – his last film as Bond – had just been released (two years late due to the pandemic). He was worldwide news – we couldn't have wished for more prominent support. We never expected anything from celebrities; we hoped that our relationship with Alison and *BBC Breakfast* would enable our message to reach a modest nationwide audience, but the unexpected backing of James Bond turbocharged everything we did.

Russ pulled up and as Mike got out of the car he said, 'Have you seen this about Daniel Craig?'

'Yeah. Look what's happening on social media! And have you seen our JustGiving page?'

The donations were flooding in.

Tim later told me he was sitting on his kitbag on Preston Station waiting for his train connection to Penrith when the story broke. No one took any notice of a man in shorts on the platform with a tear rolling down his cheek.

Shortly after getting home with Mike, Alison and Adam from the BBC arrived. We were instructed to keep Tim in a holding pattern – he was getting a lift from Penrith railway station to Morland. He parked up in Cliburn Village Hall car park, where he got changed into his purple PAPYRUS T-shirt waiting until the camera was set up. Eventually, Adam gave us the thumbs up, we called Tim in and his arrival was captured for posterity.

Our house felt full and chaotic; there was lots of chat, teas, coffees . . . and nervous laughter, with Alison and Adam asking for more interviews and footage. It was odd to think that this was only the third time that Mike, Tim and I had met in person. Here we were chatting and laughing like old mates, preparing to live in each other's pockets for the next fifteen days. 'Let's hope we get on,' I thought.

In the midst of all the chaos I was dealing with an email request from Andy Burnham's office – yes, the Metro Mayor of Greater Manchester wanted to meet us as we came through his patch. Unfortunately we couldn't find a mutually convenient time; but this incident confirmed the profile we were generating for ourselves and reassured us that our fundraising appeal was being seen and heard nationwide.

How had my life come to this? Here I was, in conversation with the Metro Mayor of Manchester's PA while talking to a BBC reporter and cameraman and getting to know two blokes with whom I was going to spend the next fortnight walking across England. Bizarre.

George arrived to wish us well and was immediately roped in for a BBC interview in the garden. George said she had been worried about Sophie's mental wellbeing; she spoke about their last conversation, the day Sophie died, when Sophie was clearly upset. George had asked her whether she was OK, but Soph replied, 'It's just a blip, Mum.' George hadn't pushed Sophie to say any more, and she reflected on the 'What if?' of not asking her daughter whether she was contemplating suicide. Something we had subsequently learned that, though very challenging to do, is exactly the way to deflect people suffering suicidal thoughts away from the route they were contemplating. What if . . .

Afternoon moved into evening as Alison and Adam completed the interview with George. They then moved on to film us as we ate our tea – Fiona scurried around in the background doing her best to remain out of shot. 'If I'd known this meal was going to get filmed, I would have made something posh!' she joked. Eventually Alison and Adam packed up, wished us goodnight and said they'd see us at the village hall the next morning. They needed to edit a package for *BBC Breakfast* – it would be broadcast a couple of times the following day before the programme came to cover our departure.

As Alison and Adam left, friends from the village piled into the house. Although it was lovely to know how much love and support we were getting, we did rather feel that we needed to focus on the task ahead and try to relax before our adventure began.

That said, it was good that Tim and Mike met Sarla, a great friend of ours from just up the road. Sarla is from a Lancashire farming family and had committed to look after us on Day 4, when the route would take us through the area near her parents' old farm.

Eventually the house cleared and we were left to our own devices. We checked our kit over and over again, reassuring ourselves that we had everything we needed. Mike had arrived carrying the three PAPYRUS flags and flagpoles that he got the charity to source. Despite my initial reticence I had to admit that, once the flags were attached to our rucksacks, they looked pretty good. I also took the opportunity to attach the PAPYRUS collection bucket to my backpack – Mike and Tim still scoffing about it being unnecessary. One way or another we were as ready as we were ever going to be. I'm not sure if you can get 'pre-match nerves' before going for a walk, but that's what I felt.

To ease a bit of the pressure we went for a wander, ending up at the village hall with the 3 Dads Walking banner Mike's mate had made for us. It was two metres long and one metre deep, with a graphic in the centre showing our route and pictures of us down the left side and Sophie, Emily and Beth down the right. It was a powerful tool that would accompany us on the route.

The banner's first home was on the wall of Morland Village Hall. We stood back to admire our work. The L-shaped line wiggling across the map in the centre certainly focused our minds on what we were about to do. We walked back home in contemplative mood.

Before we retired to bed, Tim produced a drawing by Evie, his youngest daughter. It showed us in our PAPYRUS T-shirts and shorts walking across a hilly countryside. I carefully laminated it and Tim popped it into his rucksack. He would be carrying Evie's love and support all the way back to his home in Norfolk.

Fundamentally we knew that we would all be carrying the love and support of our wives, families and friends as we walked. We were about to find out how much this would mean to us, and also discover that the people we would meet along the way would shower us with kindness, humanity and love.

We went to bed having no idea what we were letting ourselves in for – or where this walk would eventually take us.

DAY 1

Morland to Kendal

The first day of our walk dawned – a beautiful early autumn morning. I realised that this would only be the fourth day the three of us had spent together, and barely six months since we first spoke. It was remarkable to think how we had become so close, so quickly. We had already shared our most powerful and painful emotions and experiences; we had already spoken about the worst days of our lives; and we had created a plan that would help us move forward from our shattered lives. In some indefinable way, we had come to know each other very well.

Here they were in our kitchen. Tim – tall, neat and tidy, well spoken (obviously an ex-head boy!). As well as loving maps and route planning, Tim had a real eye for detail; his determination to have a contingency plan in place for any eventuality ensured we went into the walk as well prepared as we could be. Tim is also definitely the one most likely to shed a tear when listening to other people's stories of loss.

Mike – a big, burly Mancunian (although he later admitted to being born in Essex!). I think that he is the most empathetic of the three of us – he became the first to identify someone in a group who needed to talk to us. Mike is also the one who explored spirituality surrounding loss by suicide – a subject I'd never bothered to dwell upon. His crippling burden of grief, so evident when I first met him, had clearly lifted a little through our conversations and focus on planning the walk. Hopefully the next couple of weeks would help us all move forward too. Mike also has a deep voice with a proper Manc accent and a wonderful booming laugh. We got to hear plenty of that.

Because our departure was to be broadcast live on *BBC Breakfast* after 9 a.m. we had a fairly leisurely start to the day. Everything was set and ready to go after our endless packing (and repacking) from the night before. Fiona had prepared a great breakfast spread, so we made the most of it.

There was a bit of chat about the days ahead, but we had no idea what we were letting ourselves in for and absolutely no concept of how the days would pan out . . . other than the fact we had to cover 20-plus miles per day for the next fifteen days.

After breakfast, we got our kit together, put our boots on and walked out of my front door. Fiona took a photo of the three of us standing outside our house, fully kitted up, each holding a photo of our daughters. It would be a reminder to us and everyone who subsequently saw that image of why we were walking and the loss and grief that had brought us together. Everything we hoped to achieve was done in memory of Sophie, Emily and Beth.

'Are we good to go?' I asked. 'Come on then.'

We left our estate, heading for the village hall; our first steps in a walk of over 300 miles.

Walking through the village, on a road I knew so well with blokes I barely knew, it felt strange that I wouldn't be returning home for over two weeks. The streets were quiet – where was everybody? I usually bumped into someone when walking through Morland.

When we arrived at the village hall car park, I realised why we'd seen no one on the way up. It was rammed with people, mostly Morlanders, but also friends from across Cumbria and other parts of the country.

Tim spotted Richard Bland and his wife Sue – they were friends who had driven up from Stoke to see the 3 Dads off. Richard and Sue had lost their son Andrew eight years previously and had decided that they too wanted to help prevent future suicides. Richard had the brilliant idea of creating Wing Commander AB Bear, a teddy bear in RAF uniform who travelled the world in all manner of aircraft (with his own logbook), raising awareness of suicide prevention and mental-health issues. WC AB Bear was there as we began our walk.

As well as this great gaggle of folk, the centre of the car park was taken up by two fire trucks and crews from the local fire station. The word was out amongst the firefighting service that one of their own was doing a charity challenge – we'd find many other firefighters along our route in the coming days, cheering Mike on. Because of the nature of their work, firefighters are often called out to incidents involving suicide, giving them yet another reason to come out and support us.

Beyond the fire trucks we could see Alison and Adam waiting to meet us, with – or so we thought – Daniel Craig! But as we approached the group at the top of the car park, I realised it was Alan Dunn, a good friend and Mayor of Keswick, wearing a Daniel Craig mask. 'Now then, Mr Bond . . . I mean, Alan.' He didn't quite manage to carry off the James Bond look

– instead of a sharp dinner suit he was wearing walking trousers, a T-shirt and his mayoral chain. Distinctive, certainly – but not quite 007.

Adam had put the firefighters in place and successfully corralled the villagers into a cheering crowd. We were positioned with our backs to the village school, looking across the car park through a fire service guard-of-honour.

Alison was in communication with the *BBC Breakfast* producers and gave us a countdown to the start of the live broadcast, beginning with the film she and Adam had created (which had been broadcast the week before). We knew from its previous broadcast that it was emotionally charged and would engage the viewers in our story. We hoped that by going out on a Saturday morning, it would reach a new audience.

As the film finished, the broadcast shifted to Morland – we were going out live to millions of viewers on the BBC. Having been intimately involved in Sophie's story, Alison had developed a confident, caring, empathetic style of talking about suicide and suicide prevention. She asked each of us in turn about our daughters, why we were doing the walk and what we hoped to achieve. It's hard now to remember exactly who said what at the time – we just wanted to get walking!

Having spoken to the three of us and Hazel Russell from PAPYRUS, Alison stood to one side and set us on our way. As the applause rang out, several people came up and pushed cash into our bucket. We waved our goodbyes, turned round . . . and began our 300-mile walk to Norfolk. We were off!

(Except we weren't. We'd barely got out of the car park when Adam called us back. We ended up leaving and re-entering the village hall car park three times, all for the purpose of some different camera angles for broadcast. Never mind – our well-wishers clapped and cheered every time!)

Finally, we were away towards Newby, accompanied by Alan Dunn. Rachel, a Morland local, grabbed me and pushed three roses into my hand. Each stem was bound in a ribbon on which she had written one of our daughter's names; a really thoughtful gesture to mark the start of our journey across the country.

I was filled with nervous energy; months of conversation and planning had led up to this, and now here we were, taking the first steps. I was looking forward to the days ahead, sure that Mike, Tim and I would get on with each other but feeling nervous about the people we were likely to meet on the way. Would the open way we had talked about Sophie, Beth and Emily encourage others to talk to us, or would people avoid us? How would we react to the stories we were likely to hear? There was only one way to find out.

As we walked up the hill away from the village hall, a petite lady in waterproofs ran up the road to tag along for a while (and ended up walking with us for much of Day 1!). In March, Susanna had lost her thirty-six-year-old daughter Polly. Despite the dedicated care of her psychiatrist and GP, Polly had been let down by the system, which was unable to support her in the way she needed. Susanna was the first of many suicide-bereaved parents we were to meet on our walk.

We were carrying a tracker which showed our progress online in real time, which meant it was straightforward for anyone to find our location and intercept us. We were expecting to have some challenging conversations along the route and were unsure how we would respond. We had no idea what effect these stories might have on us, but we resolved to talk and share our emotions, and we pledged to keep a watchful eye on each other. We were going to spend twenty-four hours a day in each other's company – it would be up to the three of us the care for one another's mental health and wellbeing as the walking and talking progressed.

A mile along the road we came to Newby, a typical Eden Valley village; pale limestone and rust-red sandstone buildings line the single street. If the cars were removed the place would be recognisable to locals back in the nineteenth or even eighteenth century.

It was obvious that people had gathered there to see us on our way. Balloons and '*Good Luck*' messages were hung all over the place, and it seemed like most of the villagers were out on the road. I was given a huge hug by Rachel and Mark; they had lost their son Joe to a vaccine-induced thrombosis earlier that year. Their grief was palpable, almost a physical presence. We hugged and cried and shared an extended moment as we remembered our children.

Mike and Tim were approached by a couple who were in pieces, tears flooding down their cheeks, looking for some help following the recent loss of their daughter, Aimee. Barely holding things together, Aimee's mum took an order of service from her daughter's funeral from her bag and passed it to Mike. On the front cover, there was a picture of a beautiful young woman.

Mike hugged Aimee's mum and asked, 'What would you like us to do with this? Do you want me to carry Aimee with me?'

Through tears, she said, 'Yes, please . . . that would be lovely.'
Mike put the order of service in his rucksack.

As Mike and Tim said their goodbyes to Aimee's family,
Rachel and Mark released me from their embrace, our faces
running with tears. It seemed as if everyone around us was
crying. We had barely walked a mile and it was blatantly obvious that our conversations about suicide were being heard and
having a dramatic impact on those who listened.

We said our farewells and walked up the hill out of Newby,
the fresh wind drying the tears on our faces. The day began to
fall into a shape that we came to recognise. Lots of people
appeared to encourage us along, money was dropped into the
bucket, some people walked with us for short or long distances
and families shared their stories of loss, all intertwined with
plenty of laughs.

Alan played a key role as chief spirit-raiser on our first day's
walking. His natural instinct is to get people laughing, and you
can't help but smile when you look at him. Having worn his
mayoral chain while we were in front of the TV cameras, he'd
popped it into his rucksack as we started walking . . . only to
reveal a T-shirt printed with a picture of the very same chain.

Our route took us a little way up the road from Newby before
taking a track through a farmyard and into the fields beyond. As
we walked, we climbed and the views across the Eden Valley
opened up behind us. Further to the east was High Cup Nick,
one of the most stunning pieces of upland scenery in the country; formed by the Whin Sill, a massive intrusion of igneous rock
that sits under a huge swathe of northern England, here it's
exposed as a sweep of vertical cliffs that stretch around the head

of an almost hidden valley. We looked back to Cross Fell (at just under 3,000 feet the highest point on the Pennines), and Great Dunn Fell with its early warning station 'golf ball' on the summit.

Cross Fell will always have a special place in my heart. Several years ago, Sophie and I did a winter's day walk up there, and as we approached the summit the weather deteriorated. By the time we were at the top, it was close to a white-out. I took some photos of Sophie hiding from the wind behind the summit shelter, thumbs up, smiling. Despite the weather, we were having a great day out together. It's a memory that will stay with me for ever. I loved walking with Sophie. Every time I go out for a walk now, I carry a map case; as well as protecting whichever map I'm using, it contains two photos of Sophie on Cross Fell summit from that day, along with photos of two girls I'd never met, Beth and Emily.

Cross Fell, the Eden Valley – these places were home to me. It was quite an odd feeling to know I was journeying on from this familiar place and walking out into new territory, meeting new people, discovering their stories. Not quite a leap into the unknown – maybe more of a ramble.

Crossing a field full of sheep, we realised Alan was lagging behind. He'd gone off the track and was herding the sheep together. Sheep being sheep, they began to bleat.

'Listen,' said Alan. 'They're calling my name!'

'You what?'

'Listen . . .'

'Mayor, mayor, mayor, mayor . . .'

I'm not sure what Susanna made of Alan's sheep antics, but at least it got her smiling too. She'd been telling us about the struggles she was having with the Coroners Service and the challenge of being forced to live a private tragedy in a public setting. Our hearts went out to this slight lady who had decided to spend time with us and share her story of loss.

Next we reached Towcett, no more than a small collection of properties amongst dirt tracks and hedgerows. Despite the quiet setting, as we left the footpath to join the road again, more people were there to greet us. Rosemary, one of the few Towcett residents, had picked up the 3 Dads banner from the village hall, brought it up the hill and attached it to a roadside gate. She was there to give us coffee, biscuits and cake. This became a daily occurrence – no matter where we were, or how remote, someone would find us and offer cake and, increasingly often, pork pies. We posed for lots of photos and chatted with locals.

Susanna's daughter, Hannah, turned up with her kids to check that her mother was OK and still wanted to be picked up in Shap, which had been Susanna's original plan. But she was enjoying herself so much she asked to be collected later in the day. Susanna was seventy-seven, small and fragile looking. However, she was a keen, regular walker and told us that the 'old people' in her walking groups didn't walk as far or fast as she liked! I made a mental note to invite her out walking with me and Fiona when I got home.

Our route took us south on a very quiet back road, high on the ridge separating the River Lyvennet from the River Lowther, both tributaries of the River Eden. It was still a bright, clear day and we could see the Lake District fells rising to the west, the view dominated by the High Street range. This ridge runs from Pooley Bridge at the northern end of Ullswater over many subsidiary summits to High Street itself before dropping south to Windermere; a route developed and used by the Romans. I took one more look back at the Lakes, then turned my attention to the onward route – south over the Shap Fells to Kendal.

We were walking in an area of Cumbria that is often overlooked, literally and figuratively: we have the Pennines to the north and east, the Howgill Fells to the south and the ever-popular Lake District to the west. Thousands of people look down into the Eden Valley every day from these well-walked hills, but very few choose to walk here. Wandering between the picturesque villages, following the tributary rivers and streams and discovering quiet, peaceful places in the Eden Valley is an absolute delight.

We left the back roads at Winter Tarn Farm to cross the fields towards Shap. At the gate in the bottom of the field our way was barred by a large expanse of mud and a dirty great big puddle – our first water hazard. We paddled through the mud and, by clambering along fences and the gate itself, one-by-one we gained the slightly less wet ground of the next field.

Feeling bolstered by our intrepid navigation of the Winter Tarn puddle, we took the first of the 3 Dads Walking videos. Alison had asked us to take videos as we went along to get the flavour of the walk, along with the thoughts of people who joined us. Susanna and Alan became our guinea pigs. Standing in a meadow behind a high hedge, which sheltered us from the wind, I asked them why they wanted to join us.

Susanna said, 'I hope we can publicise the problem of depression and how we can prevent suicide by creating a better understanding.'

Alan's reply was, 'This charity PAPYRUS struck a chord with me because my family had a brush with suicide and I wanted to come out and support you in what you're doing.'

'How far are you going to walk with us?' I asked.

'To that fence over there!' he laughed.

It was reassuring to be told that what we were doing was important to others. We weren't voices in the wilderness, we were being heard – and more people wanted to help us spread our message of hope.

More boggy fields took us towards Shap. Dropping into the village, a familiar face came to greet us: my old mountaineering friend, Alan Hinkes. Alan is the first and only British mountaineer to climb all fourteen of the world's 8,000-metre peaks. I've known Alan for many years and have spent time on the hills with him, as well as introducing him at various events. He's close to being a 'professional' Yorkshireman and has a particularly 'Hinkesian' way of dealing with people – it involves a lot of talking! You'll often hear him state, 'You can always tell a Yorkshireman . . . but you can't tell him much!'

After we lost Sophie, Alan was one of the people who immediately stepped forward to offer help, support and love. As Alan's persona is gruff (and viewed, at times, as somewhat unreconstructed) this came as a genuine surprise. It was only after our bereavement that he told me his family had been touched by attempted suicide and that several of his friends had died by suicide. He was yet another person who was having to deal with the ripple effect of bereavement by suicide – it reaches far and wide.

Our growing band turned into the first lane in the village and rocked up at Deborah and Robert's house for our Day 1 lunch. It was a magnificent spread of sandwiches, pies, sausage rolls, fruit cake . . . Again, something we'd get used to along the entire route. We were never underfed!

As we set off again towards Shap, we took the opportunity to video Alan and ask him why he'd joined us.

'This is a charity and a cause that is close to my heart,' he said. 'I've had personal experience of suicide . . . and a number of my friends who I've lost. I think I've got an understanding of some of the issues involved.

'People say that we don't know what other people are going through . . . and we really don't. We must develop more compassion and more kindness.

'Suicide can be prevented,' he said, finally.

Talking about how he had been touched by suicide and his heartfelt plea for kindness took Tim and Mike by surprise as, up to now, they had only witnessed Alan's somewhat crusty Yorkshireness. It clearly proved Alan's point that you never know what's going on inside another person's head.

With Alan's words ringing in our ears, I thanked him and put my phone and mic back in the side-pocket of my rucksack – we marched on.

At Anderson's Village Shop and Post Office we were stopped by Bev and Dave, who gave us all HUGE bags of Pick 'n' Mix. It felt like taking on ballast! Those sweets would go a long way down the route with us (and some in Tim's daysack would even make it all the way to the finish). As we left Shap, Alan Hinkes left us to go back to his car, promising to see us again further down the road.

Next, we had to walk south along the A6 for a couple of miles, one of the few places on the entire route where we couldn't avoid a major road. Fortunately, this section was relatively quiet and had the benefit of a decent pavement running alongside it.

The A6 stretch gave us our first taste of supporters beeping their horns as they drove past. Hearing beeps and seeing people waving at us confirmed that the message we were trying to get out was being heard – it put a spring in our step and a smile on our faces. It was great to be recognised, but – and much more important – these people were making the effort to acknowledge what we were doing. I'm not sure if satisfaction is the right word to describe my emotions at the time, but I began to feel a sense of pride. We *were* being heard, money was coming in . . . maybe we could make a real difference to other people's lives. Mike's idea of carrying flags wasn't as daft as I had originally thought!

Next stop Shap Granite Works: ahead we could see the path snaking its way through mounds of stone and gravel. But before we could head off along it, a car pulled up and a lady jumped out. She put cash in our bucket and told us her son had taken his own life seventeen years earlier and the sense of loss had never left her. We listened, offered our condolences and love and shared our feelings with her.

Before she got back into the car, the driver emerged and shouted, 'I came all the way from f—king Runcorn to find you lot!' It took us a while to stop laughing – and 'f—king Runcorn' became our quote of the day.

We laughed as we made our way through the works, one of three quarries that made the name Shap synonymous with high-quality granite. These pockets of industrial activity are as much part of the Eden Valley landscape as the limestone escarpments, charming villages and the River Eden itself.

Drizzle set in and waterproofs went on as we approached Shap Summit. The weather forecast had given only 20 per cent chance of rain – but it piddled down all afternoon. We weren't too perturbed, although the views of the Cumbria Fells I'd promised Tim never appeared; in fact, all we got to see was the inside of a cloud. For some reason Tim chose this moment to check his phone and realised he hadn't turned off the JustGiving notifications: he had 2,709 unread emails (it took him some time to get his inbox back to normal!). The online donations had really started to roll in – we already had more than £160,000 on the JustGiving page.

We stopped as the path crossed its high point on Shap Fell, close to the summit of the A6 road, the original main road north to Scotland on the west side of the Pennines. Close to where we stood a stone pillar erected in the 1991 holds a tablet engraved with the following words:

This memorial pays tribute to the drivers and crews of vehicles that made possible the social and commercial links between North and South on the old and difficult route before the opening of the M6.

Shap has been long recognised as the dividing line of Cumbria; crossing from one side to the other marks a transition between distinctly different parts of the county. Today we weren't going to see much around us, but that sense of transition was clearly there.

We decided to do our first piece for the 3 Dads Walking blog (who knew that three old blokes going for a walk would need their own website, YouTube channel and a blog?). Alan Dunn and Susanna were still with us, with everyone in full waterproofs. The scene looked pretty bleak – low dark clouds spattered us with heavy drizzle, the undulating grassland around us offered no shelter from the weather and the ground was sodden – but we were all in good spirits. It might have been a tad damp, with no views and still a fair way to go, but we were all smiling and enjoying our day out.

'Come with me, said Andy. It'll be fun, said Andy,' Alan joked.

'Well, is it fun?' I asked.

'Yes!' shouted everyone.

Descending from our high point of the day we dropped into Crookdale, a sinuous valley that hunkers down green and welcoming below the exposed grass and heather-clad hills above. We were leaving the Eden Valley and briefly entering the catchment area of the River Lune. Crookdale Beck flows into Borrowdale Beck (not the famous Lake District Borrowdale – this Borrowdale is a hidden gem of the Shap Fells); Borrowdale Beck runs due east before joining the River Lune just south of Tebay. Tens of thousands of people pass this confluence daily – it's right next to the M6 and West Coast Main Line – but very few find time to visit and explore this delightful valley.

It was still raining, and there were still no views, but our group was in good spirits and the convivial nature of the walk so far continued.

Out of the blue the 3 Dads Walking phone rang. It was a journalist from *The Guardian* wanting a couple of quotes to add to the piece they had written using information from our website. I had to stand still while doing it so we didn't lose the signal (the challenges of mobile phones in the Cumbrian hills). Daniel Craig's contribution to our appeal was attracting media attention from all over the world, never mind the UK. 3 Dads Walking was taking on a life of its own.

The 3 Dads phone was an old pay-as-you-go iPhone of mine. We had decided to put a contact number on our website but, not surprisingly, none of us wanted to publish their own number. This became known as our 'burner' phone (not that we were planning anything untoward) – we carried it because we wanted to be accessible to anyone listening to our message of hope.

At High Borrow Bridge, we were met by Susanna's lift, but on foot – a neighbour of her daughter's who'd decided to leave his car at the top of the next hill rather than drive along the road to meet us. Having originally planned to walk the first seven miles with us, Susanna ended up covering close to fifteen.

When we got to the car, Susanna hugged each of us. 'You don't know how much this day has meant for me,' she said.

We had some idea. We could see that she'd been relieved to talk openly about Polly to three people who completely under-stood what she was going through. Susanna's response to walk-ing with us and talking about her loss was one we would come to see every day. As she spoke about Polly, her grief and the various challenges she was dealing with, it was plain to see that some burden was being lifted. It was as if the process of sharing these raw emotions and experiences with those who clearly understood your innermost feelings allowed a little of that emotional weight to be taken away. We found that when listening to these stories of loss and grief the weight lifted from those other bereaved parents didn't seem to land on us. We could empathise, we knew these feelings and emotions, we all shed tears and somehow there was a little more light, a little more hope in all of us.

Now we were down to the three of us, plus Alan Dunn, heading south towards Kendal. Mike took a call from Radio Manchester and was interviewed on the hoof. Where was the media interest going to come from next?

As we dropped into the Kent Valley, heading for Selside on Shap Old Road, it was Alan's turn to leave us as he'd arranged to meet his wife. He gave us all a hug and wished us well before he turned to go.

It hadn't been bright at any time in the day, but now the light was fading fast. The late start caused by our appearance on *BBC Breakfast* was catching up with us. There was nothing we could do about it – we were massively appreciative of the support the BBC team had given us, so walking a couple of miles in the dark was a small price to pay.

In the gathering gloom we had to contend with our second water hazard of the day on a lane near Watchgate; the full width of the road was flooded. Mike and Tim suggested that, being Cumbrian, I acted as a magnet for precipitation – clearly the flood was entirely down to me, not the weather we'd experienced all afternoon. As they grumbled (good-heartedly) we scrambled along the wall to avoid getting wet.

After a long day of crossing valleys and fells, our end point was a dark lay-by on the A6. Rain soaked us, vehicles thundered past, and our feet struggled to find a non-existent path on the verge. And then came the welcome sight of George, waiting for us at the appointed spot. I turned off the tracker: 23 miles. Our first day's walking was done!'

Before we knew it, George had whisked us to her house, pointed at the shower and handed out beers. Our first night's meal was largely made up of the most fantastic locally made pie from Plumgarth's Farmshop – perfect!

After tea, we sorted our kit, Fiona having transported our bags for us. I plugged in the tracker to charge it for Day 2 and was surprised to find that the signal lights were flashing – and on checking the 3 Dads Walking Open Tracking page we found that we had successfully identified George's house for anyone who cared to follow us. Not ideal. I emailed Mick at Open Tracking to ask whether we could disable the device while it was charging. Hopefully we'd get an answer tomorrow.

Other than feeling slightly weary I had a great feeling of satisfaction as we sat at George's dining table. The route had worked well, it hadn't been too far, we'd been joined and supported by loads of people, many of whom had shared their stories of loss and grief. We realised that we had created something much bigger and more far-reaching than we could ever have imagined; we were deeply moved to have created a safe space where people felt comfortable enough to share their emotions and experiences. This was completely accidental, but a great privilege to realise that we were helping other people to move forward in their lives.

Money raised (excluding Gift Aid and direct donations)
   = £200,000
Day 1 distance = 23 miles
Total distance walked = 23 miles

DAY 2

Kendal to Wennington

I woke up to find I was hugging 'Saturday', Sophie's cuddly toy dog. He was bought for her when she was small ... on a Saturday ... and he had been everywhere with Soph, on holidays and trips, even when she'd grown up. When Sophie walked out of her flat in Edinburgh on the way to take her own life, Saturday was tucked in her bed. He now stayed in George's house. She'd put him in my bed so here he was comforting me, a heart-wrenching reminder of why we were walking.

This was the first day of our new routine: waking up in an unfamiliar bed, getting up early to ensure we got to our start point in good time, packing the rucksacks, sorting the kitbags ... and, of course, breakfast.

George was up and about by the time we went downstairs. 'Just have a light breakfast now. I'll make you a second breakfast when you walk back past my house.'

We were starting just to the north of Kendal before coming through the town, then our route towards Kirkby Lonsdale would bring us back past George's front door. What a bonus – two breakfasts! Just like Tolkien's hobbits in *The Lord of the Rings*.

After our first breakfast, George ferried us back to the finish point of Day 1, the lay-by near Selside. It was a clear, still

Y

morning; dawn was approaching, mist was rising in the fields and the sky over Benson Knott was slowly losing its peachy hue. It was going to be a perfect day for walking.

I'd carried Saturday to the start point, so I gave him a farewell hug, turned on the tracker and we were off – back on the road by 7.30 a.m. Having previously lived in Kendal, and with numerous friends in the South Lakes, I wondered if anybody would venture out to see us so early on a Sunday morning – but I needn't have worried. After walking no more than 200 metres we were stopped by a shout – our first supporters of the day.

The early morning mist cleared as we entered Kendal. We picked up the old canal path and headed south, to be met by Denys and Ann, more Kendalian friends. They walked with us until we got to Kirkbie Kendal, Sophie's old school. I approached this with some trepidation: would walking past this place trigger challenging and painful emotions?

Sophie's secondary school days seemed like ancient history – so much had happened since – but walking past the building and playing fields brought back memories of my daughter as she was growing up. She was always a bright and cheerful girl with a ready smile and something to say. It never crossed our minds that this carefree teenager from Kendal could become suicidal before she turned thirty. We never saw it coming.

My concerns about walking past the school were unfounded; the memories raised were all positive. Sharing these with Mike, Tim and my friends kept me in good spirits.

A little after Kirkbie Kendal, we arrived back at George's house. We went back in for our second breakfast of bacon butties – what a way to start the day!

The route out of Kendal took the tarmacked footpath alongside the A65, which was relatively quiet before 9 a.m. on a Sunday morning. The odd car went by, most honking their horns, and a few other friends joined us for a mile or so. Stevie, a friend from my time in the outdoor trade, found us and jumped from his van crying, 'Do you want any socks?' Amongst other things he is a distributor of walking socks. We couldn't say no – new socks are always appreciated, so we popped a couple of pairs each into our rucksacks.

After Stevie left we stopped for a few moments to take on refreshment and I noticed we'd received an answer from Mick about the tracker. When it was plugged in to charge, it would always transmit, meaning that every place we stayed would be visible to the world. We felt sure this would, at the very least, infringe our host's digital privacy rights . . . but what could we do? After a bit of discussion Tim suddenly announced, 'Tinfoil! We'll wrap it in tinfoil!' We would experiment that evening.

As we approached the small village of Summerlands, a couple of cars pulled up and several people and various dogs – a collection of Labradors and golden retrievers – crossed the road and headed our way. It was Angela Allen, her daughter Tash, her sister Colleen and Tash's friend. Angela had lost her daughter Kat to suicide in November 2019, and then her husband Damian, also to suicide, eight months later. Angela and Tash's reaction to this devastating situation was to try to find something that would help others. They started a charity – Bags for Strife – which works with the emergency services and other organisations to distribute a care kit to families following the death of a loved one from suicide.

Angela and Tash realised that suicide-bereaved families often suffer a lack of support in the immediate aftermath of their loss. Bags for Strife was set up to provide this essential service; the bags contain a simple guide with links to many support services and advice about accepting help. With the guide you'll find a water bottle, sleep spray, lip balm, tissues and various other things to remind you to take care of yourself. When your world has collapsed around you, looking after yourself often gets forgotten.

To raise funds for the charity, Tash and her friend Caz had run from Leeds to Bowness (100 miles over five days). The family's story and the run had been covered by *BBC Breakfast*. We'd watched Angela and Tash talking on the Red Sofa a couple of weeks before we started our walk; they had been articulate and inspirational. We only hoped that we could emulate them.

What a privilege it was to walk with these beautiful people. They shared their story with us and we shared our stories with them, each listening intently to every detail to understand where we were all coming from and see if there were any similarities in our experiences. We discussed grief, anger, loss, sadness, love and how every emotion rolls together in the confusion following the loss of our loved ones. We all saw the pain etched in Angela's face and understood how she was feeling.

We were soon joined by Sarah Swindley with another bouncy Labrador. It was turning into Crufts! As well as being Angela's best mate, Sarah was the person who introduced me to PAPYRUS. I knew her through the Lake District Foundation, a charity aimed at inspiring visitors and businesses to support environmental and community projects throughout Cumbria – I am a trustee, and Sarah is CEO. When looking for a suicide prevention charity to support at Sophie's funeral, googling 'Suicide Prevention Charities' brought up Samaritans and Mind, followed by myriad others I didn't recognise. Being a trustee of a small charity drew me away from the big ones (they could look after themselves) – but which of the smaller charities should we pick?

I asked Sarah for advice as I knew she had a background in health charities. She immediately recommended PAPYRUS, not because she knew them from work but because one of her son's friends had taken his own life. His school had subsequently invited the charity to deliver suicide awareness and suicide prevention training to the students.

At the little village of Gatebeck, which sits on the picturesque Peasey Beck, we were intercepted by more people, who all had cash for the bucket. Tim and Mike's original thinking that what little money we received could just be stuffed into our pockets was proving to be somewhat unfounded. It was becoming clear that if I hadn't brought the bucket we would have needed considerably bigger pockets!

A run of quieter back roads took us east towards Kirkby Lonsdale, a narrow lane climbing the knobbly ridge separating the Kent and Lune valleys. Small farms peppered the landscape, and sheep and cows leisurely grazed the lush grass. The very essence of rural lowland Cumbria. The trees and hedgerows were still in full leaf although there was an occasional tinge of colour, hinting at the seasonal change. We may have been in autumn but with few fluffy clouds dotting the blue sky, and next to no wind, the day could hardly have been better for walking.

Suddenly we spotted a figure running up the hill behind us – Mr Hinkes was back! More introductions ensued, more chat and laughter. It was turning out to be a very sociable day.

Just before lunch we stopped to look back towards the Lake District fells so that Tim could take in what we'd missed the day before. The mist had cleared and the views were spectacular . . . finally. From the high ground between Morecambe Bay and the River Lune we could see right across the Cartmel and Furness peninsulas and out into the Irish Sea. All the southern and central Lake District fells were on show, from Black Combe near Millom, across the Coniston Fells to the rugged heights of the Scafell Massif.

Having spent my life walking on these mountains I felt strangely proud to be describing this view to Mike and Tim – it was like introducing my new-found friends to a member of my family. The magnitude of the view and the epic proportion of this landscape give a sense of perspective; it helps us realise that many of the issues we get hung up on aren't worth worrying about. If only Sophie had been able to see that whatever difficulty she was facing, whatever her problems and anxieties, they could all have been managed if she had seen them for what they are – insignificant in the overall scheme of things. Suicide is never the answer.

*   *   *

We turned our back on the Lakes and headed into the gentler countryside of the Yorkshire Dales, stopping for a sit down and something to eat more or less on the Kent/Lune watershed.

I videoed a short interview with Angela and Tash – and what a powerful three minutes of conversation that turned out to be.

'I don't know if you ever deal with the loss through suicide; we're living through it,' said Angela.

'We muddled through until we had the strength to turn it into something that would help other people,' Tash added. 'It's the only way to keep moving forward.'

When I asked Angela why she had come out with us, she said, 'I feel the loss of your beautiful girls and it's just amazing to support you.'

I was coming to realise that I had a potential second career as a combined interviewer and cameraman, and was well into the swing of recording anyone who would share their story with us. Before we left our lunch stop, I took a short film of Tim.

'We can't believe the impact we're having,' he said. 'People are walking with us all the time and we've raised over £200,000. We've had donations from a couple of pounds right up to £10,000. Thank you to everyone who has supported 3 Dads Walking and PAPYRUS.'

To say we were grateful was a massive understatement – we were dumbstruck by people's generosity.

We were soon back on the road with our group in tow. Shortly after setting off, we passed a couple sitting in a white open-topped Mazda. I was striding away out front and said hello as I walked past. It was five minutes later that we realised that Mike wasn't with us – he couldn't have got lost, could he?

We stopped and looked back up the lane – no sign of Mike. I was just about to give him a call when Tim's phone rang.

'Hang on,' said Mike. 'I'll be right with you.'

When he eventually caught up with us, he explained that he'd stopped to talk to the couple in the Mazda. He told us that there was something about their demeanour that had encouraged him to engage them in conversation.

'I've joined your club,' the man had said. 'My daughter-in-law took her own life a couple of months back. We don't know why. She's left our son with their two young children . . .'

Mike wasn't to know until after the walk that he was talking to Aimee's father-in-law (we'd met her mum and dad on Day 1 – and Mike was carrying Aimee's order of service). Over the next fortnight we were going to find that lots of the people who joined us were connected in ways that seemed implausible, almost unbelievable. In many ways this corroborated what we had learned; suicide doesn't discriminate, it can happen anywhere, in any family: it's 'the club no one wants to join'.

Our route rolled over the countryside towards Kirkby Lonsdale. Even though the narrow lane was bounded by hedges, we still had plenty of views over the fields and farmland, with flat-topped Ingleborough dominating the prospect ahead. With the Lake District well behind us and the Dales and Pennines ahead, the sense of transition was tangible – moving from one landscape to another was to become a fundamental feature of our walk.

Walking through the English countryside is a wonderful way to experience the changing character of the scenery. When travelling by car, bus or train, the landscape is a background that flashes by too quickly to be appreciated. Walking at three miles per hour fixes you firmly in that landscape and gives you the opportunity to take in the sights, sounds and smells, as well providing a sense of how the continually changing areas link together to create a most beautiful whole. We found that every day offered us something different, but that one thing remained the same: the sheer simple enjoyment of walking through magnificent countryside always gave an uplift to everyone's mood. Gazing over the fields, valleys and hills while putting one foot in front of another became almost meditative; without doubt walking is a powerful and effective therapy for improved mental wellbeing.

However, my mood soon took a bit of a knock, when I learned that wearing the white PAPYRUS T-shirt wasn't such a great idea. After laughing at Sarah's dog rolling in the muddiest of puddles by the roadside, I wasn't best pleased when it shook itself immediately in front of me, depositing a significant quantity of mud on to my shirt. Strangely enough, I was the only one who didn't find this funny!

I fell into step with Tash, and she asked me about Sophie and her mum, as well as how I'd met Fiona. George and I had separated when Sophie was four years old; they moved to Kendal, where George was a teacher. I saw Sophie every week, and she regularly stayed with me at home in the Eden Valley or at my parents' house near Keswick. Since my passion was the outdoors much of our time together was spent walking in the Lake District.

Fiona and I got together when Sophie was seven; my daughter immediately accepted Fiona as being part of her life, giving her the same love and affection that she gave me. Sophie continued to spend lots of time with us, so Fiona, George and I had to develop a way of managing our lives which enabled Sophie to be well loved and cared for while enabling her to spend time with both mum and dad.

Gregor was born when Sophie was ten: she and George were the first people to visit us when Fiona was still in Penrith Maternity Ward. Sophie loved Gregor, and enjoyed taking him out and about. When he was just eight years old Sophie (then eighteen) became a 'responsible adult' when she took him to Kendal Calling (Gregor's first music festival). Sophie was there with loads of her friends – they all loved it. This became an annual occurrence.

By the time Sophie turned to adulthood the relationship between me, Fiona and George had settled into an easy friendship. Despite the fact Sophie moved away to university, then subsequently onto work, the three of us saw each other on a regular basis.

Just as I was coming to the end of the tale we rounded a corner to find my ex-wife and 'the current Mrs Airey' walking towards us. It turned out that they had made their way to Kirkby Lonsdale separately because they weren't sure quite how the day would pan out. Almost as soon as they parked, they bumped into each other, worked out the way we would be approaching the town and came to find us.

As we walked into Kirkby Lonsdale, we spotted something a bit odd – loads of people lining the roadside. Was there something going on? We were a bit stunned to realise they were waiting for us! The throng began to clap and cheer as we walked past, many reaching out to shake our hands or giving us hugs – another surreal moment.

We stopped in Jubilee Park next to Devil's Bridge, a perfect place to take the weight off our feet and take on refreshment. It's a well-maintained grassy sward dotted with picnic benches and the odd tree. As well as being a visitor attraction in its own right Devil's Bridge is a well-known rendezvous for motorcyclists. There were dozens of people wandering around, many of whom came over to offer their encouragement and put money in our bucket.

After a while, Fiona said, 'Should we empty the bucket so I can take the money home?'

This was something we hadn't thought about in advance, but it was clearly necessary now. I cut the cable ties securing the lid and opened the bucket – it was almost full of notes! We tried to surreptitiously stuff all the cash into Fiona's shopping bag. She counted it on her return home – that one (partial) day's walking had raised almost £900 in cash! This was on top of the thousands that continued to be donated online, of course. We were stunned by the reach we'd achieved – it gave us plenty of food for thought and inspiration to keep going.

Two of Mike's friends, Elaine and her daughter (another Tash), turned up to see how we were getting on; they used to live in Sale but were now in Settle. Tash had been at school with Beth and insisted on buying ice-creams for us – the only problem being there was no ice-cream van anywhere nearby. After waiting a while for her to reappear, we decided that we really needed to get moving.

I stood up to put my rucksack back on and gave Fiona a big hug. 'I love you. Look after yourself.' The next time I would see my wife would be when we walked into King's Lynn, thirteen days further down the road. I knew that Fiona would miss me – and I would miss her too – but understood that she was totally supportive of everything we were doing. She had given me unwavering backing when we were planning the walk and was totally committed to doing whatever she could to help us make it to the finish.

As we continued on our way, crossing the triple-arched fourteenth-century Devil's Bridge, the throng of leather-clad motorcyclists stood to one side, many of them wishing us well and yet more pushing cash into the bucket.

We were back to being just three, as everyone who had walked with us earlier in the day needed to make their way home. This could give us a chance to decompress a little, take stock of what we'd experienced so far and have some time to just enjoy walking through this beautiful area.

Our next challenge would be to cross the busy A65, but the Sunday afternoon traffic was incessant. Eventually we saw a gap and ran. On safely reaching the other side we stepped down towards a kissing-gate that led into a field. As we pushed through the gate, we heard a shout – Tash was running towards us. She was across the road in a flash and presented us with tubs of delicious, locally made ice-cream.

We were just about to set off again when a young man with two children, a boy of about ten and a girl of around six, appeared above us, on the edge of the road. They all looked drawn. The dad said that his wife, the children's mother, had been taken by 'this dreadful disease' a couple of months before (unbeknown to us at the time, she was the beautiful Aimee pictured on the order of service in Mike's rucksack).

Our position in the field – below the road – meant that we looked directly into these children's faces. They looked confused, distraught, lost – it was unbelievably difficult to take in. We spoke to them for a little while; heaven knows what we said, as we were all overwhelmed by raw emotion. We just about held it together, and left them with our love and best wishes before we had to continue our own journey. It was all we could do.

We climbed away from Kirkby Lonsdale, walking poles tucked under our arms as we followed a footpath across a field, eating ice-cream with tears rolling down our faces. What could we say to make those kids' worlds any better? Nothing! We had to find a way we could stop other people going through this shattering experience.

The walk was becoming an incredibly powerful event. We could see that it helped people to share their stories of loss. The realisation that they were not alone gave them reassurance, and being completely open with others who knew how they were feeling gave them a sense of release. The grief of others had the potential to weigh us down or open our own deep wells of pain, so we three had to check in regularly and support each other, making sure our own mental health didn't suffer.

Quite often this came down to a brief, 'Are you OK?' We were beginning to appreciate what 'OK' could represent; it didn't have to mean that you were content or filled with joy – it could mean that you were sad or upset. The most important thing was to check that the emotions we were experiencing weren't having a detrimental impact on our overall mental well-being. It's OK to feel sad, guilty, angry, lost, disconnected . . . as long as you don't get stuck and begin to dwell on one thing. The understanding that 'OK' comes in many forms and accepting that it's normal for the emotions of grief to overwhelm without warning is a cathartic and liberating insight. It helps you to live – and to carry on living.

The conversation with Aimee's family had touched us to our core. It was hard to walk away from people who were obviously not OK. We hoped that the brief interaction with us had given the dad some hope that it was possible to put fragmented lives back into a shape that would allow his family to move forward.

As we exited the field, we left Cumbria and entered Lancashire. Back on a short section of the A65 verges, we approached Whoop Hall Hotel. At the entrance, a motorcyclist pulled up, removed his helmet and said: 'Are you the 3 Lads?'

'No, we're the 3 Dads.'

'Cancer?'

'No, suicide prevention.'

'Never mind. Here's twenty quid.'

With that, he was off.

From that moment, we wondered whether there was a group of three lads following our route across the country, questioning why no one had any cash to spare for their appeal. What would happen if our paths crossed?

Back on field paths once again, the 3 Dads Walking phone rang. It was a producer from the ITV show *Lorraine*. She said how inspirational the team found our walk and how impressed they were that three ordinary dads had managed to get the country talking about suicide prevention. She then went on to say that they would love to feature the finish of our walk live on Lorraine Kelly's show. We had to politely turn them down, saying that *BBC Breakfast* was already planning to do it. Having high-profile national television programmes queuing up to feature us was so strange; when it came down to it, we were just three blokes going for a walk. That said, we were beginning to realise what an impact our openness about our losses was starting to have.

More than six thousand people take their own lives in this country each year; we had also been told that, on average, every suicide has an impact on 135 other people. That means over eight hundred thousand people are directly affected by suicide *every* year. This doesn't consider those people who have taken their own lives but whose deaths are registered by coroners as being accidental, misadventure or as a narrative verdict (a factual statement that doesn't attribute cause to the individual). The official suicide statistics hugely understate the scale of the issue; they also don't record the thousands of people who attempt suicide and survive. There must be millions of people in the UK each year whose lives are touched by suicide, or attempted suicide, in one way or another. No wonder we were getting such a huge response.

Heading towards Wennington, we alternated between quiet country lanes and footpaths through fields. On one of the roads, we were intercepted by another two motorcyclists who'd been following our tracker and wanted to see us. One was the father of Cheyenne, who had taken her own life – he had been one of the first to donate to our JustGiving page.

Soon after leaving the motorcyclists we had to clamber onto the verge to make way for a car behind us. It drew to a halt and the window came down – Alan Hinkes again! He pulled in further along the road, got out, took more photos, walked along with us for a bit and told several non-PC jokes. It was a great way to be distracted towards the end of another long day.

We decided to film our video diary for the blog. 'What a belting day we've had,' I commented to camera.

Tim mentioned fantastic weather, fantastic people and that we were being bombarded with support, kindness, love . . . and food! We were in danger of putting on weight, despite the fact we were talking around fifty thousand steps every day.

'It's good to know that people think that what we are doing makes a difference,' Mike added. 'Powerful, powerful stories.'

The last couple of miles into Wennington seemed to go on for a long time. Physically I wasn't too weary, but the day's emotional conversations had taken their toll. The sun was setting as we were met by a local who walked us into the village centre, to be greeted by a small welcoming committee. We were more than pleased to spot Teena, our host for the night – she'd introduced herself to us at Devil's Bridge. As soon as we could leave – politely – we suggested that we should head off to our accommodation.

Teena led us round to Wennington railway station car park where she introduced us to her husband Malcolm. We chucked our rucksacks and Mike into Malcolm's van, Tim and I left with Teena, and a few minutes later arrived at their house in Burton-in-Lonsdale. Teena and Malcolm had come to our rescue when we were planning the walk. We had accommodation sorted along the whole route . . . apart from Wennington. We just couldn't find someone we knew, or a friend of a friend, who could help. When our website got up and running, we decided that we would put an appeal out on social media and within an hour Teena got back to us offering their Airbnb.

Teena said that she and Malcolm would be delighted if we joined them for an evening meal and she was more than happy to make us packed lunches for the following day. What a welcome for three strange blokes!

Teena and Malcolm were perfect hosts; the evening meal in their warm kitchen was fantastic – goulash soup followed by a chicken dish with baked potatoes and sticky toffee pudding to finish. There was more than we could eat, all this accompanied by Malcolm's excellent choice of local beer. Perfect food for three middle-aged long-distance walkers.

Before we retired to bed, I asked Teena a favour. 'Do you have any tinfoil?'

She looked a little perplexed and offered me the foil she had used to bake our potatoes.

'No, clean tinfoil. We need to wrap our tracker.'

Still looking quizzical, Teena produced tinfoil from one of the kitchen cupboards as I explained the need to 'shield' the tracker as we charged it overnight (this definitely sounded dodgy!). Once wrapped and plugged in we checked our Open Tracking page to find . . . no signal. Tim's idea worked! It made us speculate what Tim actually did in the military – was his RAF role a cover for a career as one of our spooks?!

We didn't have the capacity or energy that night to reflect on how we would cope with the physical and mental toll the walking and talking was taking on us. We already knew that we were making a positive impact on people's lives. We were quickly asleep, mentally and physically exhausted, full of food – and aware that we were making a difference.

Money raised (excluding Gift Aid and direct donations) = £235,000
Day 2 distance = 23.8 miles
Total distance walked = 46.8 miles

DAY 3

Wennington to Doeford Bridge

Before going to bed we'd agreed that since we would still be full in the morning, we would settle for a continental breakfast. At the start of Day 3, Teena produced croissants, toast, jam, fruit, yoghurt and ... bacon sandwiches! Continental breakfast, Teena-style. While we ate, Teena and Malcolm sorted that day's food into two bags each: one for lunch and another for snacks. We had enough food to get us half-way to King's Lynn, never mind the 20-something miles we were walking today!

As we carried our kit to Malcolm's van, the golden sunrise over Ingleborough promised a lovely day ahead. The previous evening we'd arrived in the dark, so we hadn't appreciated the beautiful backdrop to their house. Photos were taken of us with our banner before we headed back to Wennington.

In the railway station car park, we were joined by Bill, Sophie's uncle and my good friend. Like the three of us, he'd never walked in the Forest of Bowland, so he was keen to join us for the day to see what it was like.

We hugged Teena and Malcolm and as we walked away Malcolm was in tears ... we strode away quickly before it set us all off again. Although we'd only met the couple the previous day, sharing our stories and discussing emotional subjects over our evening meal had brought us very close in a short time. A clear manifestation of the power of talk.

For the first couple of miles out of Wennington, we followed footpaths over undulating meadows, through woodland and along quiet lanes. The air was still, the grass laden with dew. The golden dawn slowly transformed to give us clear blue skies and warm sunshine; what a fabulous start to a day I'd been looking forward to since planning the route. We chatted amiably as we walked, Tim and Mike finding out more about Bill. I'd known Bill since the 1980s when I first went out with his sister. After George and I split Bill and I remained firm friends, regularly going on walks that were always filled with conversation, debate and laughter.

Shortly after 8 a.m., I took a call from BBC Radio Cumbria, live on the *Mike Zeller Breakfast Show*. Tim took a couple more calls, the first from BBC Radio Norfolk who would call him at 3.40 p.m. for a live interview. The second was from his wife Sue. Tim had recently moved house and the lights had all blown upstairs. Despite the fact that Tim was up a hill in Lancashire 260 miles from home, he needed to sort it. While Mike, Bill and I focused on the beautiful morning views, Tim was making calls to Mark, his housebuilder. The problem turned out to have a silver lining – Mark had seen the TV coverage and donated!

We continued the gentle climb, regaining the road at Alcocks Farm, where we were met by a couple in a car. The man got out and greeted us.

'I was planning to walk with you, is that alright?'

Of course it was. Our new friend was Martin, a farmer from Lancashire; his daughter Tilly had taken her own life four weeks earlier and he was in the rawest state of grief. A friend had seen 3 Dads Walking on the TV and had mentioned us to him. He immediately decided that he needed to meet us so he could discover how we had begun to deal with the loss of our own daughters.

Martin was a lovely bloke, completely down to earth, and one of those farmers who is rooted in his place. His grief and confusion were clear to see, and the pain of his loss was etched on his face. He walked with a stave he had cut himself and had a gait that was most certainly agricultural. He looked like he was built to tramp across the countryside in the most economical manner.

As he fell into step with us, Martin told us about Tilly. Hers was another suicide that came out of the blue; another family not given the chance to seek help; another family shattered. We shared our stories and told him how we had come to the conclusion that we needed to create something positive from our losses.

Bill and Martin had much in common – Bill was a retired farmer, so they had the chance to chew the fat on all things agricultural.

'Where in Cumbria did you farm?' Martin asked Bill.

'I didn't farm in Cumbria, I just moved there. I farmed in Northumberland.'

'Where in Northumberland?'

'Wooler.'

'I know a bloke in Wooler, I sometimes see when I'm over there,' said Martin.

'Who's that?'

'Shorty.'

I burst out laughing. 'Shorty?! You know Shorty?!'

Shorty is the partner of George – Bill's sister, my ex-wife, Sophie's mum! It took a while for us all to stop chuckling over the coincidence.

We had been climbing gently for an hour or so in perfect weather, with blue skies offering breathtaking views. We stopped for a brew at Harterbeck Farm, and I took off my boots. I had to wring out my socks – the heavy morning dew on the grass had worked its way over the top of my boots and my socks were soaked. That's when I realised my schoolboy error . . . I'd not packed any spare socks in my rucksack.

I can't say I was particularly bothered at the time, as I'd walked with wet socks in the past. As long as they were made of merino wool it had been fine . . . up until today. Today would be the day when, for the first time in years, a wet sock would cause a significant and possibly walk-ending blister.

Strapped back into my boots and wet socks, we left the tarmacked road, picking up the Hornby Road – a track with a gentle climb into the heart of the Forest of Bowland, an ancient route that linked the Vale of Lune to the West Riding of Yorkshire. The air was clear, and the views opened up behind us. We were able to look back on our route of the previous two days and contemplate how far we'd come.

We looked out over the Vale of Lune, Ingleborough, Whernside and Pen-y-Ghent, the Yorkshire Three Peaks to our north-east and, further away to the north-west, the distant Lake District fells. This would be the last sight of my home ground; once we went over today's high point, the Lakes would be lost from sight.

Transition was the recurring theme in our journey: the changes in the English countryside over relatively short distances, the topography, the field boundaries, the type of agriculture, the architecture. This geographical transition reflected our emotional pilgrimage. Trying to find a way from the raw gaping hole of the initial loss, through anger, guilt, deep sadness and betrayal to some form of acceptance; whether you like it or not you have to find some way of being able to live your life. It can never be the same again – but it is fundamentally important to find a way to live *with* your grief because it will never go away.

The easy uphill gradient allowed us to cover the ground at some pace, and also enabled plenty of conversation. One or other of us was always alongside Martin. We hoped that we were helping him.

We told him how our world-shattering losses had changed our lives, how we slowly got back to living again, how that had created a desire to do something to help others, the way circumstances and our children had brought us together and ultimately led us to be walking over the Forest of Bowland.

Tim had heard about the Forest of Bowland from his eldest daughter who had completed her Duke of Edinburgh Gold expedition there and told him how beautiful the place was. Tim had presumed the Forest of Bowland would have trees but there were none. It transpired that 'Forest' was an ancient word for an area preserved for hunting, and didn't necessarily mean the landscape would be wooded.

We enjoyed sweeping views over the rolling moorland as we strode along the well-made track, eventually stopping for lunch at Salter Fell, our high point of the day. I asked Martin whether he would be happy to talk in front of the camera – he was, and I asked him why he'd joined us today.

'I recently lost my daughter to suicide and I need to understand why. I've got loads of unanswered questions,' he said. 'These like-minded people have all experienced the same thing. Talking about it really helps.'

'What's it been like walking with us?' I asked.

'I've really enjoyed it. We're all on the same wavelength. We've told our own stories and it's helped a lot. If it helps raise money for PAPYRUS that will be good. When I was brought up, we didn't talk about this. It was pushed into the closet, but this has opened my eyes.'

Martin's eloquent account summed up every conversation we had had with other suicide-bereaved people; sharing our stories with people who were going through the same experience was very powerful. Talking about our loved ones could never bring them back, but these conversations gave us all strength.

We took the opportunity to record our daily video diary. Mike began by saying how stunning the area was before Tim became more contemplative, saying, 'Today has been a day of reflection. Of walking and talking. Some conversations are really difficult, but they're so valuable to us and other people.'

Mike responded, 'People are reaching out to us. They believe in what we're doing. They believe that promoting open and supportive conversations with young people is the right thing to do.'

I agreed. 'The mantra of the day has been "Keep talking – talk, talk, talk".'

'Yes.' said Tim 'It's very uncomplicated.'

Mike signed off, 'We've had wonderful support so far. Thank you – it's much appreciated.'

Although I'd begun to feel a bit of friction on the sole of my right foot, it didn't feel like much, so I ignored it. A mile or so after our lunch stop we turned off the track onto an indistinct footpath that dropped into the Whitendale Valley. Walking through waist-high ferns and grasses, this spectacular V-shaped valley offered a change from the moorland track we had been on all morning.

As we reached the valley floor, the path dropped onto a lane where we were joined by Debbie, a friend of mine from Kendal, and Gary, a colleague of Tim's. They'd bumped into each other further down the valley and struck up a conversation, and quickly realised they were out looking for the same three blokes.

Debbie and Gary walked with us along the track as it followed the River Dunsop towards the hamlet of Dunsop Bridge. Here we met Jon – another mate of mine, a member of the Bowland Pennine Mountain Rescue Team. He was our lift and landlord for the night, so we were very happy to see him!

Our planned brief stop for refreshment at Dunsop Bridge turned into something of an extended hiatus. Tim had arranged to do an interview with Radio Norfolk during the afternoon, not realising that we would have no phone or 4G signal, so he asked at the nearby café whether he could piggyback on their Wi-Fi – they said yes, but it meant that we couldn't move on until the interview was completed. Unfortunately, rather than putting Tim on air immediately as they'd said they would,

Radio Norfolk proceeded to play two songs and do a travel report!

While waiting for Tim, Mike did an TV interview with Paul Crone for Granada, the ITV Northwest regional news. Paul was a very eccentric and lively character who was an old sparring partner of Dutch – Peter Holland, the PAPYRUS Media Manager. They had worked together in local news media for many years.

As Mike and Tim were doing their media duties, I checked my feet; my left foot was fine, but the underside of my right foot was developing a blister, right on the fleshy part behind my middle toe. I couldn't recall ever getting a blister there before. There was nothing I could do other than put my soggy socks and boots back on and keep going.

Interviews done, we said our goodbyes to Debbie and Gary. We were, now back to the group of five who had crossed the Hornby Road – the three of us, along with Bill and Martin. We were walking through the fields alongside the River Hodder, a much more pastoral scene than the upland landscape we had traversed earlier in the day. The heather-clad moorland dotted with shooting butts had been replaced by open pastures stocked with sheep and cattle grazing alongside the meandering river.

Bill became the gate-opener-in-chief. Mike piped up with 'Bill . . . Gates!' At the time, we thought this was hilarious (we'd obviously had too long a day).

Our forced stop at Dunsop Bridge meant that we approached Whitewell as dusk began to fall. It was a little frustrating to know that we would finish walking that day in the dark, but nature did provide a consolation: a barn owl silently glided across our path as we walked along the road. For the next few minutes, we watched as the owl meticulously searched for its next meal. This ghost-like bird soundlessly worked its way back and forth across a couple of meadows seeking out its chosen prey: voles, shrews, mice. It was a wonderful way to be escorted to The Inn At Whitewell as the light faded.

Charles Bowman, the owner of The Inn, had generously offered to feed 3 Dads Walking but – unfortunately – our walk didn't finish there. Because we needed to make Day 5 into Salford shorter, we had extended Days 3 and 4. Our finishing point was three miles further down the valley at Doeford Bridge, where we had arranged to meet Jon, who would bring us back to the Inn.

After having photos of the five of us taken outside the pub, Martin and Bill went inside to await their lifts. It had been a real pleasure to walk with the two men; Martin looked like a different person now, compared to the drawn and crushed bloke who'd joined us that morning. It was good to watch Martin and Bill chatting amicably together as they went into the pub. Talking is good.

When I thought about our time walking and talking with Martin, I realised that our time with Susanna on Day 1 had become something of a template for what happened every time we met someone who had suffered the loss of a child to suicide.

At first, we would talk about their child and the circumstances surrounding their suicide, then we would move on to the aftermath, the pain and anguish we all suffered, and begin to discuss how we manage to keep on living. We'd then talk about how we'd got to where we were. Eventually the conversation would drift away from suicide and the impact it was having on us – walking through the English country-side ensured that we were continually distracted by the changing vistas around us. Sooner or later, we'd find ourselves talking about topics other than suicide and suicide prevention: the views, friends and family, news, politics, the weather, local history, sport, films, books, TV – you name it, we'd talk about it.

We turned away from the pub and set off into the gathering twilight. Over the next three miles, it got dark, wet and muddy (Mike and Tim jokingly blamed this on me, of course). Walking with our path illuminated by headtorches, it seemed to take an age to get to the rendezvous point – but we made it. It was quite a relief to get to the bridge and find Jon waiting for us.

We piled rucksacks and tired bodies into Jon's Fiesta and away we went at breakneck speed! We wondered if he was channelling his inner Colin McRae. In the back of the car, Mike and I were struck dumb, and in the front, Tim thought he was reliving his time as an RAF Tornado navigator.

After our short white-knuckle ride, we arrived back at The Inn At Whitewell . . . in one piece! We staggered into the pub to be greeted by Dutch and his wife, the Dutchess. We joined their table, ordering beers and food – a steak for me, and fish and chips for Mike and Tim. The food was courtesy of the pub and our drinks were covered by Dutch.

On finishing our meal, we thanked the staff at The Inn and took our life in our hands again, trusting Jon to drive us to our accommodation – Smelt Mill, the Bowland Mountain Rescue Team's base on the south side of their territory, a row of old terraced houses that had been converted into a communication centre, garage and bunkhouse. We were very grateful that the team had readily offered us the use of their facilities.

We were in bunkbeds on the first floor at the top of a flight of steep stairs, and the toilets, showers and seating area were on the ground floor. Going up and down these stairs really hurt our tired legs! That said, the place was small but perfectly formed. The living space had a few soft sofas and was heated by a toasty woodburning stove – having been well fed and watered at Whitewell, the warmth of the room and the comfy seats soon had us preparing for bed.

Just before we retired, I rechecked my feet. The soggy sock in my right boot had done a great job of inducing a blister, about the size of a penny, on the fleshy part by the ball of my foot. It didn't look good. When I stood up, it felt like I was standing on a pea. All I could do was ensure that it was protected once we started walking in the morning.

When we were planning the walk we discussed numerous hypothetical scenarios, including what would happen if one of us couldn't continue. We'd decided that if one of us was incapacitated the other two would carry on. That night I went to bed wondering if the problem I was having with my foot would force us to make a decision I didn't want to contemplate.

Since Sophie's death in 2018 my life had taken an abrupt change of direction; I had chosen to become immersed in the world of suicide prevention. I had become determined to keep going, keep talking, to make a difference. This had brought me here, in a bunkbed sharing a cramped room with two other suicide-bereaved dads who were as determined as me to do something positive. However, I now had a growing doubt about my ability to make it to the end of our walk. Was this small but extremely painful injury going to prevent me from walking to Norfolk? All I could do was protect the wound as best I could, grit my teeth and carry on. We had over 250 miles to go . . .

Money raised (excluding Gift Aid and direct donations)
= £242,885
Day 3 distance = 22.8 miles
Total distance walked = 69.6 miles

DAY 4

Doeford Bridge to Darwen

I woke to Tim's cheery greeting of, 'Morning, chap!' He went on, 'My God, you were snoring well last night.' I'd been blissfully unaware, but Mike agreed that I had been making a bit of a din. Sorry, chaps.

The limited space in the bunkroom meant we were on top of each other as we sorted our kit. Amongst the chaos of three men sorting rucksacks, kitbags and provisions for the day, I inspected the sole of my right foot. The blister was unburst, but the flesh around it was looking sore. I took some tape and padding out of our first aid kit and applied protection as best I could. After putting my boots on I stood up gingerly. It didn't feel great. In fact, it felt very uncomfortable and quite painful. I popped a couple of Ibuprofen. 'It'll be fine,' I thought.

We picked up our rucksacks and headed out to Jon's car, the Flying Fiesta – and thankfully arrived at Doeford Bridge without mishap! There we were both surprised and pleased to find Sarla (our friend from Morland who'd volunteered to look after us on Day 4): she'd been due to meet us at our morning coffee stop, but had decided to come and see us off. She was going to support us on Day 4, crossing the broad Ribble Valley and onto the hills to the west of Blackburn before climbing Darwen Hill and dropping off the moors close to Edgworth. With well over

3,000 feet of climbing in total it was going to be a tough day (especially for my foot).

We bade Jon and Sarla farewell at 7.30 a.m. and found our chosen footpath which led into a field. After walking a hundred metres or so we realised there was no obvious way out of it: no sign, no gate, no stile. Not a good start . . .

Here's when the OS Maps app on our phones proved its worth. As part of the planning process, we had created digital versions of our daily routes. All we needed to do was open the app and press the locate button; this would show us exactly where we were, and we could retrace our steps to intercept the footpath marked on the digital map. A bit of searching led us to a collapsed stile and wobbly plank over a muddy patch, hidden under an untrimmed hedge. No wonder we couldn't find it.

In field number two, the map showed that the footpath ran directly to a lane at the far end. In reality we found that it had been blocked by a new-build house, so we had to make up our own route to eventually regain the track we wanted. These two fields set the tone for the day – the Lancastrian footpaths we used weren't that well signposted or maintained.

Our first climb of the day was onto Longridge Fell: a short, sharp ascent to a trigonometry (trig) point (a stone or concrete pillar installed by Ordnance Survey as a fixed point from which surveys were conducted). It should've given us great views back to the Forest of Bowland and out towards the Irish Sea; unfortunately, as we plodded up the steep slope the clouds descended and cloaked the ridge . . . although as we came through forestry on the south side of the fell we caught a glimpse of the view over the broad Ribble Valley to the hills beyond Blackburn, our destination for today's walk. One climb done; three more to go.

We walked onwards towards Ribchester Bridge, but not before we came to another stile that was hidden by an over-grown hedge and an unsigned right of way through a large farm. Again, the OS locate button pointed us in the right direction. We couldn't understand why the farm owners didn't make sure footpaths across their land were clearly signposted; surely they would prefer walkers to stay on the correct path rather than wander off aimlessly?

Our route from Longridge Fell sloped gently to the south; we walked through farmyards, meadows and coppices as we made our way gradually towards the River Ribble. Coming down the lane at New Row we could see a vision waving a PAPYRUS flag at the road junction – it was Sarla. We found that she had secured a roadside bench, attached the 3 Dads banner to the hedge behind it and was on hand to offer tea, coffee, cake and whatever else we needed. I removed my right boot and inspected the damage. The blister had burst – that was good, wasn't it? The pressure had been released and it no longer felt like I had a pea in my boot, but the blister had been so deep that the flesh beneath the loose skin was red raw. I applied a fresh dressing and took another Ibuprofen. There wasn't much more that I could do; I had to keep walking.

This was going to be painful, but pain can be managed and wounds heal. Having come so far stopping was never going to be an option. I was determined to make it (on foot) all the way to Norfolk. Because we spoke about our girls every day, the feeling of Sophie being with me was palpable. It was as if she was there, whispering in my ear, 'Go on, Dad, you can do this.' As I put the first aid kit back into my rucksack I looked at the photo of Sophie I was carrying. 'Yes, Soph,' I thought. 'I *can* do this.'

Despite Sarla's best efforts to force feed us her tea loaf, we made our excuses and headed on our way. We had plenty of downhill still to go towards the river and crossed lots of fields – mostly without any waymarks or signs – but we were happy with our route-finding. Tim and I had fallen into a comfortable routine, with one of us regularly checking the route on the OS app, cross-checking with the other to determine the correct way, distance covered and, most importantly, how far to go. Mike left us to it; we had discovered that navigation wasn't his strong point.

On we went, enjoying each other's company – the morning's walk was filled with laughter until Tim began to express his frustration at the Dominic Cummings fiasco (the government adviser who flouted the rules of lockdown, quoting his love for his family as the reason) not least because Tim – while following the rules – had lost his daughter during the pandemic. As he stomped on, his justified anger descended into a full-blown rant about Cummings and his lack of adherence to the rules. Despite Tim's diatribe being ultra-serious, once Mike pointed out how he was reminded of Basil Fawlty from the BBC series *Fawlty Towers*, we burst out laughing . . . and took quite a while to stop.

We knew that a BBC news crew would be waiting for us at Ribchester Bridge, so we pushed on to get there at the agreed time. Unfortunately (no doubt talking too much) we missed the footpath that would take us directly to the bridge and had to complete a half-mile diversion (everyone checking our route via the website could see we'd gone off course too).

The BBC crew were at the bridge. They'd obviously been following our tracker, as they had the camera pointing down the wrong (but right) road. The interview took a little while because several people stopped to give us cash, and the TV crew used the opportunity to interview them about why they wanted to support us. It all felt a bit surreal.

Sarla was there to check we were OK. She'd also commandeered a couple of road maintenance signs and used them to hold the 3 Dads banner on the approach to the river crossing – if you were travelling over Ribchester Bridge that day, you couldn't avoid noticing it.

Aware we were running behind time, we wanted to get away, but just before we set off, one of the women who'd stopped said that she'd noticed that our planned route took us away from the Ribble up the course of a Roman road. She told us that it was a very muddy path and we would do better heading further up the A-road before turning right. It sounded sensible, so that's what we did – it's always good to listen to local knowledge.

As we walked up the road the BBC camerawoman kept leap-frogging us in her van to take 'action shots' of us three middle-aged men walking along. As we turned off the road we saw Steve, a friend of mine from my time in the outdoor trade, who'd used our tracker to find us. He gave us more cash for the bucket and a big hug. 'I was seeing a client in Preston this morning and just had to come out and see you,' said Steve. 'You, Mike and Tim are doing a wonderful thing. You're all over the telly and people are listening to what you're saying.'

He went on, 'Keep up this great work. You're saving lives.'

Steve's unexpected arrival and his kind words prompted me to a few tears. I gave him another big hug as we set off again.

Although we'd started the day on our own, in the last half hour before reaching Ribchester Bridge we'd been approached by loads of people offering encouragement, giving us cash and expressing gratitude for what we were doing. It made me think about the wider impact we were having across the country; if we could introduce PAPYRUS to more families and prompt some conversations about suicide prevention, we knew we could save lives. All these interactions showed us that our voices were being heard.

Climbing away from the Ribble Valley on quiet lanes towards Mellor, Mike, who had been checking his phone, said, 'Someone's sent us a poem.'

To which Tim replied, 'Don't read the poem, Mike.'

'Don't read the poem,' I echoed. Both of us realised that, if the poem was remotely good, it would provoke a tearful breakdown – but Mike read the poem:

Our Girls

We can still hear all the giggles,
See the smiles and feel the love
For our gorgeous girls who left us
Yet have given us a shove
To step out into all weathers
As the road ahead uncurls.
We're out walking,
We're out talking,
We're out walking with our girls.

We three know the depths of sorrow.
We've lost count of all the tears
But we've found our hearts and legs again
And hope to crush the fears
Of the lonely, frightened, helpless
As their turmoil twists and swirls.
We're out walking,
We're out talking,
We're out walking with our girls.

So, we're striding down the country.
If you see us, give a wave.
Even better, find your wallet
Or look up our 'giving' page.
If we help a few and save them
As these scenes of life unfurl.
Now you're talking!
We're out walking.
We're out walking for our girls.

For Beth, Emily and Sophie
Every good wish, Helen Taylor, Coventry

By the time Mike got to the end of the first verse we had stopped walking; by the end we were all in floods of tears. We leant on a gate and had a really good cry.

Wow. What a lovely, thoughtful poem. We were incredibly touched and decided that we would have to thank Helen for her wonderful words.

Once we pulled ourselves together, we got moving again along a very tidy driveway which gave way to a rather muddy, unloved piece of ground. We checked the OS app – we were on the right track, on a footpath still going uphill, but it was obviously not well used. The conditions underfoot became progressively worse until we reached a paddock by a house; the way was completely blocked by electric fences. We rechecked the map – we were definitely on the right of way. So we climbed over the electric fences . . . and only two of us got a shock (Tim's longer legs helped him!).

The house had a number of 'Private/Keep Out' signs, along with one portraying a snarling dog and the words, 'This dog can reach the gate in 10 seconds, how fast can you get there?' We got the feeling that the owner didn't particularly like people walking through his land. (On our return home we reported the blockage to the Lancashire Public Rights of Way Officer who had the footpath reinstated.)

Our country is blessed with thousands of miles of public rights of way as well as huge areas of open access land. It is incredibly important to maintain and defend these rights of access; we all benefit by being able to walk in and enjoy our countryside – the three of us are living proof of the restorative powers that direct connection to the countryside can bestow.

Sitting on the crest of our second ridge of the day was Mellor, the village where Sarla said she'd set up our lunch stop. Our path crossed a couple of fields on Mellor Moor, still showing the faint outline of a Roman camp, with views to the west overlooking the huge aerodrome of Samlesbury – two distinctly different military installations, separated by two millennia. As we approached the village we saw Sarla madly waving her PAPYRUS flag. What a welcome! She led us through the narrow streets to The Millstone, where she had arranged to use the pub's picnic benches for our lunch stop. She had also told a couple of workmen who were digging up the road that they had to stop when we arrived – which they did.

Together with her sister Margaret – with whom she was staying for a couple of nights – Sarla had produced enough food to feed a small army. We made a good effort, eating all kinds of delights – the highlight being Margaret's sausage rolls with chilli jam. As we sat outside the pub, more people came up to talk to us, some who had lost loved ones to suicide, others who wanted to wish us well. We made sure everyone was offered something to eat – there was more than enough to go round.

Just before we left Mellor, a car screeched to a halt in front of us (which was a bit of a shock for the driver of the car just behind). A woman jumped out, narrowly avoiding getting run over by the second vehicle, and shouted, 'I've seen you on the telly! Let me give you some money.' Mike and Tim pointed to the bucket on my back, into which she poured a purse-full of coins.

Mike and Tim laughed. 'Andy *loves* change!'

Funnily enough I didn't laugh quite as much as the other two – it was more ballast to carry!

Our brief conversation with this lady revealed that she had lost her son to suicide five years previously, hence the emergency stop. With so many people stepping forward to share their stories with us it was blatantly obvious that suicide was everywhere. The question we began to ask was, 'Why aren't we talking about it?'

In the UK, we seem to have chosen to ignore the biggest killer of under thirty-fives in the country. Imagine if two hundred school children died annually in school bus accidents, or if eighteen hundred young people died every year drinking contaminated alco-pops. The powers that be would react immediately, inquiries would be held, research done, answers found and lives saved. However, because suicide is hidden behind stigma and taboo those deaths are seen as individual tragedies. It's only when you stand back and see the bigger picture that you begin to understand that we, as a society, are blinkered to the biggest risk in our young people's lives. We need to get real. We need to SHOUT about this. We are allowing lives to be lost unnecessarily. Something needs to be done.

Over the remainder of the walk ideas would begin to form as we started to realise that WE needed to do something. We were developing an overview of how suicide was devastating families across the country; we couldn't ignore what we were seeing. We refused to stand by and let preventable deaths continue to happen . . . but what could we do?

As we walked out of Mellor, the 3 Dads Walking phone rang. I answered with a cheerful, 'Hello, 3 Dads Walking.'

I knew immediately that this was going to be serious. Here was a woman in distress, her words pouring out amongst sobs and cries. She was calling to ask for help with her son, who was feeling suicidal. She had seen us on TV, searched for our website and dialled our number. It sounded like she was at breaking point. It was good that she had reached out, but we weren't (and still aren't) suicide-prevention specialists – we were just three blokes walking across a field in Lancashire.

I listened until she stopped talking and then carefully explained that we weren't the ones who could help her, but we knew people who would. I directed her to HOPELINE247, reading the number off my wristband before saying goodbye and wishing her and her son well. We looked at each other and realised that we had just appeared on the front line of suicide prevention – we might have just helped save a young man's life. The key was not to try and be the expert, to have the answers, but to know where help could be found. We could signpost those in need of help and advice and direct them to the most relevant place.

HOPELINE247 is staffed by fully trained mental-health professionals who are there for young people in times of crisis and concerned others who are looking for support. They can help create a safe plan that will enable those who are suffering to deal with their suicidal thoughts and plot a way forward to a safe and satisfying life. They are lifesaving superheroes.

Throughout the day we were regularly being updated by Dutch. Heart Breakfast wanted an interview for Amanda Holden and Jamie Theakston's radio show – they would call back later. In addition, *The Times* newspaper wanted to cover the story in its Saturday supplement and Tim had been offered up – the reporter would call tomorrow at 7 a.m.

A short downhill section was followed by another climb, this time towards Billinge Hill and Witton Country Park where we joined the Witton Weavers Way, a National Trail that conveniently followed our overall direction of travel south. We were now a couple of miles away from the centre of Blackburn, an industrial town nestled into the hills north of Manchester, but despite the proximity of the urban area the countryside we were walking through was peaceful and pleasant. We got a view from the ridge looking across the north Lancashire plain over Preston to Blackpool and the Fylde coast, with the southern Lakeland fells still in sight. You don't need to get far away from a town to feel completely immersed in the natural environment.

We walked through the forested country park, the path zigzagging between mature oak trees. We'd not seen anyone else out walking but then, close to the River Darwen, a woman approached us. We said our hellos as we passed each other. She walked on a few yards before turning to shout, 'It's you, isn't it? I've seen you on the telly!'

'Yes, it's us!' we replied as she came back to drop more cash in our bucket.

We crossed the River Darwen and the railway line close to Cherry Tree Station, where we were met by Dutch along with Harry Biggs-Davison, chair of the PAPYRUS trustees. Harry wanted to walk with us for a little while and he took the opportunity to tell us that our fundraising had now reached £314,000 on JustGiving and around £60,000 more from direct donations.

We walked and talked with Harry. He told us about the death of his son Patrick, and the challenges he and his family had faced in the run-up to Patrick's suicide. We all have different stories but the outcome is the same – shattered lives left behind. All of us wanted to help other families avoid going through the same harrowing situation.

As we climbed away from Cherry Tree we walked through a new housing estate, still on the Witton Weavers Way. We came to a barrier: the estate was being extended. Metal fences barred the way and a sign said the closure was in place due to heavy machinery being used across the site. We looked up the route – we only had to cross 400 metres . . . should we pull back the barrier and run for it?

Before we had chance to act, a bloke in a hard hat and hi-vis jacket appeared, 'You can't go through there,' he said. 'It's closed.'

'But we're walking to King's Lynn and our path goes through here,' I said. 'Are you telling us you're blocking our 300-mile charity walk?'

'You'll have to go to the site office. Back down the hill.'

We discussed our options (including barging past the hi-vis man) and decided that finding the site office was the right thing to do. We turned around and trundled down the hill. We shouted up to the office window, asking for the site manager, and several faces appeared through doors and windows.

Tim said, 'We're the 3 Dads Walking. Our daughters all killed themselves and you're stopping our charity walk to King's Lynn. We need to get across your site.'

Taking on board our flags, our cause and our request, one of the construction workers said, 'I've seen you on the telly.' With that, several people came down to talk to us. It was quickly agreed that we could be escorted along the closed path – the one thing they wanted in return was a photo of us standing outside their sales office! We duly obliged.

As we walked through the estate one of the guys told Tim that his best friend had killed himself a year earlier, so our walk had particular poignancy for him (suicide is particularly high among construction workers – 507 took their own lives in 2021, according to the British Safety Council).

We continued on our way, but it wasn't too long till we were in trouble again. Almost immediately after crossing the next road, we were off route once again – another farm with no footpath signs. We could see the remains of a stile but it had been thrown to one side. After a bit of to-ing-and-fro-ing we plumped for a gate into a field.

Away we went . . . the wrong way. It took a while for the penny to drop, but by the time it did we'd almost reached the bottom of the field and could see the track we needed, just over the tall hedge. There had to be a gate, but there wasn't. It was a *long* field and we really couldn't be bothered to trail all the way back, so we decided to climb the barbed-wire fence separating us from the field which held the path. We now had four middle-aged blokes trying to do something they'd rather not – and certainly were no longer built for. Unfortunately, Harry videoed our efforts, so our less-than-graceful fence-climbing skills have been saved for posterity! Amazingly we all cleared the barrier without ripping our clothes or damaging ourselves (other than our dignity taking a bit of a knock). At least we were back on track.

On leaving Cherry Tree we had picked up the Witton Weavers Way again. We were delighted to be following a National Trail as we came to the final section of the day. The last few miles would be in darkness, so having good underfoot conditions and a waymarked route would be of great benefit.

We dropped across a field to cross a brook in a small wood before beginning a gentle climb through more meadows towards the village of Tockholes. This was the start of the longest climb of our day – all the way to the top of Darwen Hill.

We arrived at the village hall in Tockholes for a quick pitstop with Sarla before our ascent of the hills and the moor beyond . . . Before we finished our food stop it started to rain, gently at first, but the threatening sky promised a proper soaking. Rather than wait till it got worse, we put on our waterproof jackets and pants again.

A quick check of my foot confirmed what I'd feared: the flesh around the burst blister was looking very raw. It hurt, but what could I do? I redressed it, put new socks on and popped a couple of Ibuprofen.

As we were getting our kit sorted, Harry told us that although he'd love to keep going he needed to get to the station to catch his train back to London – he'd come up on the train that morning, a several hundred-mile round trip to go for a walk with us – what a star! I'd been delighted to be told that Harry was going to walk with us, but astonished to discover the lengths he'd gone to in order to walk with us that day. More hugs all round before he left us.

Over the small rise beyond Tockholes we dropped down to Earnsdale Reservoir then joined a lane which took us onto the lower slopes of Darwen Hill. The light was beginning to fade and the summit was shrouded in mist (we were getting used to this). We knew that our high point was going to be Darwen Tower, an 85-foot octagonal tower erected in 1898 to commemorate Queen Victoria's Jubilee and celebrate the locals gaining access to the moors. The view from the top was said to be stupendous, reaching from the Peak District across North Yorkshire and back to the Lake District, before taking in the more distant mountains of North Wales and across the Irish Sea to the Isle of Man. We fell into silence as we climbed, each of us breathing deeply on our own path to the top. The Darwen Tower remained invisible until we were right on top of it – our view, once again, the inside of a cloud.

Tim reached the summit – 1,220 feet above sea level – first, and gleefully pointed out that the Norfolk flatlander had beaten the northern hill folk! After a couple of photos in the gathering gloom we set off. However, it wasn't long till Tim hurried back to the top – in his victorious excitement he'd left his walking poles leaning against the trig point.

Walking in the dark with headtorches in the lashing rain wasn't the most pleasurable way to negotiate the last few miles of our hardest day. I tried to put brain and body into autopilot; there was nothing I could do to make the next section any easier so I needed to ignore my tiredness and the throbbing pain in my foot and just do it! Tim led the way for the simple reason that his headtorch, a gift from his good friend Rich (who would support us near the end of the walk), was by far the brightest.

Unfortunately the Witton Weavers Way let us down once it turned away from Darwen Tower. Despite being a National Trail it reduced to a narrow groove containing trip hazards every few yards, the path mostly hidden under long wet grass.

Tim and I constantly checked the navigation. We couldn't afford to get it wrong up there on the exposed moorland. We seemed to be moving at a snail's pace – but at least we were still moving.

Our path took us through a small forest as the darkness deepened. Rain blurred our vision and soaked the path, while branches snagged our PAPYRUS flags. Staggering over this boggy ground provoked a colourful string of expletives.

At that moment, the 3 Dads Walking phone rang – I answered and it was a chap who wanted to congratulate us on our achievement and tell us how inspirational we were ... lovely, but possibly not the best timing. Our telephone supporter was hugely enthusiastic about everything we were doing, so I struggled to get a word in. Eventually I managed to thank him for his call but explained that even though it was 7.30 p.m. and dark, we were still walking, stuck in a forest and *still* an hour away from the pub.

On we staggered, out of the forest and onto the moor, micronavigating our way through the wet, windy conditions. We eventually picked up the track that led to Cadshaw Farm and our rendezvous with Sarla ... and there she was! A sight for sore eyes. We got to her car at 8.30 p.m. – thirteen hours after we'd started, having ascended four separate ridges and climbed over 3,200 feet. What a day! As for the Witton Weavers Way ... if we ever met a Witton Weaver, we would know where to stick his loom!

On the drive to the pub, I felt guilty about the call I had cut short earlier so called back. It turned out that the caller was Swasie Turner, a Liverpudlian police officer who'd lost his career and right leg to an act of violence in the line of duty. Swasie had since pushed his wheelchair thousands of miles, all over the world to raise huge amounts for charity. He'd seen 3 Dads Walking and wanted to praise us for our efforts and contribute to our appeal. It was humbling to know that this committed fundraiser felt urged to congratulate us on our efforts. Thank you, Swasie.

Sarla had booked us a table at the Toby Inn, Edgworth – it was a huge relief to be sat down in a warm and welcoming pub after our long and tiring day. And there was more: one of the staff told us that not only would the pub cover all our food and drink, they would also match the value of our meal with a dona-tion to our JustGiving page! It was in our interest to eat and drink as much as we could! But we were so exhausted that we only ordered a pizza and beer each. The pub refused to bring us so little, so added garlic bread and chips. We managed to eat most of it, but when it came to Tim's second pint of beer, he was beaten. Neither I nor Mike could help him out, so we walked away from half a pint. Unheard of.

Before we left, the bar staff wanted a photo with us. We obliged, as we couldn't believe these young people wanted to be seen or associated with us. We were just about to leave the pub when the staff member who'd served us opened up. 'I lost my best friend to suicide last year,' he said. No wonder he'd gone out of his way to help us.

Comfort greeted us at the beautiful Quarlton Fold Farm. Today had been particularly challenging; we had covered close to 25 miles and climbed over 3,200 feet (much of it in the rain, and the last two hours in the dark). When we had planned the walk, Day 4 had always looked likely to be the toughest; I certainly hoped so, because I felt physically exhausted and so tired that my brain seemed full of mush. I needed sleep before I could contemplate the 200+ miles we still had to cover.

When we walked out of Morland I barely knew Mike and Tim. Now, after covering almost 100 miles in their company, I'd come to know more about the character and personalities of these men and I knew that they would be friends for life. Meeting Mike and Tim was entirely down to Sophie making the worst decision of her life. I would have loved never to have had the opportunity to meet them . . . but that wasn't an option. I would be up and walking with them again in the morning – and Sophie would have loved them.

Before falling asleep, I inspected my foot. The blister now looked more like an open wound. It was bloody sore. I couldn't think of anything more I could do with it other than keep it clean and well padded. It looked like I'd be taking more Ibuprofen tomorrow.

Lights out, eyes shut . . . sleep.

Money raised (excluding Gift Aid and direct donations)
    = £251,297
Day 4 distance = 24.8 miles
Total distance walked = 94.4 miles

PART TWO

Mike and Beth

Never in a million years would I have ever imagined my youngest daughter Beth taking her own life. However, on 28 March 2020, she did just that, plunging her family and friends into the most unimaginable grief. She was seventeen years and eight months old.

Where do we go from here? The easy option for me would be to lie down and die. Believe me I want to. Kill myself, give up on life, drink myself into oblivion and f—k the world for dealing us such a cruel blow. Dramatic, I know, but so true.

However, it's not that easy. Beth left behind family and friends who love and miss her deeply, but still have their own lives to live. I am part of their world whether I like it or not. The thought of them going through this pain again wracks me with guilt. But Beth's actions have left a huge fallout. The word 'devastation' does not even come close. Moving forward without my little girl is too hard to comprehend.

The truth is I have never written in my life, but there are so many words in my head and I feel the need to share them. The story of Beth Palmer needs to be told. Too many precious young lives are being lost. My aim is to diary every emotion and feeling as we try to move forward with Beth's memory and make a 'new normal'. Make no mistake, she was a big character and her loss is being felt deeply.

Now that we are reluctant members of this new 'club' it is clear we are not alone on this deeply rutted road. I hope young adults will read this and reconsider making decisions that allow no second chance. Beth fell into despair when I believe there was hope. A wonderful life lay ahead for this beautiful young woman. If only she could have seen it.

Since Beth's passing, time has moved on as if I am in a dream. A nightmare with no end. No waking and getting on with life. Utter shock and disbelief have overwhelmed once normal happy family stuff.

It is very easy to get lost in your own despair and we all grieve on different levels. Helen [Beth's mum and my wife] and I are prime examples. I need to talk, constantly going over the same things on a loop. Up to ten unofficial counsellors in a day. Helen is quiet, spending time on Beth's bed, often crying. Both of us are simply heartbroken inside.

Our daughter Emily, the other family member living at home, has found some sort of solace with her boyfriend Matt, who has been so good. We do worry about Em, though, as she is being so brave – we suspect it is to protect her mum and dad. Watch her, we will. Her little sister was an enormous part of her life.

Saturday 28 March

I had been on nights and had walked Monty, our dog, with Helen in the morning before falling asleep downstairs on the sofa. Around midday I was roused by a scream that at first my groggy mind attributed to Beth messing around with Monty. Further screams became more desperate. I leapt upstairs, but my fire-service experience told me it was too late – my baby had gone.

A living hell then takes over. Everything you love and take for granted is turned upside down. Your home, your haven, your safe place is full of green and black uniforms.

Emotions smash through your body: shock, disbelief, anguish, magnified a thousandfold. Question after question from face-less people.

Trying to protect Helen and Emily is my first instinct but as the realisation hits, I am rendered useless. Great tearless sobs rip through my body. Emily cries for her little sister.

The rest of the day is surreal. Important people come and go. Who they are or were, I could not say. Pointless questions that do nothing to bring Beth back. Helen and I could not even cry – the shock was too great.

Making phone calls to relatives was so tough. The first I made to Helen's brother, Dave. You start the call with 'Hiya mate, how are ya?' – then you tell him his beloved niece has taken her own life. This is the 'ripple effect' – the shock and disbelief begin to reach out.

Dave tells Auntie Donna, then cousins, Jess and Daisy. Nana and Grandad are next. Then it is my sister, Auntie Lindsey, with Uncle Ally and cousin Brodie in Scotland, followed by Beth's half-sister, Charley. All are beside themselves.

Social distancing takes a back seat as family and friends gather and give solace the best they can, until they gradually melt away and only Helen, Emily, Matt, me – and a crushing realisation that Beth is no more – remain.

Thursday 9 April

Funeral.

My beautiful Beth, my darling girl.

From the moment I set eyes on you I loved you with all my heart, always have done and always will.

Your life was full of fun, family, mischief, friends, dark fruits, dance, fake tan, laughter, music and your utterly beautiful voice, but above everything your life was and still is full of love.

I know you have found peace, I know you are all around us.

Bethany Harriet, I love you more than anything in the world.

Night, night and God Bless X

By Helen, Beth's mum

Covid-19 had been a massive factor in Beth's death. Its impact was felt at the funeral too, with only ten close family members allowed in the chapel. To be cremating your daughter, who just over a week ago was filling the family home with music and laughter, smashes you with an anguish and sadness completely off the scale.

Friends, family and workmates lined the route. All socially distanced. My fire colleagues and the police also paid tribute. The outpouring of love was truly astounding. I cried my eyes out while my brother-in-law drove us there and back.

In fact, everything about the day was beautiful, but inside I

114

was screaming, 'Beth – what the f—k have you done? Everyone loves you – yet you've thrown everything away.'

Saturday 18 April

Four forty-five in the morning, and the sleeping tablets have released me from their dreamless grip. I lie next to Helen, not moving, listening and feeling her anguish as she sleeps. Anger starts to creep through me, each question unanswered:

- Why my family?
- What have we done to deserve this?
- How can we survive the pain?
- How can I regain enough strength to carry on?

Then my sights turn to Beth:

- How could you do this to the very beings who loved you more than life itself and who I know you loved back?
- How could you plunge us into a world of grief with seemingly no end?
- How could you throw away all your dreams?
- How could you let us discover you like we did?

I get out of bed and make my early counselling call to my sister Lindsey. I vent quite unfairly to her and she gives all the right answers, as she always does. It is becoming increasingly obvious talking helps, but there are no real solutions. We are on the Road of Grief – and it's a foul place.

Monty the dog gets walked very early. I want to avoid people. The angry internal rantings at Beth continue. Truly, I thought she was stronger than this. I stand by the waterpark and let out a silent scream. Tears will not come today.

Still, before 7.30 I am back home and start writing. The days seem so long, especially with the lockdown – nothing to look forward to but a bit of decorating.

The house is still full of sympathy cards. Helen has read them all and wept at the beautiful words. It is not for me – they just remind me of a beautiful daughter who made a rash decision and threw her life away.

Helen went shopping this morning. I selfishly didn't want to. I just did not want to talk to anyone else. Masked and gloved up against the Covid-19 virus, she felt relieved she was not instantly recognisable to the other Aldi customers.

It is tough in the outside world away from lockdown because Beth is everywhere. Helen broke down when she came home. Passing the Metrolink station Beth used so often was too much.

Deep sadness is a term I would use to describe my mood at present, with the occasional black hole when the Diazepam wears off. All normal aspects of grief, I hear you say – but so tough to deal with.

Afternoon naps were once a guilty pleasure, but today images of Beth turn through my mind like a never-ending picture show. I seek Helen and find her once again on Beth's bed, snuggling a jumper that still smells of our daughter's perfume. My coping mechanisms are very different. I avoid looking at photos, listening to her recordings, reading bereavement cards and looking at Facebook. I am pushing my little girl to the back of my mind.

I ring my eldest daughter, Charley, regretfully making her cry by going over old ground. Sometimes grief is selfish and you become inconsiderate of other grieving souls. My work colleague Russ is my next call and he listens patiently, giving advice and encouragement. After hanging up I return to the same lonely place. Time for another Diazepam.

Days seem to last for ever and I am sent into another black hole by inadvertently clicking on Facebook and bringing up a picture of Beth and Alice, a good friend, with the text, 'Miss you so much my angel'. Must try to be more careful.

Speak to Linz, Ally, Charley and Neil P., a work colleague and good friend. All are wonderfully patient listening to my ramblings.

Helen and Emily occupy themselves making cookies. Glad they are having some fun.

Cannot wait for Zopiclone dreamless sleep time.

Guilt in spades . . .

Sunday 19 April

The Zopiclone gradually loses its grip on my dreamless sleep. Subconsciously, I see Beth silhouetted at the open door, backlit by the salt lamp. Silently she turns and moves away. Maybe not wanting a confrontation.

3.30 a.m. Another f—king day.

Helen is not beside me. She is in Beth's bed seeking some sort of solace from her dead baby's smells and soft fabric.

Upon shutting my eyes last night, I felt today was not going to be good. My mood confirms this. Trying to doze, Beth dominates my thoughts. Seeing her through life sinks me into another black hole of what I suppose is despair. The little girl I loved so much has taken her own life. This is a grim reality.

My now normal morning routine takes over. Diazepam and a call to Scotland for Lindsey's counsel. Same questions, same answers. It does help me to talk, but as soon as the call ends I am back in the 'now'. And it's shit.

Walking Monty on this beautiful morning is not therapy. Always a deep thinker, I chew things over. The demons get bigger every day. I have issues with no real solution other than to 'man up' and 'push on through', ultimately moving past the grief onto a new life beyond Beth.

A proud young dad with a double buggy walks by with a cheery, 'Hello'.

I let out a stifled sob.

Being scared is something different for me. I have been worried many times, but now I am really scared for my family. They all seem so fragile. Beth was taken so easily, and the thought of losing someone else is unbearable.

Once big, strong Dad, I now feel weak both mentally and physically. In my role as protector, I must have failed Beth. Blame is not something I am trying to place squarely upon my own shoulders or anyone else's, but my mind is still full of guilt. Beth's decision to leave a world that loved her may never be understood, but every day is an internal search for clues.

The feeling that my mental health is on the edge is with me every minute. Without Diazepam and Zopiclone it is doubtful I would be out of bed. Black holes are appearing more often. I will speak to the doctor tomorrow, but I know what she will say:

- Your grief is no different from anyone else in this same situation.
- All the seven stages are being worked through.
- It will never totally go away.
- I think we should lower your Diazepam prescription.
- Have you tried one of the help lines?

None of this will be music to my ears.

The Covid-19 lockdown has kept us isolated, protecting us from the very thing I blame for pushing Beth over the edge. I know Em and Matt are bored 'shitless'. Helen and I move around each other, afraid to say the wrong thing. Home has become a very lonely place.

Dark places exist within us all, even in the bravest souls. My eldest daughter Charley has been such a comfort to me, especially in the days immediately after Beth took her life. Unable even to get out of bed, I was consumed by shock and disbelief. She nursed me, soothed me and stroked my head, putting her own grief to one side despite suffering from her own long-running mental-health issues.

Today she rang me consumed by sadness. TV images of lockdown and what families and communities are doing to support each other had brought the anguish back in spades. The father in me was stirred. My big girl needed me and wanted to know I was OK. Out of my black hole I crawled and, with everything I could muster, I set about changing her mindset. Talking about the future, as so many of my friends have done with me. It felt good to be needed. From now on I shall monitor Charley and boyfriend Gaz carefully.

The days are long after getting up so early, but even the attempted afternoon nap is aborted after Beth disrupts it with continuous memories.

Speaking to Neil P. and Suze kills some time, but I am afraid the monster of the black hole is pulling me back in.

Cousins Daisy and Jess visit with Donna. It's great to see Emily laugh, but sitting with them is too much and I retreat further into the house. Images of past happy family gatherings fill my head and I do not want them to see the depressed figure I have become.

Helen is being so brave and is basically getting on with it. We do discuss my condition quite openly. Doctor tomorrow.

Monday 20 April

4 a.m. Here we go again. A new day.

Helen is beside me. Silent in her sleep. Monty must have heard me stir. He jumps from Beth's bed, landing with a thump, then makes his way into our room, burrowing in beside me. Despite being a small and smelly Jack Russell cross, he is a huge comfort.

Consciously I try to push Beth into a corner in my mind and lie still. It is no good: vivid images make me jump in my half-sleep. Denying a beloved daughter and literally turning her pictures to the wall is my coping mechanism. Not Helen's – she needs to see and feel her life. Still we remain on different planets.

The night before, I sat and had tea with Helen, Em and Matt before trying to watch *Guardians of the Galaxy 2*. Everyone laughed and pretended, but again I felt alone in my black hole. Beth loved these family nights.

Following my 'Groundhog Day' routine, I get dressed, go downstairs and phone Lindsey. Once again, she listens and gently consoles as the same subjects are revisited. Ranting about Beth's rash decision is common. Anger wells up and over, then my sister mops it up.

Helen is up early and we walk Monty together. Another beautiful morning in lockdown, but sadness keeps pace with us. Things act as triggers to spark emotions. Today a child's sunhat left on a fence brings an image of baby Beth at Euro Disney. Tears run freely.

Worrying about Emily is constant. She stands tall with the support of Matt. Always tough on the outside, I know the loss is devastating. Coping for her means looking forward. I decorated Em's room the week after Beth left. It gave Em a fresh start and occupied my mind. Yesterday she threw out her JLS dolls. No going back – but I do wish they were all little girls again.

An email pings up and offers a mental health instructor's course. A strange coincidence. My initial reaction is to accept, to help the world and prevent families from going through this atomic bomb of pain. The truth is, mentally I am not ready.

Feeling my mood darken, I ring Chaplain George, who I knew from work. His gentle advice and encouragement always give comfort. Not having faith in a god after Beth died had been a dilemma. Desperately needing to believe she had been welcomed somewhere beautiful by a divine being, I had to let God in. George again listens to my despair and anguish without judgement, putting me, if only temporarily, back on track.

Doctor Allen is next, getting a full emotional report on my mental state. Straight to the point again: 'You are going through the natural process of grief. Are you thinking of hurting yourself?'

Honest answer: 'Turning out the lights has crossed my mind, but I couldn't do this to the rest of my family and friends.' Remember, I am a survivor of bereavement by suicide and am now living in the ruins.

Diazepam and Zopiclone stay on the menu, with a little Mirtazapine for a nightcap.

Reporter Mel Barham texts about an interview I did a week or so ago for *Granada Reports*. Article should go out tomorrow. Mel met Helen, Emily and Beth a few years ago in connection with my row across the Atlantic, raising funds for Francis House Children's Hospice in Didsbury (I needed a challenge at the time), and stayed in touch. They want to include an expert on suicide, Jess from the Martin Gallier Project. We speak and find common ground. She recommends Debbie from The Barbara Bettle Foundation for support. I text and leave a message.

Helen, Em and Matt head off for a meeting in the garden – socially distanced, of course – with Nana and Grandad. Not wanting to upset them by seeing their broken son-in-law, I stay at home and doze fitfully on Beth's bed.

Debbie rings and says that all our pain is natural grief. I've heard this before, and it's clearly too early for counselling, which leaves a sense of hopelessness. However, she offers ongoing support for the family.

Calls continue with Charley and Lindsey. Again, covering old ground. My Samsung is becoming a lifeline.

Tuesday 21 April

The new night-time cocktail of Zopiclone and Mirtazapine knocks me into a deep, heavy sleep with welcome images of normality ... but Mr Grief gives me a shake at 4 a.m., and it's time for a piss. Space-walking into the bathroom I wobble, directing the dark brown flow into the toilet bowl. Memo to self, must drink more water.

Still groggy, I return to bed. Helen and Monty are both there, still and silent. I wonder if H is feigning sleep or just keeping her eyes shut to block out the 'living hell' that is our new world.

The residual effect of the drugs allows me to delay the new routine of the Lindsey counselling call and the dog-walking game of avoiding people at all costs. Less than a month ago things were so different: hangover, Americano, walk Monty, muse on life's now meaningless problems, talk to anyone, big breakfast, jobs ... and see the girls late morning, sat at the breakfast bar.

Happy days.

Gone for ever.

Eventually I give up and, still spaced-out, get dressed, text Lindsey and get Monty ready. Not even 7 a.m. I feel apprehensive and wonder if this feeling is shame – people thinking 'this man's daughter was so miserable she took her own life'.

Like an alien amongst mankind for the first time, I go for a fast walk around the block. Did she turn away? – the friendly lady with the nervous spaniel. Always chatty, but not today. Unsurprisingly, people sometimes pretend they haven't seen you, rather than see and feel your grief. The world looks the same but it feels very strange, like a parallel universe.

Helen and Em watched a *Thor* movie last night. It has become a routine for them. Glad they were together, I retreated to bed. Dark fingers were pulling me into the now-familiar black hole. Grief is foul. It grinds you down, laying you naked and vulnerable to all your emotions. No hiding places. No answers. No nothing.

My mobile rang three times while I lay, eyes tight shut against my misery – Neil P., Russ and Charley, all trying to take away some of the acute emotional pain.

Avoiding Facebook, I am now out of the loop. Finding no comfort in tributes, I do not look. A world without Beth is a sadder place for many of her friends and I do worry about their mental health. Whether the Caroline Flack affair had any bearing on Beth's decision may never be known, but suicide is not glamorous. At all levels it is hideous.

Healer Adam, one of Guy Griffiths' contacts, emails with an appointment for 9.30 a.m. tomorrow. Guy – one of my Atlantic rowing mates – is very spiritual. I am not, but at this stage I am willing to try anything. Nothing ventured, nothing gained!

Granada reporter Mel texts. The article I filmed is ready and will go out today. Too painful for me to watch. I just hope it does some good.

Helen returns some bowls to our friends Suze and Horse – many people have been bringing us food – and comes home in tears. Last time, Helen was there to pick up her youngest daughter. Landmines of emotion explode everywhere when you tread in Beth's steps.

Charley visits and we sit out in the sun chatting. Messages

start to come through from the Granada Report praising my efforts. I go cold, remembering why I've done the interview. Diazepam had shut me off. I was the dad whose beautiful, talented daughter had taken her own life, thrown away a glittering future and throat-punched her family into a spiral of grief. The black hole was once again beckoning.

Steve, Beth's college tutor, rang and spoke to Helen. Never saw this coming – tribute concert to be arranged for one of the best students in forty years of teaching, he said.

Anguish filled me to the brim, silently screaming: '*Beth, what the f—k have you done?*'

Wednesday 22 April

4.15 a.m. Beth had been with me most of the night. A last-minute gig had meant we had to run around looking for her gear. Nothing unusual in that, other than it was just a dream. She was just ashes in a pot, in a bag, in her room. The waves of sadness crept back. This time just over neck-deep.

Made the effort for Em and Helen last night and attended movie night. *Black Panther* was on the bill. A superhero taking on an evil foe and overcoming incredible odds to finally win the day. How pathetic did I feel? Once I felt strong. A firefighter, triathlete, ocean rower and, most important, a proud father to three girls. Now self-loathing, weak both mentally and physically after four weeks of zero exercise. Looking in the mirror, a withered old man looks back. Unkempt hair, saggy skin . . . and wearing the same clothes every day.

A memory comes back. Beth, Grandad, Helen and I attended

a Queen tribute concert in a local theatre. A seated venue with pissed people wanting to dance soured the atmosphere. A heated discussion with one individual resulted in me getting into a fight, ably supported by my sidekick Beth. She had not been speaking to me for two weeks after a minor falling-out. Now we were Batman and Robin.

Adam the healer is an interesting character. Looking a little like Jesus, he sits on the other end of a Skype call. Determined to remain open-minded, I settle back and listen to his spiritual noises – a little like a seagull with a rumbling stomach. I tell him a little of the family history at the start of the session, but he soon reflects on my deep sadness before starting on my inner pathways with what must be a divine energy Dyson. Vortex healing is a divine healing art from the Merlin lineage. Powerful stuff – if you believe.

Adam made contact with Beth. Tears rolled down my face. Is this all bollocks, or not? He described her deep sorrow. Before realising the consequences, she had taken herself away in a fit of worthlessness. Basically she 'f—ked up'! Beth's sadness was taken away by Adam's Vortex noises and replaced by love. Her happy childhood had been another subject as well as her love for her sisters. She was now moving onward on a journey to peace.

Exhausted after ninety minutes of this I was incredibly emotional. My mind remains open to the existence of Merlin.

Friday 24 April

My head keeps going under, but I am still swimming. Determined to stay positive, I banish Beth to the corners of my mind and avoid taking even a glance at her pictures. Survival is the name of the game.

Helen and I shake off the effects of the Zopiclone and walk Monty on a glorious spring morning. People cheerily socially distance and wish one another good day. The world keeps on spinning through our grief.

Shopping is next. H does Aldi while I head to the Pound Shop for bird food, of all things. A black hole opens up as I remember Beth dancing in the town square at Christmas. Even being out with an anti-virus face mask makes me uncomfortable. Someone might recognise me.

Unbeknown to me, Em had been talking on social media to Annabel, from Norfolk, who had also recently lost her sister, Emily, to suicide. Out of the blue I receive a text from Annabel's dad – Tim – and call back. We talk for hours. Our grief is mirrored. The circumstances are uncannily similar. Tim's daughter Emily had taken her own life just four days before Beth. Lockdown had again played its part. Truly tragic. We share each other's pain. Both our families are living a nightmare and have long, tough journeys ahead. A bond is formed, and we agree to try and help each other.

The rest of the day is spent in the garden. The glorious weather means hot tub, sunbathing, circuit training and barbecue. It all seems surreal as I look up at Beth's window and wish with all my heart she would stand up and look out.

It is four weeks since she took her own life.

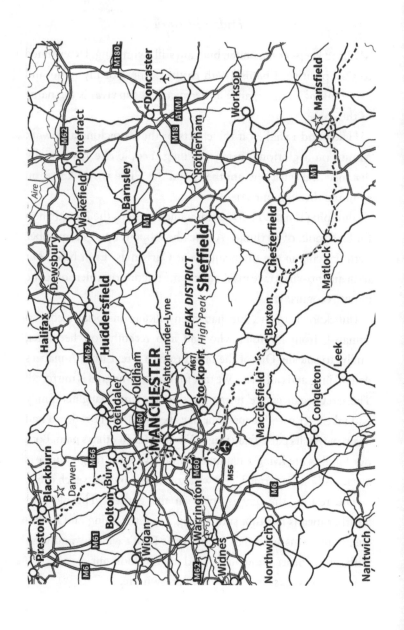

DAY 5

Darwen to Media City

I lay still in the darkness, my full bladder not allowing me to go back to sleep and my thoughts wandering over the last year or so. Beth as a physical presence was gone. She had taken her own life. Right in front of me she had fallen into despair and decided this world was too miserable to exist in. All the things I did, as a father, to keep her safe and help her make sensible decisions, meant nothing. I didn't even get the chance to fight the metaphorical demon that had made her world seem so worthless.

Being angry at Beth – and at myself for not seeing her inner anguish – was a daily event that was (and still is) part of complex grief. It tied my guts in knots so tight I felt as if I might rip myself apart. It was, perhaps, a true reflection of total heartbreak.

Sliding my hand from the covers I reached for my mobile to check the time. A big mistake.

'Morning, chap!'

A cheery greeting came from the single bed next to mine as the bedside light was switched on. Tim's big beaming face smiled down at me with 'I am awake, awake, awake' written all over it.

It was impossible to be annoyed by Tim. His affable RAF persona, straight out of the Battle of Britain, exuded enthusiasm and the 'stiff upper lip' attitude of the military. He really is a great guy – his love for his family is obvious in everything he does – and, like me, his grief was his reason to walk and talk. Emily's suicide had unexpectedly thrown us together with Andy in some sort of bizarre Monty Python Quest.

It was 5 a.m. and we could have had another hour in bed but no, the map was out, and I was being organised. Media City in Salford was today's objective, but first we had to sort out the area we'd turned into an emergency drying room after our soaking up on Darwen Hill the night before. All kinds of walking paraphernalia adorned radiators and any available hanging space. The towel rail boasted a selection of gaiters, gloves, hats and a brilliant brand of underwear, Comfyballs (kindly donated, and which certainly lived up to its name) – anything other than towels. Despite being on our knees when we arrived the night before we'd placed our wet boots carefully by the radiators, taking care not to mark the freshly painted walls. Not surprisingly the atmosphere was humid, with a slightly musty aroma.

Andy had been allocated the other room with a kingsize bed. We all agreed that, to save us from his snoring, this was for the best.

Just after 7 a.m., Tim took a phone call from *The Times* – while sitting on the toilet. He thought they were calling to arrange a time for an interview later in the day, but no, it was NOW! Much to my amusement, I could hear Tim's refined voice – 'Hello, Tim Owen' – before he launched into the most eloquent of answers to the interviewer's questioning, despite his somewhat inappropriate situation.

The Times said they would feature 3 Dads Walking in their Saturday magazine, so he had to make time to talk to them – even after having extricated himself from the bathroom – but he had to ring off when Hilary Ramwell (the Quarlton Fold Farm proprietor) appeared with a pile of bacon sandwiches, and Russ McCulloch (our transport and bag carrier for the day) turned up to take us back to our starting point. Tim arranged to speak to *The Times* again later that morning.

Russ was a Manchester Airport Fire Service buddy of mine for over twenty years. He was short in stature, with the temperament of a Jack Russell – and a big heart. He had known Beth since she was born, and when she died the shock had literally knocked him off his feet. His commitment to support my family in the aftermath truly showed what a loyal friend he was. We had always tended to wind each other up and had often fallen out, but he stood tall; well, as tall as 5 feet 6 inches could. Russ also had his own family pressures with his much-loved autistic son Finley.

Back at Cadshaw Farm, our end point on Day 4, the weather was significantly better – dry and bright, with a little low cloud on the hills. Some familiar faces were waiting: John Sulek and Simon Connolly from Manchester Airport Fire Service, Russ's wife Andrea McCulloch and her friend Lorraine Jones.

The early pace was swift, mainly due to John's long legs; walking and talking was effortless for him, but I was thinking, '*Bloody hell, John, give us a break!*'

Soon we dropped down to Turton Bottoms and Jumbles

Country Park set within the beautiful West Pennine Moors. A pretty place and well worth a visit, especially on an early autumn day as the leaves start turning russet and reflect upon the surface of the water in the reservoir.

Climbing the opposite side of the valley we took a short cut. We came off the Bolton Rotary Way as we passed Walsh Fold Farm, and onto the road – it would save a couple of hundred metres of walking and that was a psychological bonus. The Rotary Way is a 50-mile-plus circular footpath that circles the whole of Bolton borough, created as part of the 2005 Rotary Centenary Project.

We were joined by another airport firefighter, Matty Obersby, with coffee and more food. Matty joined the fire service as a cadet at sixteen and was a little wayward (to say the least). However, his cheeky character and big smile always won through, resulting in a promotion to Crew Manager. He'd become my partner on the first-response medical vehicle and we'd spent hours talking about our kids. I think he saw a similarity between the two of us. Although he was still a little wild, he was a doting father to two beautiful little girls and Beth's suicide had hit him very hard.

We climbed away from the road, passing very close to Quarlton Fold Farm where the mischievous Matty had arranged to set off some purple and teal flares (reflecting the colours of the PAPYRUS logo) on either side of our path. Despite the fact we had to walk through the smoke, choking, it made for a great photo opportunity and was used by *The Times*. (It was definitely a better image than Tim sitting on the toilet.)

The path became indistinct and we ended up in a marshy, boggy area, much to Tim's annoyance. Having discussed footwear that morning and been told the walk was on well-defined tracks all day, Tim had elected to try out his new trail trainers. Much to our amusement he ended up getting his well-pedicured feet wet.

As we climbed the hill at Affetside on the course of a Roman road, the mist turned into heavier rain. Our sights were set on Bury, but first we had to pause and talk to the dozens of locals who had come out to wish us well and offer their support. Yet again, one was an old friend of Andy's. The Cumbrian certainly had a far-reaching network of acquaintances. This was Norma, whom he knew from the theatre in Keswick in the 1980s. I had no idea Andy was a thespian and tried to picture him in a Shakespearean role.

Again, we were joined by bereaved parents – a married couple, both head teachers, who'd lost their seventeen-year-old son. Walking and listening, we empathised with the utter devastation and grief that they were trying to deal with. In many ways it was an honour to listen to such stories. We were not qualified in any way to give advice, but we had lived experience. It was becoming clear that the realisation that you were not alone and that there was someone who felt the same way as you did help those in pain to process the unimaginable.

At the top of Affetside, 900 feet above sea level, the splendid views over Bolton and Bury were denied us by the mist (again!). Tim returned to his call with *The Times* and spent much of the next section of the walk with his ear pinned to his phone, talking passionately about the whole experience.

I listened to excerpts and thought about families who were, tragically, about to lose their precious children. Some would know their youngsters were struggling, but others would be living in ignorant bliss of the hell that was about to befall them. What was the answer? How could we help them? As we walked on I went over and over these questions in my mind. I'm sure it was the same for Andy and Tim.

Arriving on the outskirts of Bury, Andy spotted a well-wisher wearing a Manchester City hat and naturally fell into conversation about football. Before long, this well-wisher said, 'Do you fancy a coffee?'

I did, and immediately said 'yes', daring to hope he would have a proper coffee machine that would produce a frothy cappuccino.

Our new-found friend promptly called his wife. 'Get the kettle on, I've got 3 Dads coming for coffee in five minutes. We need ... five, six, seven ... eight cups!'

Mr Man City hat steered us slightly off the route into a nearby housing estate and a family home where the kettle was well and truly on. Sadly, no cappuccino – but the biscuits made up for it.

Tim stood outside leaning on the wheelie bin, still talking to *The Times*. As we left, our City friend suggested an onward route that would avoid the mud on the lane we'd planned to use. Good local knowledge was helping us once more.

From the centre of Bury, we picked up the Irwell Sculpture Trail. Originating in Bacup and 33 miles long (and the largest sculpture route in the UK, featuring over seventy works of art) it would take us straight into Salford following the

River Irwell – a perfect way to avoid road-walking. I'd recced the route some weeks earlier and knew it would be flat and fast.

Our lunch stop was at Radcliffe. Food was supplied by Russ and involved some very healthy options, including beetroot and pine nuts. We sat on the Bury Council roadside benches, eating our packed lunches and tending our feet. The chance to wiggle our bare toes by an A road in a small Lancashire town could now be classed as a luxury.

Back walking, we were soon joined by a lady we'd met on Day 1 (sadly her name had not been noted) and her friend. She explained that her flowery-mouthed driver (who had coined the term 'F—king Runcorn') was her brother. She'd been mortified to think that he'd offended us so was reassured to discover that his outburst had kept us laughing for quite a while.

She spoke to us about the loss of her son seventeen years previously and how her grief hadn't gone away – just changed. This was something we were discovering for ourselves. Her friend shared with me that the bereaved mum had never talked about her grief, but because we 3 Dads had been so open with our own experiences, it had given her the confidence to do the same.

I was to learn far more about 'postvention' a little while later from Suicide Bereavement UK, an organisation run by a lovely and very driven lady called Dr Sharon McDonnell. SB UK offers courses and education that are invaluable in dealing with suicide-related post-traumatic grief. SB UK states – and Andy has already mentioned – that more than 135 people are affected by a single suicide. In Beth's case, I would say that number was far higher. She was a real character with an extended network of friendship groups. Also, SB UK say that those closest to the suicide are 80–300 per cent more likely to take their own lives. I can relate to that.

We entered Prestwich Forest Park, 200 hectares of woodland and open space, and found a quiet place where Andy video-interviewed John Sulek. John was a little reticent because he wasn't sure he would be able to say anything relevant, but Andy just had to ask him one question: 'What's your relationship to 3 Dads Walking and why have you come along?'

In just under two minutes, John nailed the essence of 3 Dads Walking – he talked about needing to know more about suicide and suicide prevention so he could better support me. He said that both his dad and his grandfather had taken their own lives and talked about his love for his daughters. 'I think that what you're doing should be embedded in any school curriculum,' he said, finally.

We crossed the Irwell and headed into suburban Salford. Amid the hustle and bustle of the long drag down Langworthy Road we passed two youths, one having a cigarette and the other eating chips: Gregor (Andy's son) and his mate Joe from Liverpool University. I had met Gregor at a PAPYRUS Champions training course, which resulted in my contacting Andy – strange to think what that chance meeting had led to! He is a likeable lad with a fondness for beer and roll-up ciga-rettes – we were finishing today's walk in the Seven Bro7hers Bar, so the timing of his support for us was perfect.

As we approached Media City, I explained to Tim and Andy that we needed to enter the Piazza from a specific direction because I knew that the BBC's cameras would be set up pointing across the bridge. This would provide a grand entrance and allow the 'small' crowd of family, friends and media to see us coming. I also knew we would pass under one of the big screens displaying Evie's drawing of we 3 Dads and PAPYRUS. I thought it was a great plan – but for some reason it seemed to throw Andy and Tim.

Andy made the point that as we were arriving from the north, we didn't need to cross any bridges to get into Media City. Trying to explain that it only involved a few hundred yards of detour – and was for artistic effect – was met with some resistance. I was getting frustrated and had to bite my lip.

Both the BBC and Granada had set up on the bridge for what was to be a pretty awesome shot, and the other two dads just did not get it. The long miles were taking their toll on Andy's feet. Unbeknown to us he was developing a huge blister on the ball of his right foot, and was stubbornly carrying on regardless.

I kept myself focused amid the barrage of 'Why?!' and 'Wrong side!' responses and kept the group moving towards The Lowry, where we stopped for a toilet break. As we approached the front door, the security guard recognised 3 Dads Walking and pointed us at the closest loos. Crossing the large foyer in all our walking gear, rucksacks and flags included, we were applauded by the staff who were getting the place ready for an evening event.

We crossed the Manchester Ship Canal before passing in front of the Imperial War Museum North and approached Media City Bridge from the 'wrong side' – and got the green light and action signal from the TV crews. One way or another, we were going to get there.

We could see that the camera crews were surrounded by dozens of people. Friends and family were there, together with the PAPYRUS team and random people who had been caught up in the event.

As we got nearer, Helen let Monty off his lead. Wearing a jaunty PAPYRUS neckerchief, he was the first to welcome us to Media City. Andy and Tim were not sure whether the small black-and-white terrier was in attack mode or running to greet me. We walked in, three abreast, to a warm welcome of cheers and hugs before doing yet another – short – interview for the BBC.

Monty the dog is a poodle-Jack Russell cross. He is now ten years old, with some terrible habits, bad smells, a ball obsession and a very uncertain temper. Beth loved him and used to sneak him into her bed. Tim and Andy were never sure of his intentions and treated him with due respect, a bit like you might treat a senior Peaky Blinder.

People use the phrase 'dogs are just animals', but to me they are precious souls. After Beth, Monty was the reason I got up in the morning. He lay on the bed with me, curled up with a comforting warmth. He willed me to get up and walk with him even though I could hardly remember how to breathe. He wanted me to live and loved me unconditionally, as he did the rest of the family, every day. I'm certain he would lay down his life for those he loves. He is a small dog with a huge heart.

Eventually, we made it into Media City Piazza where *Sinking Feeling*, a new animation commissioned by PAPYRUS, was playing on the large screens. We had to stand and watch. This was followed by some images of 3 Dads Walking, as well as Evie's 'Good Luck' drawing. It was very moving.

We then retired to the Seven Bro7hers Brewing Company Media City Bar (highly recommended). We were very weary, but it was amazing how much better a few beers and a burger each made us feel. I sat with boots and socks off, not caring how bad my feet smelt. The bar was packed full of friends old and new who wanted to be a part of our story. It felt truly humbling.

The team at Seven Bro7hers included Keith and Alison. Keith is one of the seven brothers who created the company, and has become a good friend. He also likes to test his new beer samples on me, and that's no bad thing! Alison's children, Izzy and Harry, were childhood friends of Beth and her sister Emily. We shared some wonderful years with them at our caravan at Goodenbergh Country Holiday Park, near Bentham in North Yorkshire. The four of them played 'Harry Potter' in the woods and were out all day, just as kids should. They even smelled of the outdoors. I knew Beth was truly happy there when she was too young and innocent to be polluted by the pressures of life. How I wish I could turn the clock back.

Andy introduced his mate Neil Bradley to me and Tim. Neil is head of Mammut UK; and he'd supported 3 Dads Walking with a range of outdoor clothing and equipment. Tim and I were keen to express our thanks. He asked if we needed any more gear, so I tried my luck on another pair of boots in a slightly larger size. Walking this sort of distance every day you learn things about your body, and the fact that my feet seemed to swell slightly and touch the end of the toe box as the day progressed leads me to recommend the following: always get boots half a size too big and trim your toenails, or you risk them turning black and falling off. Just as mine eventually did. Not pretty.

I was joined by Charley and Gaz, Beth's cousin Jess and boyfriend Liam, Neil Harris and Kelly, a suicide support worker who'd stuck with me through some really dark days. Kelly worked for Greater Manchester (formerly Suicide) Bereavement Information Service. She was a huge support for me in the early days, post-Beth. Just having someone who knew how to signpost some kind of way forward was so important. She also provided a kind, empathetic, listening ear.

Claire Brook was also there. Claire was a Human Resources solicitor who hosted a suicide-prevention webinar during lockdown, to which Andy contributed. Andy was introduced to her by her sister Annette – one of the mums who met 3 Dads Walking near Shap Summit on Day 1.

A convivial evening was had by all, but before we began to flag too much, we took our leave and headed to my house. It had been a hard day's walking, mainly on tracks – we certainly all felt it in our knees and, in Andy's case, his feet. The blister situation was getting serious, but he kept it very much to himself. Some tough days lay ahead – but the Cumbrian was to prove he was made of stern, if not a little grumpy, stuff.

Money raised (excluding Gift Aid and direct donations)
   = £256,000
Day 5 distance = 23.2 miles
Total distance walked = 117.6 miles

DAY 6

Media City to Poynton

It felt strange to be back in my own bed. Waking in the early hours, I thought about the seismic shift that had taken place in my life. I was once a dad, doing dad things for Beth – taxi driver, unofficial roadie, an entity simply addressed with, 'Dad, could you . . .?'

How I longed for those days. Her cheeky comments followed by 'I love you Dad', because she knew she could always get away with it. I would always pull a pained face, but in truth I never cared because I was proud of my little girl and watching her perform – she had a wonderful singing voice – made me feel so special. Now I was a bereaved father carrying a huge boulder of grief on a journey with two other bereaved dads. How had this happened?

Our house was a large, late-Victorian affair – home to a market gardener at the end of the nineteenth century – which we'd bought as a rundown shell. I toiled over it for many years, turning it into what I hoped would be the vibrant family home where Emily and Beth could grow up until they spread their wings. I never foresaw angel wings.

Andy had always been banished to the basement when he'd stayed with us in Sale. Beth's music studio had been down there, but it was now converted into a guest room. The last time I'd heard her voice – a full-gusto version of 'I Will Always Love You' – it had defeated the sound insulation and could clearly be heard on the ground floor. Whitney Houston was not her style, but for some reason that night it was her choice. The last words I would ever hear her sing.

Andy was a great fan of the subterranean room – the perfect place in which to practise his now-legendary snoring technique. Alone. Tim, on the other hand, was upstairs in the spare room next to Beth's. Always a light sleeper, not having to share a room with the noisy Cumbrian came as a welcome break.

The salt lamp was still lit in Beth's room at night and spread a warm glow through the door, that was always left open. It had become a ritual for Helen and me, a light to guide our lost daughter back to us in the dark. This didn't seem to bother Tim; he was certainly not afraid of ghosts. He understood it.

We were up early for a light breakfast at about 6.15; the car was due at 7 a.m. Day 6 was to be a big one. The walking was to be brutal, both in distance and underfoot: 26 miles, nine hours of walking on mainly tarmac, a route I had recced. Flat, hard surfaces were always gruelling. You'd think they would be faster and easier, but they wore you down, rewarding you with sore feet and blisters. Not really what our Cumbrian friend needed.

I was already feeling very emotional, and trying hard to keep it from the others – but Andy and Tim seemed oblivious, chatting happily. This was my hometown, the place where Beth had grown up and lived for all of her seventeen years and eight months. Today's walk was likely to be a full-on emotional rollercoaster – and I knew it.

A car from the BBC came to collect us – a Jaguar. We piled in, wearing our walking kit and boots, along with our rucksacks with PAPYRUS flags sticking out of them. The car interior was luxurious and smelt of leather. I did wonder if it had a drinks cabinet, but maybe that was just for rock stars. By the time we arrived at Media City, Tim and Andy were laughing and joking about not getting out – they were just too comfortable.

We eventually got ourselves together and headed towards the BBC. As we approached Quay House we were stopped by a security guard demanding to know what we were doing.

'We're 3 Dads Walking and we've been invited to sit on the *BBC Breakfast* sofa.'

'Ah. I thought you were some kind of demonstration.' At least this confirmed that the flags were drawing attention.

After going up a couple of floors, we were led to the waiting area outside the studio where Tim was pleased to see Evanna Lynch, who played Luna Lovegood in *Harry Potter*. Tim's daughter Evie was a huge fan, and would later be amazed that her dad had sat on the same Red Sofa as her idol.

Considering how passionately we all felt about what we were doing, and the message we wanted to get across, we were surprisingly relaxed. We entered the studio and sat on the Red Sofa opposite Naga Munchetty and Charlie Stayt. They smiled and went out of their way to make us feel comfortable before the live interview. As we chatted, Alison and Adam's film was running – we could see it on the monitors, but the sound was down (probably a good thing).

We were on! I consciously brought my knees a little closer together – Helen had told me off for 'manspreading' on our previous appearance. We were asked about the girls, PAPYRUS, how we'd got together and how the walk was going. We had plenty to say and they gave us the time to talk. It felt like we were covering everything we wanted to say, and they wanted to listen. When asked about who was supplying the food each day all three of us appealed for people to stop bringing it! We were on for over twenty minutes – amazing coverage during prime time on the *BBC Breakfast* show.

When we finished, both Naga and Charlie thanked us for talking to them and wished us well on the rest of the walk. Before we went on *BBC Breakfast*, our JustGiving total before Gift Aid was £256,000. Later that day, the total had increased by nearly £40,000 to £293,000, which included an anonymous donation of £5,000 to Andy. It was incredible – especially as more donations were being received directly by PAPYRUS.

Outside we met Martin Hibbert, the next guest on *Breakfast*. He was a survivor of the Manchester Arena bombing at the Ariana Grande concert in May 2017; in fact, he was the closest person to the blast who'd survived. He was paralysed from the waist down and had come to the BBC to talk about his planned climb of Kilimanjaro, the highest mountain in Africa. We were a bit stunned. It put our wander across the country into perspective. We chatted with Martin and he was keen to have a photo taken with us (it felt like it should have been the other way round).

Before we left, I was invited to do an interview with Mike Sweeney on BBC Radio Manchester, and disappeared into the studio for ten minutes while Tim and Andy waited outside.

I was very impressed with Sweeney, as he was affectionately known (and not just because he was wearing shorts in October). A journeyman presenter who'd been on many stations, he was the ultimate professional. Sadly, he'd lost his sister to suicide many years before and his interview really came from the heart. Here was someone else still carrying the grief and questions that arise in the aftermath of suicide.

The clock was ticking, and we needed to leave. I shook Sweeney's hand and hurried back to Tim and Andy, who'd been stopped by Richard Frediani, the Editor of *BBC Breakfast*, who said, 'We've got this. We're right behind you.' He made it clear that he and his team would do everything within their power to help us keep spreading the word about suicide prevention.

Finally, all our media commitments were done, and we could head for the exit. Quite a few people were waiting for us outside. Claire Benson was there – a long-term friend and ex-work colleague of Helen, babysitter of my Emily and Beth and the person who introduced me to PAPYRUS. She was a member of Bee Vocal, a mental-health choir based in Manchester, and something of a mental-health activist who'd been deeply affected by Beth's suicide. She'd stepped up to give great support to me and Helen.

Horse (aka Keith Hancock) was an Essex boy, and someone with whom I was always guaranteed to get into trouble after a few beers. He was also a sure-fire bet to say the wrong thing, at the wrong time, but he had a heart of gold. Why was he known as Horse? Well, not just because he had a long face.

Suze was Horse's long-suffering wife. Even with her stern half-German heritage, she struggled to keep him in check. She was one of those who'd lent me an ear and council when I was in my darkest place.

In the crowd I also spotted Tegan, Suze and Horse's daughter and Beth's friend, sisters Freya and Scarlett Bratt, also friends of Beth's, and my work colleague and friend Danny McGuinness.

As we said our hellos, Andy's phone rang – it was one of Andy Burnham's assistants. He said that the mayor was stuck in traffic and running a little behind schedule. Our Andy thanked him for his call in his direct Cumbrian way and pointed out that Mr Burnham should have had a pretty good idea about the traffic situation in Manchester. He told him that we'd be gone by the time they arrived. With that, we were off. It's funny how some things turn out. You'd have thought that standing up the Mayor of Manchester would have burnt a bridge there and then, but all credit to Andy Burnham: he has since become one of our greatest supporters.

We retraced our steps from the day before, crossing Media City Bridge and passing the Imperial War Museum North, where my next-door neighbour Danielle worked. She and the staff had come out to wish us well. Around the next corner, Keith and Alison from Seven Bro7hers Brewery waited outside their new premises – yet more smiling faces and more messages of good luck came our way.

We'd just got into our stride when we were stopped again, this time at Old Trafford (I'm a Manchester United fan). Approaching the East Stand, we could see a fire appliance and firefighters, a couple of TV crews, dozens of well-wishers and Neil Harris, a good friend and a United Youth coach who'd arranged the visit. At the centre of this throng stood a diminutive chap whom Andy and I recognised immediately – Lou

Macari, the Manchester United legend whose career spanned from the days of Bobby Charlton, George Best and Dennis Law (the 'United Trinity') to playing with Steve Coppell and Bryan Robson. I fondly remember his poster on my chipboard wall back in my childhood.

Lou gave the 3 Dads a wonderfully warm welcome. We talked about our girls and the walk. Lou told us about his son Jonathan, who took his own life in 1999 – it turned out we were all members of that same club we never wanted to join. He asked us about the donation that Daniel Craig had made. 'Right,' he said, 'I'll give you ten thousand and ONE pounds. I don't want to be beaten by James Bond!'

We spent quite a while talking to the various journalists who were there. The BBC did not interview us, as the conversation they'd already filmed with Lou said it all. I then managed to reduce the MUTV reporter (Manchester United has its own premium TV channel) and his cameraman to tears.

We had our photos taken beneath the statue of the United Trinity before we were led into the stadium for more photos and conversation. Lou told us about his charitable work in Stoke, where his Macari Foundation was currently looking after forty-seven homeless people, many of whom were struggling with mental-health issues. He told us how he was inspired to do this after driving past a group of homeless people close to his home, then going back to talk to them about their situation. He knew that he could help them.

As we left Old Trafford, we picked up more people who wanted to walk with us. Quite a troop followed the canal-side path towards Sale with plenty of chat and laughter along the way.

Richard, who'd started with us at Media City, talked about the loss of his father to suicide in 1953 and the shame and stigma felt by his family back then. It was clear that his father had come back from World War II suffering from PTSD and unable to cope with his return to civilian life. In conversation with Tim, it transpired that Richard's sister also lived in Shouldham and would be joining the walk further along the way. It was such a small world.

Reaching Sale Waterside, I was blown away by the reception – there were hundreds of people, including loads of school children and yet more firefighters. Walking through the applauding and cheering supporters was the most surreal moment of the journey so far. But while I was overawed at the turnout, I was not surprised. This was my hometown, after all, and Beth was so loved, and touched so many people. Again, it was so hard not to cry.

It was here we were joined by Beth's grandad David, eighty years old and fit as a flea, acting as an outrider on his cycle. He'd been so close to Beth – they were soulmates – and felt her death acutely. Part of this pain comes from the fact that things have happened out of the natural order. A wonderful nana and grandad should never lose a beautiful granddaughter who they doted on.

And Monty was there once again, sporting his PAPYRUS bandana.

As we re-joined the road, our group swelled to well over one hundred – lots of people were intent on staying with us as we walked through Sale. Our first destination was Beth's primary school, St Anne's. We turned onto Trinity Road, and as we headed down it even more people came into view. It turned out that the entire school population had come out to welcome us, the road lined on both sides with the staff and pupils of all ages. Many of the children held up pictures they'd drawn expressing messages of good luck and love; many mentioned Beth, Emily and Sophie. We walked along, tears streaming down our faces, thanking as many people as we could.

Fortunately for us, it wasn't long after leaving St Anne's that we arrived at my house. Horse was stationed on the drive with instructions to keep people out so we could sit and have lunch in peace (we needed it). After such an emotional couple of hours it was good to be inside, away from people, quietly contemplating what we'd just experienced. We had never imagined this when we started talking about 3 Dads Walking – how the hell had we managed to mobilise so many people to come out and show us their support? The most powerful thing was seeing so many young people lining our route.

Physically recharged and mentally refreshed, we said our goodbyes to Helen and went back out onto the road. Our supporters were still waiting so away we went, soon meeting Craig Fleming, a colleague of mine. Shortly after getting going again we turned onto Norris Road, home to Beth's secondary school, Sale High. Again, the whole school was outside waiting for us. As we approached, we could hear singing – 'Tomorrow' from *Annie* (Beth had played Annie in the school performance in 2018). Walking up to the gates we saw large images of Beth on stage, and students holding up posters bearing all our girls' names.

In tears again, all three dads stood behind the students holding the posters while photos were taken and the school children continued to sing. It was powerful and emotive stuff.

We had fewer people in tow by now, but still a healthy number. Before long we were onto Brooks Drive and making good time towards the airport. As we reached the bottom of the road, Andy said, 'Shouldn't we have turned left back there? That's where our route goes.'

I explained that this was a quicker route – albeit on a road – and would save us time. The surface was new, there was a narrow verge on which to take refuge, the weather was dry, and it was only about 400 metres long. I had walked the road in my recce and in my considered opinion it was safe, so long as everyone kept their eyes open.

Andy was not happy and recalled inspecting this section on Google Maps and deciding it was too dangerous to walk along – it was a rat run, he said, with no footpath and narrow verges. A heated conflab ensued.

Days earlier I'd explained to the other two that I'd made some alterations to the route on this section, but it had been too late to change them on the digital OS maps they'd already downloaded. They'd obviously not taken this on board. I could feel my temper rising as Tim joined in and agreed with Andy. I could see that some of our supporters were starting to feel uncomfortable. It had already been a very emotional day, and I was only just holding myself together. I think people could tell.

We pressed on down Whitecarr Lane in awkward silence,

apart from the occasional shout of 'Car!' when we hopped up onto the verge. We soon emerged at the end unscathed.

Safe in Newall Green, Wythenshawe, we worked through the estate and made our way towards the airport. Much to my frustration, this seemed to surprise Andy again. I'd made no secret of the fact that Manchester Airport staff were going to greet us as we made our way towards the A555.

Next the group entered the edge of Newall Green and crossed the bridge before arriving at Painswick Park. Once again, Tim and Andy questioned the route – this time concerned about getting our feet wet. Through gritted teeth I explained that crossing the park involved no more than a path through grass and then over some playing fields, and wouldn't result in wet trainers. It proved to be the case, but I was starting to feel a little dejected. The highly emotional day was taking its toll – but considering I was half-way through a relentless 300-plus-mile walk with two virtual strangers it was probably inevitable.

However, my spirits lifted a little when I saw the reception outside Terminal 3 when we eventually got to the airport. There were plenty of colleagues, and Helen had made the trip too. They brought us coffee and chat – although it would have been even better if they'd found us something to sit on. More firefighters appeared, including Matty, who did his smoke flare trick again. Fire appliances were decked with PAPYRUS flags. The throng also included many of the airport management team, including Karen Smart, Rad Taylor and the Fire Service Manager, Neil Gyllenship. I was touched by the effort. It really meant so much.

I have worked at Manchester Airport since 1987, when I took a temporary job as an airport hand before moving to security and then to the fire service in 1996. In thirty-four years, the airport has changed so much, supporting me through many different phases of my life: two marriages, three daughters and now Beth's suicide.

When my daughter died my colleagues wanted to support me, but really didn't know how. Many had known me since I'd started and we'd talked about our kids, sharing our hopes and dreams for them, never foreseeing an end like this. I know Beth's death hit many of them hard – and when I came back to work, they shared their own experiences of their children's mental health.

Work is now an ongoing struggle for me, and aspects of my profession make every day difficult. Suicide changes you as a person. Your tolerance levels and coping mechanisms are not the same. The fire service management team do not have a manual on how to deal with a grief-stricken father of a seventeen-year-old girl who took her own life, but they do their best with a compassion for which I am grateful.

Unfortunately the next stage of our route followed the footpath/cycleway alongside the A555 – it was the most direct way to Poynton, but it was awful for walking. It was on tarmac, noisy and unforgiving underfoot. With vehicles hammering past at 50mph, it was hard to hold a conversation – and in Andy's case extremely painful, with his blisters now becoming open wounds. It wasn't a nice way to cover any distance, never mind six-and-a-half miles!

In all challenges there are times when you must dig deep, and this was it. It was obvious we were all hurting emotionally and physically. We didn't walk together, each of us accompanied by our own group of supporters. Doing my best to appear upbeat I was hiding an inner sadness that was now becoming a very dark place.

I stopped to address a hot spot on the ball of my left foot and let the others carry on, knowing I could catch up again. Only Al Demmy stayed with me. It was good to sit on a grassy bank, inspect my foot, put a dressing on a developing blister – and basically recalibrate.

The monotony was broken briefly at Stanley Green, where we were met by more family and friends. After a few minutes chatting and taking on more food, we had to return to the purgatory of the A555.

My brother-in-law Dave joined us for a few miles. Dave was a life-long Manchester City supporter who'd been in the airport Fire Service when I'd started going out with his sister. He'd been clearly unimpressed with me back then, but after twenty-five years he'd got used to the idea. Dave was the first person I phoned when Beth died. His immediate pain and horror will haunt me for ever.

At long last we spotted a sign for Poynton. Andy was visibly flagging, and his feet were obviously in bits. My insistence that we needed to continue on to Brookside Garden Centre did not go down well. Again, I'd mentioned it in advance, and it'd gone unheeded. The Mayor of Bramhall, a Stockport Tourism reporter and hopefully Stockport Superheroes were going to meet us there. I'd walked this diversion as part of the recce but now, after so many miles, it seemed never-ending – and Tim was getting calls and messages to say we were off-route, which really didn't help.

We approached the garden centre, Andy with a distinct limp. There were people waiting for us, including Charley and Gaz, but it was obvious the Superheroes and Stockport Tourism hadn't turned up (and the mayor had already joined us on the A555). There had been no reason for the diversion. I was embarrassed and very pissed off. Andy was furious. To walk a pointless mile or so out of the way on feet like raw meat was too much for the Cumbrian. He vented his anger on me.

I had to dig deep to keep my temper in check. I was full of grief, hurt and injustice, and the day had been a rollercoaster. I'd tried my best – but was now getting 'shit' from a bloke who hadn't, as far as I could tell, looked after his feet.

A dark pit of depression was opening for me. I'd felt every step of the diversion too. Watching Andy hobble and feeling his anger pushed me into a pretty dark place. Andy was furious, Tim was quiet, and I was in a black hole. 3 Dads Walking were going in three different directions.

The Cumbrian limped off and I left him to it, too weary to argue. A bit of space would be good for us both. There were still 180 miles ahead of us, and we had to keep going.

First things first, we had to get to our accommodation. That night we were staying at Charley and Gaz's house, which unfortunately was right across town.

Gaz pointed out a route that would cut the corner and avoid the centre of Poynton, saving us some distance. We reluctantly decided that we needed to go into the centre just in case anyone who was following our tracker would be daft enough to be waiting there for us at that late hour. On we marched, each dad in a separate group, people talking to us but not getting much back.

A large group of people was waiting for us at the crossroads in the town centre. It was a good job we hadn't missed it. We talked to everyone, had photos taken with the mayor (who was still with us), and then headed off on the final leg (with Andy on his last one).

Finally, we were there, packs off, boots off, into the house. Andy collapsed onto the sofa and lifted his weary (and throbbing) feet off the floor. It was obvious they were REALLY hurting. He took off his socks before Horse burst into the living room. His reaction was classic Horse: 'F—king hell, look at the state of his f—king feet!' he said in his strong Essex accent.

A couple of seconds' tense silence were followed by a tirade from Andy: they were his feet, and he would do with them as he wished. I was glad they were not my feet. The blister was now a nasty open wound, and I was worried. Andy's ability to carry on would be sorely tested.

After the final supporters of the day left, the house seemed much calmer. Showers were had, kit rearranged and Andy strapped his injured foot (while no doubt contemplating how much it was going to hurt over the following nine days).

As I lay on the sofa, my bed for the night, Andy came in and, out of the blue, enveloped me in a great bear-hug. No words were needed. This was an incredible journey for us all, pushing us to the limits both physically and emotionally. With that he went to the bedroom that he was sharing with Charley and

Gaz's pet snakes. Tim and I thought a little time alone with his feet and a few pythons might do him some good.

I certainly was finding the challenge of the walk mentally very tough – even more than physically, on the whole. The world of grief was often solitary, and I was used to being alone with my thoughts. Now I was with Tim and Andy 24/7. Don't get me wrong – I was becoming increasingly fond of both men, but my tolerance levels were more fragile these days.

The friction with Andy had left me exhausted, and I soon fell into a fitful sleep on my daughter's sofa.

Money raised (excluding Gift Aid and direct donations)
= £293,000
Day 6 distance = 23 miles
Total distance walked = 140.6 miles

DAY 7

Poynton to Buxton

Day 7 may have been the shortest day in terms of mileage, but for Tim and his family it would be the most difficult. Day 7 was 15 October, and it would have been Emily's twenty-first birthday. Just eighteen months ago Tim could never have imagined that this is what he would be doing on his daughter's birthday: he would be arranging a party, or worrying about her going out too late or drinking too much. But all those scenarios had disappeared. He now had to support his family through another difficult anniversary while in the middle of a 300-mile walk. These significant dates, once the source of such joy, have to be navigated with care. The emotions can literally knock you sideways. Andy and I knew this, and resolved to be there for him. We truly understood how emotionally painful this anniversary could be.

David, one of Tim's work colleagues, was also helping. He had generously offered to sort accommodation in a luxury hotel and spa in Buxton, not only for us but also for our wives plus Evie, Tim's youngest. This sort of support, from people who understand, helps with the pain and complex emotions that are always with you.

The OS route planner confirmed the distance as 14.2 miles, with plenty of climbing, but we knew we would walk more

– the digital planner didn't account for the extra distance covered when we were walking on gradients as opposed to flat ground.

As the day dawned, the brightening sky was cloudless. It was cold, but looked like it was going to be a perfect day for our walk into the Peak District. Despite yesterday's trials and tribulations, I was feeling a little better within myself after Andy's hug and a good night's sleep. The sunshine made everything appear shiny and new.

Tim and I were keeping a circumspect eye on Andy's progress. After Horse's 'expert assessment' of his foot we were more than a little concerned. The last thing we wanted was to be down to 2 Dads Walking. The pace was left to Andy as he hobbled on uncomplainingly and in surprisingly good humour (no doubt helped by a cocktail of painkillers).

We'd barely gone 100 metres before we were joined by Nigel, a Poynton local who'd walked the last few miles with us the previous evening, and a woman who emerged from a car by the roadside and introduced herself as Shelly. She'd got her husband to bring her from their home in West Kirkby (on the Wirral, 55 miles away) because she'd been inspired by the open way we'd been talking about mental health and suicide prevention. To our surprise – we'd only just met, after all – she ticked us off for starting late. Eh? It was 7.30 a.m. – it clearly stated on our website that we would start every day at 7.30 a.m.

'Except for 15 October when you'll start at 6 a.m.,' said Shelly. 'That's today!'

Ah . . .

'You've read it wrong,' Andy replied. 'It says DAY 15 – our last day – not the fifteenth.'

Shelly wasn't impressed with our argument – she suggested our use of English could have been a bit clearer. It turned out that she was a teacher, so she knew best . . . She and her husband had been sitting in their car for an hour and a half waiting for our tracker to be turned on – whoops! Fortunately, Shelly turned out to be a lovely woman who didn't hold a grudge – we were forgiven.

Away we went alongside the Cheshire Ring Canal as the sun flooded light across the Cheshire Plain. Inside two miles, the first climb of the day began – we had about 1,000 feet to gain, initially through Lyme Park, a National Trust property. We reached the gates of the park shortly before 8.30 a.m. to find them locked. After a brief discussion about climbing over Nigel pointed out that there was a gate along the road that was always open. This proved to be a real winner. Instead of following the drive through woods towards the main house, our diversion quickly rose above the trees, giving us a stunning vista. We stood with the sun on our backs looking across the Cheshire Plain to the Irish Sea, the North Wales mountains, and the hills of Lancashire we'd crossed two days before. It was beautiful and everyone was smiling. The tensions of the day before were forgotten – and the prospect of a short day with a spa hotel, wives and food waiting at the end certainly served to lift the spirits.

Approaching Lyme House, we re-joined our planned route, bypassing the house and ascending through woods towards the deer park where we were greeted by the bellowing of red deer stags in rut. Stags on either side of the path were doing their best to stake their claim to the hinds – it was a magical section of our walk. We hadn't known that there would be red deer around and it was a great privilege to experience them on such a gorgeous morning. But all things must pass. We climbed over the stile at the top of the park and left the deer in peace.

As we walked on Shelly told us more about herself: she was a teacher in a school for children suffering from extreme anxiety. These children were unable to attend mainstream school, and many couldn't even leave their houses. Shelly spent most of her time going into homes, spending time talking to and helping parents cope with the situation. She was effectively a social worker who also happened to be a teacher; an angel dropping in to help make some sense of the turmoil.

Shelly was going to walk with us the whole way to Buxton. As we travelled along the track on Sponds Hill under a bright blue sky, it felt like we were well on our way towards King's Lynn.

At the next road crossing, Nigel took his leave and began to retrace his steps to Poynton. Our group didn't get any smaller, though; waiting for us here were Andy and Liz from Stoke-on-Trent. They'd lost their daughter Sinead to suicide in July. Andy had struggled to keep going, but when he saw us on *BBC Breakfast* he decided he needed to come along to walk with us.

We dropped into the Kettleshulme Valley, Andy and Liz circulating between us as we exchanged stories and talked about the crushing devastation of losing a child. We shared the feeling of your life ending and the slow realisation that the world was going on as normal around you – and that somehow you needed to keep going.

Andy and Liz readily agreed to do a short interview about their loss and how they found walking with us. Our Andy asked a couple of questions, and we secured another powerful video. Stoke Andy talked about how down he was after losing Sinead and his struggle to keep going. Our appearance on television had inspired him and talking to us had showed that there was hope for the future – that it was possible to move forward positively. He and Liz found us to be 'real down-to-earth guys who we can relate to'.

When we crossed the stream in the valley bottom, Andy and Liz left us to return to their car and we were joined by Peter, a man clearly drawn with grief. Together, we began the steady climb towards Pym's Chair, not only the high point of the day but also the high point of the entire walk (it would be all downhill from there!).

The road up to Pym's Chair is steep and rises to a challenging 1,545 feet. It's popular with cyclists, and we were passed by countless Lycra-clad beings in all shapes and sizes relishing the pain of the Peak District's own Alpe d'Huez. Not quite as spectacular as the French Alps, perhaps, but the beautiful moorland with its green and golds stretching to distant hills certainly has its own appeal.

As we plodded up the road, a chap on a recumbent trike descended towards us. As he got closer, Andy shouted something about it being amazing who you found on these rural roads – it was Paul Hallinan, a mate of his who had lost his right leg to cancer and had become a great advocate for disabled access to the countryside. The trike Paul was riding was electric, so he easily managed the steep road towards Pym's

Chair. We managed to get a short video of him pedalling his machine through a road-wide puddle as the walkers skirted round it on the grass verges.

Close to the car park at the road's high point, we were joined by Peter's wife and their dog. Also there to greet us were Richard Bland and his teddy bear, Wing Commander AB Bear, who – with Richard's wife Sue – had come to see us off in Morland on Day 1! The hilltop car park was our lunch stop and very sociable it was too. We took the time to take two videos: one with Richard and the other with Peter.

Richard talked about losing his son Andrew, how that had led to the creation of the #BEARFORCE and the work he was doing to get people to reach out for help. His mantra was 'TALK, TALK, TALK'. Wing Commander AB Bear accompanied us on the rest of the journey to Buxton, attached to Tim's rucksack.

Peter talked about the loss of his son Jamie two years earlier, and how painful the grief still was. He saw that 3 Dads Walking was enabling people to have more open conversations about mental health and suicide prevention and he wanted to lend his support. He was also keen to talk about NOT suffering on your own – the fact that his son felt that he had to sort all his problems by himself rather than ask for help meant he didn't feel able to reach out. Peter's message was identical to Richard's – when feeling down and suicidal, the road to recovery begins by talking to someone about how you feel.

Our long descent into the Goyt Valley was filled with plenty of chat and laughter, fuelled by the perfect weather and views of the endlessly rolling hills. On crossing the dam of Errwood

Reservoir we faced the final climb of the day – 600 feet of ascent – before we began the downhill section to Buxton. The climb went by surprisingly fast and before we knew it, we were heading down.

The last mile was on a tarmac footpath and the extra pressure created by walking downhill, especially on the hard surface, made Andy's right foot extremely painful. Even though it had been a relatively short day, he was hobbling quite badly and despite his still upbeat humour I could tell he was really suffering.

As we passed the 'Welcome to Buxton' sign, we knew we were almost there; our accommodation that night had been donated by the Buxton Crescent Hotel, a newly refurbished spa hotel right in the centre of town (and more importantly, at the end of the road we were on).

As we were passing some shops, a car came to a sudden stop in a lay-by next to us. The doors opened and a woman jumped out.

'I'm Helen Taylor,' she said. 'I've come to find you!'

It was Helen who'd sent us the poem 'Our Girls' on Day 4 . She gave us all a hug – it was wonderful to be able to thank her in person. Talking to Tim, it became clear that Helen lived close to where he grew up in Coventry; it turned out that her house was only 300 metres away from Tim's childhood home and no more than half a mile away from where his mum and dad live now! That small world again.

As Tim talked to Helen, I saw Andy's wife Fiona coming down the road – and it looked like she meant business. Fi had been talking to a local pharmacist about blisters and she was carrying a large bag full of footcare products. It appeared the Cumbrian was going to get the pedicure of his life.

Rather than stand blocking the pavement, we suggested that we head to our accommodation: a grand late-eighteenth-century Grade 1 listed building and now, after major restoration, a luxury 5-star spa hotel.

Waiting for us outside with Sue and Evie was my Helen. I could see the pain of the last eighteen months since Beth left us etched in her face. Once she would have been the first to laugh and poke fun – especially at me – but life was different now. Losing her youngest daughter and soulmate has changed her for ever. This is true grief and she will carry a Beth-sized hole in her heart for the rest of her days.

We all had a chance to chat to poet Helen before she made her excuses and left us to get checked in. Andy was literally hauled off by Fi for a thorough inspection of his foot.

I couldn't wait to make the most of the spa and was in the pool with Helen within thirty minutes of arrival. It was heaven, swimming between the indoor and outdoor pools and letting weary muscles get pounded by the water jets. We could have done with this at the end of each day.

Tim, Sue and Evie joined us, and it was great to see the little girl have fun as only a kid can in a swimming pool. Helen and I went back to the room to get ready for dinner, and my 'I'll just have five minutes on the bed' quickly lapsed into a deep state of unconsciousness.

It was good to see Helen, although she looked so tired. Our twenty-three-year marriage, once so strong, was being sorely tested by the forces of grief – they could certainly break a family apart. In losing a child to suicide, you can become isolated in your own world of pain; you retreat into a bubble of coping mechanisms that help you get through. To have a few hours rest and relaxation with my wife in the beautiful Buxton Crescent Hotel was such a tonic for us. Nothing that had gone before was forgotten, of course – but this felt so good.

Andy didn't make it to the swimming pool. His struggle with his blistered foot was becoming very real. He'd hidden behind good humour all day, gritting his teeth and getting on with it, but his foot was, as Horse had so eloquently described it the night before, 'a f—king state!'

Out of Andy's earshot, Tim and I had been in discussion all day about a contingency plan if the Cumbrian had to give up. Luckily, Fiona was on the ball and after Andy had showered, she took him (slowly) to the pharmacy she'd discovered earlier. It looked like a shop from the Edwardian era, she said later, but with a twenty-first-century pharmacist. He looked at Andy's wound, discussed the best way to dress it and how to look after it as the walk went on. Andy was relieved that he didn't talk about taking weight off it or stopping walking.

Helen and I eventually joined the others for dinner (my five-minute nap having gone on a little longer than intended): the 3 Dads, our wives and Tim's youngest daughter Evie. At nearly eleven, she was Manchester United- and football-mad. Little did she know we had a surprise for her.

Helen had sourced a pair of Manchester United Adidas football boots in Evie's size. Even through our own grief, witnessing the true joy of a child receiving a gift that meant so much was so special. They do say that being kind to others can help those who are grieving. Evie spent the whole evening chatting to us – and wearing the boots.

It was a great evening. Tim, Sue and Evie smiled and joked with all of us, despite it being such a difficult day: Emily's twenty-first birthday. They were all still hurting, crying inside as we all were, reeling from the indescribable pain, but the power of our shared bond and mutual support helped. That knowing look, the need never to explain or justify your feelings, knowing there was understanding, love and support, was so important. I guess Tim and his family knew we had all gone through those milestones, and would continue to do so for as long as we lived, but it was comforting to know our friendship had supported them through this very poignant day.

Money raised (excluding Gift Aid and direct donations)
  = £309,000
Day 7 distance = 15.3 miles
Total distance walked = 155.9 miles

DAY 8

Buxton to Matlock

Helen was still in bed and gave me an affectionate grunt as I kissed her goodbye after breakfast. She was exhausted. The toll of losing a child to suicide is immense; every day is like carrying a great boulder of grief. Helen and I could never quite get a grip on it before it shifted into a more awkward position. I wanted her to take the opportunity to have a lie-in and maybe get a massage in the hotel's health club before she left.

An efficient laying out of walking kit the night before led to my smooth transformation into the teal-coloured Dad, and I was soon heading down to reception to meet the others. There was already quite a crowd gathering outside the hotel; the morning was cool, but dry. Alice Bannister was there with her mum Anna and huge Great Dane puppy, Wellington. They'd travelled that morning from their home in Castleton.

As well as being a college friend of Beth's, Alice ran her own record label, Hope Valley Records, and had signed Beth only months before her death. They'd started to record what was to be their first album, but then Covid hit. It is hard to know how this beautiful and talented young woman could process the loss of her soulmate whom she also believed was an amazing talent. I saw them sing together at a couple of gigs and the contrast between Beth's soulful voice and Alice's sweet harmonies was spellbinding. Their version of 'Cherry Wine' by Hozier could silence a room full of noisy drinkers . . . before they exploded into a huge round of applause.

I always felt such immense pride when Beth sang but, looking back on it, perhaps even then all was not well with my youngest daughter. Maybe her refusal to change her guitar strings and or look at new equipment were signs of her losing some kind of hope. Those thoughts still haunt me.

Sadly, only one album track was completed: 'Pixel Screens'. This incredible song about teenage angst was also written by Beth and is a constant reminder of what my little girl could have achieved if only she could have seen hope beyond her despair. The lyrics possibly tell the story of a young woman falling out with life, ambition and love. Her life had been so simple when she was little.

This ain't love, no
Don't tell me that this was <u>worth</u> the wait
All it gave me was somebody's <u>heart</u> to break
Am I somebody
'Cos somebody's <u>gonna</u> get hurt
And I know that you want her
So you kick me to the dirt
Played <u>dirty</u> just to get hurt
And I've <u>never</u> been so hurt
No I've <u>never</u> felt so bad
Even <u>though</u> you didn't want that
Can't help it if I feel bad
We've got our <u>issues</u> we've got our faults

But I'd rather this way
Than live in the day
When you don't call me up
I'm down
I'm trying my best
Boy give me a rest
It's my patience you test
Just wanna fool around
Oooh oooh
This ain't love no
Not even close to shit that I once dreamed
Spot the difference between me and pixel screens
What I gotta do to get a drink
Cos I'm gonna get wavy
And now you're not my baby
There's no way that you can save me
Set sail and call me navy
And there's nothing you can pay me
Because I've never felt so bad
Even though you didn't want that
Can't help it if I feel bad
We've got our issues, we've got our faults
But I'd rather this way
Than live in the day
When you don't call me up
I'm down
I'm trying my best
Boy give me a rest
It's my patience you test

Just <u>wanna</u> fool around
Oooh oooh
Stop <u>looking</u> at me now
Stop <u>looking</u> at me now
You know that I'm no clown
Stop <u>looking</u> at me now
Stop <u>looking</u> at me now
Stop <u>looking</u> at me now

Alice was determined the song should be heard and courageously produced it to raise funds for Beth's JustGiving page. The page raised over £17,000, and we used it to fund courses on suicide awareness and prevention. 'Pixel Screens' by Beth Palmer went on to become #1 in the iTunes Singer/Songwriter Charts.

Sadly, Alice was no stranger to suicide, after losing both her auntie and grandma to it, and she bravely agreed to be interviewed with Anna in the hotel reception. I was left in awe at the frankness of both mother and daughter.

Outside the hotel, a very relieved Wing Commander Tim was handing Wing Commander AB Bear back to Richard Bland. Babysitting the precious bear all the way from Pym's Chair the day before had been a great responsibility (especially considering Tim's RAF connection).

We were greeted by Mark Liddell with his thirteen-year-old son Zac and nephew Sam Harris, Helen's godson. They'd come from Sale to walk the whole day with us. Sixteen years old, 6 feet 6 inches tall, another Sir David Attenborough in the making and an excellent Peter Crouch-style footballer,

Sam is a young man with a heart of gold. Having known Beth all his life, he felt her passing deeply, but he'd galvanised himself into a fundraising effort that had produced over £1,300 for PAPYRUS.

Mark, Zac and Sam had done lots of walking together. This was going to be Zac's longest-ever day out, so Mark had created a JustGiving page entitled '*Zac & Sam's 23-Mile Hike – Supporting 3 Dads Walking*'. Zac is a beautiful human being. His tales of kings and queens through the ages made the miles tick by – it is remarkable how much knowledge he retains (unlike me: I struggle with my own mobile number).

As we set off, Alice and her friend joined us. Alice is Day 1 Susanna's daughter; she lives in Macclesfield and wanted to walk the Monsal Trail with us. Away we all went, through Buxton, heading up the A6 before turning east across fields towards the Trail. At the second farm, we had a bit of a verbal kerfuffle when the farmer insisted the right of way did not pass through his property. Andy and Tim checked their maps and decided that it most certainly did. They turned their backs on the farmer and, pointing the way with walking poles, led our tribe along the path marked on the OS map.

We hadn't gone too far before we found the path blocked and had to use a side lane to get back to the road that the farmer had tried to send us along – but that wasn't the point! Tim and Andy were determined that we needed to exercise our right of way, even though it would, much to my amusement, turn out to be impassable.

Often a point of conflict between landowners and ramblers, footpaths are clearly marked on OS maps. However, if they are not well trodden and kept clear you can end up with lost walkers wandering over private land. Result: frayed tempers.

Over one stile, our merry band entered a field full of cows. They were quickly developing an interest in us and were quite boisterous to the point that we thought they could become aggressive. I adopted a defensive posture, squaring up to and facing off the bovines and talking gently to them, while having my walking poles ready to fend them off. The group was ushered quickly towards the next stile to exit the field. Tim was probably quickest, as he was wearing a bright-red cap that his father had very sensibly insisted he use to keep the sun off his very fair-skinned head. It could be a red rag to a bull.

It was one of those awkward stiles that wobbled a bit, with overhanging bushes to snag backpacks and flags, thus slowing down our exit. I continued to face the cows down, making soothing noises at them as the rest of the group made their escape. This wasn't bravery on my part, but a shift in attitude that has come with complex grief. Once a field of unpredictable cattle would have had me running for the nearest gate, but that desire for self-preservation has gone. I really don't care like I used to, and my attitude towards a field of skittish bovines has changed.

Across a few more fields we came to the top of the embankment overlooking Wye Dale – it was beautiful in the early morning stillness. The only problem was that the heavy dew on the long grass was penetrating our boots. No matter how good the Gortex system on your footwear, constant soaking can end up playing havoc with the state of your feet. Ask Andy. Regular sock-changing was needed.

As we walked and contemplated the loveliness of the Peak District landscape, Tim pointed out some quarry buildings hunkered in the valley bottom. 'I recognise these! It was one of our training targets!' He obviously saw the countryside from a different perspective – a military one.

Our path took a winding route, passing under a railway bridge before reaching the Monsal Trail, a cycling, horse-riding and walking trail constructed from a section of the former Manchester, Buxton, Matlock and Midland Junction Railway, which was built by the Midland Railway in 1863 to link Manchester with London.

The Trail would take us all the way to Bakewell – nine miles gently downhill. What a great way to spend the next three hours. Our chatty band headed off down the disused railway line, which closed in 1968.

As the conversation ebbed and flowed, we learnt that Alice was a bioengineer who'd worked to produce one of the Covid vaccines – we were all suitably grateful. Zac kept us entertained demonstrating his incredible knowledge of Russian monarchy through the ages, whilst Sam chatted about his hopes for university and a career in zoology.

We remembered that we should take some footage using the BBC camera we were given at our last visit to the Red Sofa . . . and so we gave it to Sam. Our thinking was that even though us oldies might struggle to use it, a sixteen-year-old wildlife enthusiast would understand it immediately. He did and spent the rest of the day taking short videos for the BBC, the best of which were taken as the group walked through one of the tunnels that are a feature of the trail. Not as much fun as filming David

Attenborough with the mountain gorillas of Uganda, perhaps, but good practice nevertheless.

At Millers Dale, we decided a coffee/tea stop was in order. Set in a former railway building, and offering tasty refreshments for walkers and cyclists, we were transported back to the bygone days of steam. Fiona and Tim ordered takeaway drinks – this was the only time on the entire route when we had to pay for anything (it was quite nice to be incognito for a change!). It was pleasant to take a bit of a time out to watch the world go by; since it was a Saturday, the Monsal Trail was busy with walkers and cyclists.

We kept good time and were soon at Monsal Head, directly above Monsal Dale and the River Wye, and one of the most photographed viewpoints in Derbyshire. We'd arranged to meet David and his wife Lisa there. David was Tim's army equivalent for the East of England – he was the one who sorted out our wonderful accommodation in Buxton, and had even insisted on paying for our meals.

When we arrived at the agreed rendezvous, we were surprised to find that the car park was a couple of hundred feet above the Trail, at the point it entered the 490-metre Headstone Tunnel. Tim called David to check to see if he was in the car park (he was) . . . in a flash, David and Lisa were coming down the zigzag path towards us. Close behind were Sue and Evie – they were on their way back to King's Lynn and wanted to see Tim before heading home.

Andy took off his boot and Fiona redressed his wound (all caught on video, so you can see how rough she was with him). Just as he'd laced up again, a couple pushed through the group

– it was Richard and Rachel Pollard. Andy had shared a flat with Richard at university forty years previously, and they hadn't seen each other for about fifteen years. Amazingly the couple were there by chance. They had seen the 3 Dads on TV over the previous days, but although they were in Derbyshire for a weekend walking holiday, they hadn't realised that they would be anywhere near the route. They just happened to be walking along that part of the Monsal Trail that afternoon – a lovely coincidence. Andy seemed to have friends and acquaintances everywhere.

Our extended stop had to come to an end. After hugs and goodbyes, away we went through the tunnel.

It wasn't long before our numbers swelled again. As we rounded the next corner we saw George, Bill and Cherry coming in the opposite direction; they had parked in Bakewell and walked north along the Monsal Trail to meet us. They were also there to be Fiona's lift back to Buxton. Towards the end of the trail, just to the south-east of Bakewell, we had another short break and did a bit of filming. Mark and Zac reflected on why they walked: the exercise, to develop a respect for the outdoors and to help build positive mental health. Zac said he was walking with us because he wanted to support us, to raise money for PAPYRUS and because he just loved walking – and told us that he'd just walked his thousandth mile in a year! He was very proud of himself and quite right too. Sam, meanwhile, explained that as well as raising funds for PAPYRUS, he wanted to send a message to teenagers that there is always a different option to suicide. 'Suicide is a permanent solution to a temporary problem,' he said. 'There always is a way out, no matter how hard it seems.'

Before we put our rucksacks back on, Mark pulled the 3 Dads together so that we could present Zac with a certificate celebrating his thousandth mile. The thirteen-year-old accepted it with a broad grin.

It was time to move on. We said goodbye to Fiona, George, Bill and his partner, Cherry . . . and hello to Richard Hildebrand, a Bakewell local. We talked to Richard about our planned route and he suggested sticking to a farm track (not marked as a right of way) that would save us about a mile – we immediately liked him. He was one of those good sorts who was involved in all kinds of groups and activities in his community, including being a DJ on the local radio station, S41 Radio.

Richard's route was excellent – we saved quite a climb and made good progress through Combs Farm towards Rowsley. Dropping into the village, we met Lucy and Chris – Lucy is Andy's niece – as they walked up the road with their dog. Before Andy could cross the road to hug them, they said, 'Don't hug us. The girls have Covid!' Lucy's daughters were staying with their father, and she hadn't seen them since they had tested positive, but as she worked in the NHS she wanted to be as safe as possible.

Another family joined us as we crossed the River Derwent. Of course, Andy soon discovered that the mother's best friend was married to Justin Farnan, a mate of his from Keswick. The world kept getting smaller.

Immediately after crossing the river at Darley Bridge, the gang turned left to follow the minor road, which was also the Derwent Valley Heritage Way.

Tim and I began to speculate about how many people Andy

didn't know when we found out that the next couple to join us used to rent a flat belonging to his brother and played on the same pub quiz team in the Lake District as Andy. Claire and (another) Andy had moved away from the Lakes years before and now lived near Matlock. They'd seen the 3 Dads Walking story on TV and decided they needed to come along, put some cash in the bucket and say hello.

We had our final brief stop of the day at Darley Bridge, next to the dark waters of the Derwent. All our recent followers departed, leaving us with Mark, Zac and Sam. We were joined by George, a friend and Chaplain of Manchester Airport airport, who helped me through some of the darkest times following Beth's death. When I first speculated about a potential walk, George and his wife Libby – the Bishop of Derby – had immediately offered their house as a place to stay.

I now ashamedly admit that I used to avoid Chaplain George on his fire-station visits, hiding in the locker room until he'd gone. I was not a man of faith or God, but Beth's death led me to ask questions. What happens when we die? Is that that it? Does everything turn black and then nothing? Or is there more?

Soon after we lost Beth, Guy, an old Atlantic rowing friend, had contacted me to offer his condolences. An ex-army officer, he had always been spiritual – and, not 'getting it', I had always turned the other way when he'd talked about it on board *Britannia 3* in the middle of the Pond, hundreds, if not thousands, of miles from land. Now, however, it was different. I needed to look beyond the black-and-white world I existed in with Beth and explore the possibility of an afterlife – and maybe even a heaven.

Guy recommended a book, *Proof of Heaven, A Neuro-surgeon's Journey into the Afterlife* by Dr Eben Alexander. It blew my mind and raised the possibility that I could see my little girl again on the other side. I was the world's greatest cynic; for me to believe in what I could not actually see was unheard of.

The weight of evidence for an afterlife was massive. There are so many books, organisations, personal accounts and documentaries recounting the heavenly experiences of those who had been through Near Death Experiences (NDEs). Individuals who have had a close shave with death and who recall momentarily leaving their bodies and travelling to a beautiful place of peace and love that feels like home, even seeing deceased loved ones and interacting with a divine presence.

When talking to family and friends on the subject, they too admit to experiences that they will not recount in public for fear of being labelled as 'bonkers'. Their tales bear such a similarity to the others I have researched that I am now convinced there is something beyond. Maybe we are 'spirits having a human journey', and the other side is home. Anyway, if I do meet Beth again, my beautiful little girl will get a kick up the arse before I envelope her in a never-ending hug.

The last couple of miles of the day took us through riverside meadows to Matlock Bridge. We said our thanks and goodbyes to Mark, Zac and Sam before getting into Chaplain George's car. Zac and Sam were still smiling, despite having done their longest-ever single-day walk.

It turned out the Bishop of Derby's house wasn't in Derby but in Duffield, a twenty-five-minute drive along the Derwent Valley. On arrival, Libby gave us a warm welcome. Despite the house being a 'working' property it was incredibly homely. We were soon ensconced in our rooms – Andy in the Church Commissioner's Room and I had a whole floor to myself. Andy was particularly pleased to see that his en-suite bathroom actually had a bath – it gave him the first opportunity since damaging his feet to give them a good, long soak. Luxury.

After we had something to eat I videoed a short interview with George where he talked about my 'profound journey' and how privileged he was to 'metaphorically walk' with me through my darkest times. George also mentioned that they'd lost a family member to suicide and that one of his family was a suicide survivor. He reflected on the lack of support for people struggling with their mental health and lack of openness and honesty surrounding suicide and suicide prevention. 'It's only when we are honest that we can address those issues,' he said.

Money raised (excluding Gift Aid and direct donations)
   = £319,000
Day 8 distance = 22.9 miles
Total distance walked = 178.8 miles

DAY 9

Matlock to Mansfield

After a comfortable night we woke to a rather damp start to Day 9. After we'd gathered our kit together, we unrolled the 3 Dads Walking banner and stood outside with Chaplain George, Libby acting as photographer. We insisted on having a photo with Libby too, so she quickly disappeared into the house and came back ... as a BISHOP! She was wearing jeans from the waist down and Bishop-wear from the waist up – a purple tunic and a *massive* silver cross! It was reminiscent of Clark Kent nipping into a telephone box and reappearing as Superman.

George soon had us back at Matlock railway station. For the first time we were setting off into unknown territory; the planned route for the next two days went across landscapes none of us knew. Interesting times to come, I thought.

The first few miles east followed the A615, fortunately on a roadside pavement. On reaching Tansley, we turned onto footpaths through fields. We were soon joined by a couple who wanted to walk with us: Keith and Mikey Pierce. They had no direct experience of suicide, but they'd seen our story and we were using footpaths near their home that they walked regularly.

As we crossed a ridge near Wheatcroft, the view opened over north Nottinghamshire. We were leaving the hills behind; the climbing was done and the flatlands were beckoning. It felt like we were making proper progress now.

As we descended, we encountered a few young cows. Once again, I undertook cow duty, but this time the animals were much more placid, with one taking a particular liking to us and following until we crossed the stile into the next field. It looked quite sad as we moved away into the distance.

The morning had been intermittently damp, so we were wearing our lightweight waterproof jackets supplied by Mammut; these had proved to be very effective in keeping out the rain. On reaching Wessington, we sat in the bus shelter to have some food and drink. We looked like three vagrants, but a number of people chatted with us, and more cash went into our bucket.

Andy took the chance to check on his feet – they were still not looking good, and he was still struggling. Tim and I were concerned as we had over 100 miles to walk and the hardened Cumbrian was hurting . . . badly. I dispensed more painkillers.

As we entered the small village of Shirland, we were met by a couple who walked with us for a while. They lived nearby and invited us in for coffee, tea, snacks and cake, which we consumed in their back garden. They were retired police officers and had been involved in many suicide incidents, so they saw our walk and suicide-prevention message as vitally important.

Suicide has a ripple effect, with close family and loved ones at the epicentre and those such as the police and other emergency services a little further out. The point our new friends were making was that they still carried the trauma of attending such incidents. Through all the hell of losing Beth I still remember the face of a young constable. He was kind, considerate and professional to the last, but I saw despair and disbelief etched on his face. These amazing people we turn to in often the worst times are human – and being witness to such grief day in, day out, can be such a colossal burden to carry.

We'd struggled with planning part of today's route; the paths between the Peak District and Newark just didn't go in the right direction. After a lot of googling and searching on Google Maps, Andy discovered a recently opened nature reserve that wasn't marked on the OS map. The Blackwell Trail was only a few miles long, but it linked to footpaths at either end which enabled us to join everything together and keep us going in the right direction.

As we approached the start of the Blackwell Trail at West-houses, we met Dale, a man who'd followed our tracker and wanted to walk with us. The first thing he did was propose a change – he said that our planned route would take us down a wet and muddy lane, so he suggested we divert a little way south to stay on a drier path. We agreed – and Dale led the way.

He explained that the Blackwell Trail was a multi-user route, with walkers, cyclists and horses all coexisting on the same path. There was so much planting of new trees and shrubs it was hard to see that it had once been an industrialised land-scape; a wooden sculpture of a miner gives a clue as to the area's former life under the Blackwell Colliery Company. The path follows the old mineral railway that served the pits and coking ovens.

As we walked along, two women rushed towards us, one of them shouting, 'I have to give you a hug!' It was Julie and her daughter, who lived not far away. Julie was a massively enthu-siastic supporter of 3 Dads Walking and talked with such passion as we walked along. Yet again, we were a bit stunned with the reaction we were getting from the people we met along the way.

I was always up for a hug. This walk was bringing out the best in people. I was finding that laughing and joking was becoming easier with the kindness being shown, but still within lurked the never-ending sadness that I would not be going home to my little girl. They say 'there's is no place like home' – but mine no longer felt like the place of sanctuary it once had.

I fell into step again with the group across these old coal lands.

Life is full of characters, and we were meeting so many. Just when you thought the tracker had run out of surprises it would produce another. There was no time to get lost in your own thoughts – and perhaps that was a good thing. As we moved through a secluded section on the path we could see a figure with a small dog dancing about and waving at us just a short way ahead. We looked at each other and could not help but smile – this person was obviously delighted to see us. The figure turned out to be a very tall, elderly gentlemen with a very ancient mongrel. He was another Tim who had driven from Coventry to meet us – he'd lost his nineteen-year-old daughter Nikki to suicide in 1987. Tim was very charming and erudite.

Coventry Tim explained that he'd read *The Times* feature the previous day and was impressed to see how we were reaching out to people and talking about our loss. He said, 'Reaching out is very difficult because people are often afraid to talk.' He talked about grief and how it changes over time and how he hoped that by doing this walk, we would have something that would help us by the time we reached the end. As we finished recording him, we turned to see Dale standing behind us in floods of tears.

It turned out that Coventry Tim had been a teacher and also an actor – it showed. It looked like he had wandered off stage to meet us and he was eloquence personified. We left him in the nature reserve and headed onwards.

Traffic roared by us as on an unavoidable section of the A38, the noise and hard surface under our feet magnifying any discomfort. Two miles later, just before we escaped from the road, we were stopped by two men: the younger one sullen and the older one stressed. They were father and son and had driven down from Leeds to talk to us; the father was desperately worried – he explained that his son suffered from severe psychotic episodes and that he didn't know where to turn.

It was obvious that this desperate father would do anything to help his son, but every road was proving to be a dead end. I reflected on Beth and the fact I did not even have the chance to fight for her and get the help she so obviously needed.

'What can we do to help?' we asked, but the father continued, now focusing on his son's medical history.

We kept asking what he thought we could do to help him, pointing out that we weren't mental-health experts, just 3 Dads Walking. We tried to talk to him about PAPYRUS and HOPELINE247, but we weren't sure if he was listening to us.

As we turned off the A38 we saw the man and his son get back into their car and drive off – we wondered what the future had in store for them. It was clear to us that they'd been let down by or lost somewhere in our overstretched mental-health care system. It all seemed desperately sad.

Daylight was turning to dusk – it was proving to be a long day. Our lift – Nigel, another old friend of Andy's, who was helping us out tonight – was nearby and we were in need of respite. We realised that we were – incredibly – just shy of the 200-mile mark. It was hard to believe we were two thirds of the way there.

When we arrived at Nigel's car, Dale thanked us for allowing him to walk so far with us. Yet another walking companion going back to his life. I wondered how these people would remember us in years to come. So many people were coming and going, some telling the most heartbreaking tales and carrying such grief. Talking was proving to be a powerful tool in processing the aftermath, and the fact that myself, Andy and Tim could provide such a platform was helping us too.

During the drive towards Newark, Nigel explained the sleeping arrangements. Because he and his wife were helping his elderly mother-in-law, they were unsurprisingly cautious about Covid. They were happy for us to shower in their house but didn't want us to spend time inside or sleep there – we could use the shed instead.

Andy had stayed with Nigel many times before (although never in the shed). He knew it was a big shed, but it had been a cluttered and mucky workshop when he'd last seen it. What were we letting ourselves in for?

It was dark when we arrived, and Nigel said that there was room for two in the shed and that the other bed was in his classic VW campervan. I volunteered for the van immediately . . . To our relief the shed was no longer a workshop. It was brightly lit and warm, there was a large table covered in bottles of beer and wine – it felt cosy. Before we did anything, Nigel insisted that we order our food – a takeaway curry. That meant we could get a shower while he nipped into town to pick it up. What a great plan!

The four of us sat in peaceful companionship, enjoying superb food and beer in what became known as 'Nigel's Stable' (which seemed religiously appropriate after being in the Bishop's house the night before).

We were then shown the next room in the shed, which was accessed by a separate external door. Here was everything Nigel thought we would need for breakfast and packed lunches the following day, plus tea and coffee-making facilities . . . and even more alcohol. An adjacent outside tap provided drinking water. The supplies Nigel had in would have lasted us the entire walk.

Nigel's final surprise was our outside toilet, which was in a shed with no light and a few resident spiders. It had a mirror and a small sink with a cold-water tap fashioned from a piece of copper piping. It was all perfectly usable, if a little nippy!

Eventually we ran out of steam and needed to sleep. Nigel retired to his warm house, taking our boots with him to dry them out. I collected a duvet and went out to the campervan, leaving Tim and Andy with two mattresses sitting on top of two single wooden bedframes.

I was happy to be getting a bit of 'me' time. The camper had no power and was a little chilly, but I double-layered my clothing and the duvet was nice and heavy. I fell asleep almost immediately, without the aid of the sleeping pills I had become so reliant on (I'd left them back home in Sale – I wanted to keep a clear head on the walk). All the walking, talking and fresh air had taken me to a very different place at night-time. Too exhausted to think about much apart from the next day, I was resting better than I had done since before Beth had gone.

Being a long way from home and the life I once knew felt so surreal – almost as if I was living in a dream. The walk had become so much more than a fund-raising exercise for PAPYRUS – it was now some kind of quest to stop young people giving up on life. With every conversation along the way we were learning more, and finding out that those loved ones who were left to grieve believed far more could be done.

We need to protect our precious children from their greatest danger: themselves.

Money raised (excluding Gift Aid and direct donations)
    = £323,000
Day 9 distance = 21 miles
Total distance walked = 199.8 miles

PART THREE

Tim and Emily

CHAPTER THIRTEEN

Tim and Emily

My beautiful daughter Emily was the reason I was walking. Her decision, just eighteen months earlier, had totally devastated so many lives. Nobody had been immune to the pain – family, friends, colleagues – and looking back it was impossible not to question everything I had ever done as a father.

Emily had always been a bit different from her siblings. She could be wonderfully loving, generous and affectionate, but then she could snap at the slightest thing and become incredibly angry, even from a very early age. The simplest request – 'Could you put your socks on?' – could result in an outburst.

When she was young, her behaviour was put down to 'the terrible twos' by our GP. Later we sought support from her primary school. Although her teachers never experienced her angry behaviour she did struggle with reading, which led to a diagnosis of dyslexia when she was ten. This gave her additional time in exams and support in her education, but she still tussled with her emotions.

In her early teens Emily's behaviour became worse, much worse, and her mental health was very poor – it led to a very dark time in all our lives. My wife, Sue, and our children, Annie, Tom and Evie, all loved her deeply. She was so beautiful, clever, caring, generous and talented ... but just struggled with life.

Only her closest friends and family were aware of just how tough everything was for her. She struggled with routine things – going to school became a huge issue; rowing on a Saturday morning at a local club where she excelled, attending various athletic events, again for a local club. Just getting her there could lead to massive emotional outbursts, which she felt really bad about later. As her attendance at school became erratic she sank further. A number of suicide attempts saw her hospitalised, and she was placed under the care of CAMHS (Child and Adolescent Mental Health Services). We were in crisis as a family. Although we were supported by a range of organisations – including social services and her high school, who were both unbelievably good – her mental health was really suffering. It was a horrific time – but then we had a breakthrough.

One of our friends in the village was a retired psychologist and she asked if Em had ever been assessed for autism. 'No,' had been our simple reply. She suggested we look at the National Autistic Society's website. At the time there was a basic questionnaire which gave a score; the level of that score indicated if you should seek an assessment. Our score indicated that Em should be assessed. We asked several family members to complete the assessment, without Em knowing, and all produced the same result – Em should seek a formal assessment for autism.

We spoke to our GP and CAMHS, and it was clear that any assessment through the NHS could take months, if not years. So we asked our GP if he could refer Em privately to one of the National Autistic Society's assessment centres – the Lorna Wing Centre in Bromley.

A few weeks later we took the journey south to Kent. The professional – but so tremendously caring – staff of the Lorna Wing Centre interviewed us separately. After a morning of interviews, we took time out for lunch and upon our return the doctors sat us down. Although there were more tests to do, it was obvious to them that Em had high-functioning autism, and they were amazed that she had managed to cope for so long without specialised support. While the diagnosis was a relief to us – we now knew what we were dealing with – it ripped Em apart. She was a fifteen-year-old who had just been told that her brain functioned differently from the majority of people – she looked destroyed. If only she had been given an assessment and diagnosis in her early years, she could have been given the support she so desperately needed from the start.

After the diagnosis, we bought every book and read every article we could find on high-functioning autism. It was clear that parenting a young person with autism was so different from that of a neuro-typical child.

The diagnosis unlocked further invaluable support from school and external education providers. Em worked hard to rebuild her life and, with help, she gained GCSEs and attended art college, gaining a BTEC. One of her coping strategies had been to go to the gym and she decided to complete a Sports Fitness apprenticeship. She learnt to drive and passed her theory and practical tests first time round – driving was her gateway to freedom.

She'd worked in our community pub part-time for a couple of years, and after finishing her apprenticeship, Em worked there on a full-time basis. She was the life and soul of the place. On a Thursday night I would often meet friends in the pub, and Em would be there holding court behind the bar. Her behaviour could still be erratic, but we knew more about how to deal with it, recognising when she needed time out and space to reduce the sensory load on her brain. But then came Covid.

We'd been listening to the news and watching as the virus spread around the world. With family in northern Italy, the epicentre of the outbreak in Europe, we had a feel for how bad it could get. The incredibly caring Em had said she would volunteer as part of the Covid response and was thinking about a career caring for people within the NHS, something she would have been so good at.

And then we started to cough . . .

That Monday, 16 March 2020, Em was at the gym and we phoned her. 'You'll need to come home as we need to go into isolation as a family,' we said.

Em was annoyed – she hung up. But she called back within a minute. 'What do we need? I'll nip to the supermarket and get some food.'

We gave her a list and she called me from half-way round the shop: 'Dad – can you transfer me some money as I don't think I have enough in my bank account to pay?'

'Of course, how much?' I replied, and transferred £60 straight away.

She arrived back home around an hour later in her bright red Mini with £120 worth of shopping, including loads of chocolate, crisps and other goodies – a typical nineteen-year-old's shop!

But she was upset. She told us that while she was queuing with the trolley, an older couple had told her off, in front of other shoppers, for buying so much. They incorrectly presumed she was a young single person being selfish and hoarding food. They never gave Em the chance to explain that she was doing a big shop for her family of six and that the food would need to last the next week or so. She was devastated and in tears that strangers could be so nasty. I would love to meet that couple and explain how their comments so adversely impacted Em. Comments are made all the time online, and occasionally – as per Em's encounter – face-to-face, but do we ever know what people are actually going through and what impact a needless comment will have? If they had given Em the chance to explain they would have ended up praising her, as a young person, for being so caring and supportive of her family. Words really matter – and at that particular time, they really mattered to Em.

We relaxed into our isolated state over the next two days. Em and her brother, Tom, and sister, Evie, spent the time eating much of the chocolate she'd bought and watching films. Em seemed to be in a happy place. And then everything changed.

On 18 March, Em was in an agitated state from the minute she woke up. The mechanisms she used to cope with her autism were all being denied her. She was angry. She saw her job in the pub disappearing and her two main outlets for dealing with life – driving her car and working out in the gym – both stopping. She felt she was being prevented from doing anything, from doing the normal stuff young people do. She asked us if she could go up to the beach with our dog – we said that she couldn't. At the time, if you had Covid symptoms, you weren't allowed out. And everyone followed the government's rules – right?

This was just too much for Emily and she walked out of our house. I heard the door slam, a routine thing when she was under pressure. When this sort of thing happened the CAMHS specialists had told us not to go chasing after her as it would inflame the situation. So we just let her go into the garden to calm down – and that was the last time we spoke to her. We found her fifteen minutes later. She had attempted to take her own life.

She was rushed to hospital in an ambulance, unconscious. Those minutes are too painful to write about but I remember screams, my family, police, ambulance staff in a haze of tears and devastation.

Could it get any worse? Oh yes.

As she had been displaying Covid symptoms, she went straight onto the critical-care Covid ward on life support where no visitors were allowed. We then endured a horrendous two days before we could visit Em after she tested negative for Covid – she just had a common cold. She'd attempted to take her life because of a common cold.

During those two days we phoned the critical-care ward and received regular updates. These initially offered us some hope, but as time went on, the hope started to disappear. Once Em was Covid-free we were finally allowed to visit, so that evening, Friday 20 March, we did. She looked beautiful, just sleeping, with her nails done perfectly and her hair carefully brushed. There were various tubes connected to her, keeping her alive.

We sat down with the medical staff who slowly, carefully and compassionately explained to us that 'the injuries Emily has sustained are too great and she is unable to breathe on her own'.

They went on to explain how 'the life-support machine is keeping her alive at the moment', and then we heard those words 'there is no chance of survival'.

We were utterly devastated, absolutely destroyed – our world was falling apart. How could this be happening to us?

As we sat, the NHS staff returned to their amazing care of Em, compassionately talking to her as they tenderly washed her face and arranged her beautiful long blonde hair.

In amongst all this they sensitively broached the subject of organ donation. It transpired that she had signed the organ donor register when she was eleven. In this absolutely horrific situation, we now had a glimmer of hope – other families' lives would be transformed by Em's organ donations. A final typically selfless and generous act.

Over the next forty hours, attempts were made to contact organ recipients who were a potential match. Hospital operating theatres and staff were lined up, and specialist organ donation vehicles were assigned to transport Em's lifesaving organs across the country. This whole process was complicated by the fact that many of the staff required to carry out the organ donation process had been reassigned to Covid wards. As we counted down our last hours and minutes with Em, the specialist team kept us informed every time a recipient was located, bringing us some comfort. This drawn-out and difficult process extended Em's final time with us by a few more hours – so, so worth it.

Finally, on Sunday 22 March, Emily's life support was switched off and we held her as she passed away.

There are no words to explain the pain of that moment, and the aftermath. I felt totally lost, numb and isolated, my world a living nightmare, normality smashed. Simple daily activities – getting up, washing, preparing food, exercising, just breathing, just existing – required so much effort. Everything felt like being faced with an enormous mountain to climb, but with no idea of how or where to start. As a dad, I was meant to know what to do in rough times; I was meant to have some wisdom to give to my family, to guide them through life. I had nothing to offer.

In my RAF career, I'd had some pretty extreme and dangerous experiences. But in every case I'd been subject to some form of training, a building-block approach of increasing challenge, which had given me the tools to deal with it. However, I had not been trained to deal with the suicide of my daughter, and I knew, very early on, that I needed help and support. That was perhaps the most important decision I made.

I remembered I'd seen a video by Admiral William McRaven, a now-retired United States Navy four-star admiral who commanded special forces. He'd given a speech at the University of Texas in 2014 about ten lessons he'd learned from basic training, and for some unknown reason his speech had always stuck with me. His first lesson was simple: make your bed. If you can accomplish that first task of the day well, then the rest of the day has a better chance of going the same way. If you go to bed that night having done nothing else, you can look at that bed and realise that you did accomplish something that day.

That was my first step – to make my bed – and I did; in fact, I made everyone's beds. Simple: but a start to existing in my new reality.

I reached out for help from whoever I could, given the Covid restrictions and the fact that nobody was allowed in our house. We could not hug or touch family and friends – comfort from normal human contact just wasn't available.

The RAF were superb; they'd even offered us accommodation and food when Em was in hospital. We were scared of going shopping and catching Covid, preventing us from attending Em's funeral. So locals and friends from the RAF kept delivering supplies to us. We would meet them on the drive, standing two metres away, always with tears in our eyes. Our friends just wanted to help and take the pain away, but they couldn't. However, their love and support were so welcome.

Welfare support came from the fantastic charity MIND, who sent round Steve, a suicide-bereavement support worker. We also had Alex, the RAF Padre, and Carol from the military charity SSAFA. This face-to-face support – even outside and at distance – was essential, and I hate to think where we would have been without it. I owe so much to these three amazing people.

Emily's funeral took place on 2 April, a short ceremony at the King's Lynn crematorium with six family members. Rich, a good friend whose family was like a second family to Em, asked if the funeral cortège of a VW campervan hearse and two cars could go the long way round the village, and past his house.

The roads in the village are basically a loop from where we live: to the playing fields, up another road to the green. The cortège departed our house and drove past the swings where Em had played, the football pitch where she'd been a member of the club, past the pub where she'd worked and the primary school she'd attended. It felt like the whole village had come to say goodbye. Hundreds of people were outside their houses, in their gardens, on the village green doing their permitted thirty minutes of exercise. Em's whole life had been in the village and this was their chance to say goodbye. I was driving behind the VW campervan and Em, with tears rolling down my cheeks and my eyes focused ahead. I dared not look at all those people, knowing if I caught their eyes and saw their tears it would just crush me. I was in a parallel universe – this wasn't really happening – just a really, really bad dream.

The funeral service lasted twenty-five minutes, with no wake or celebration of Emily's life. We were back home by 10.30 a.m., devastated. This is a word I use repeatedly – but it does not adequately describe how I or the rest of my family felt.

Utterly heartbroken, Sue cried out: 'That's it, she's gone, and no one will remember her in a year's time.'

Those words stuck with me.

We continued to exist, our horrific new world of devastating grief in isolation only interrupted by food deliveries, friends bringing supplies, family and friends calling us, and our three sources of professional support: Steve, Carol and Padre Alex.

And then, a month after Em died, my eldest daughter Annie approached me and quietly uttered the words a dad normally doesn't want to hear. 'Dad, I have been talking to this man in Manchester!'

I was horrified and confused, especially as Annie has always been the mature and sensible one. 'What?!'

'No, Dad – it's OK, it's another family like us. They've lost a daughter too.'

Annie then explained how she had seen the story of Mike's daughter Beth on social media and she'd reached out to him and his family. She gave me his number and I messaged him:

Mike, I am so sorry to hear about your daughter, Beth. Please do accept my condolences as a father in a similar situation. My daughter, Annabel, shared your story from a media article the other day and gave me your number. We are on the journey with you but think we are a couple of weeks ahead as Emily passed on 22 March. As dads in a similar position, it would be an honour to talk. You and your family are in my thoughts. Tim.

To my surprise, Mike responded immediately:

Tim, thank you. Our hearts go out to you and yours for Emily. Annabel is incredibly brave. Same awful journey indeed. Glad to talk anytime really. Just text first. Mike.

The following day we spoke for the first time: two dads, 200 miles apart, but totally lost about how to move forward and how to live. We spoke about our lives, families and daughters, both asking the same questions to which we will never have an answer.

We spoke for over an hour. We agreed that we should call each other, whatever time of day or night, if we felt we needed to chat. That offer of peer support from someone who really understood what I was going through was an absolute gamechanger for me.

A few weeks later, we needed to sort through Emily's belongings. It was too soon, but my mother-in-law had broken her leg and needed to come and stay with us – in Em's old room – so we had the most painful task of sorting through her belongings. As we did, most of the time in tears, I found a note from Emily which she'd placed in her cloth shopping bag, overlooked by the police: her final letter to us. In the beautifully crafted letter, two sentences stood out: *'The last thing I'd like to ask of you is don't be ashamed of what I have done. I don't mind people knowing about what happened to me if it will help them before it's too late.'*

I could never be ashamed of Em; and – incredibly – here she was, giving us the green light to use what had happened to help other people. I was absolutely devastated, crushed again – this was Em speaking to me, six weeks after she'd gone. But her words really resonated with me, and I knew that I needed to do something.

I just wasn't sure what.

I called Mike and told him what I'd found. Over the next few months, he and I spoke regularly about our families and how we were (or were not) dealing with the situation. Mike spoke about a charity called PAPYRUS, explaining that it was a small but growing suicide-prevention charity based near him in Warrington.

In trying to understand what Beth had done, Mike had

booked himself onto some courses offered by the charity. This was the first time I heard that suicide is the biggest killer of under-thirty-fives and that around two hundred school-aged children take their own lives every year. Mike and I spoke about these statistics – imagine if a school of two hundred children was destroyed every year in the UK. There would be outrage and an outpouring of national grief. Instead, these young people die individually, leaving their families isolated and destroyed in the aftermath.

Mike told me that PAPYRUS ran a suicide-prevention hotline called HOPELINEUK (since renamed HOPELINE247), staffed by professionals trained to talk to someone in crisis, or to their family, friends or anyone who could be classified as 'a concerned other'. Why had I never heard of this? What if I or Em had known this support was available? Would she have reached out? Would a simple phone call in her time of crisis have saved her?

Steve, my MIND support worker, had recommended a course called the Anchor Project. This was an eight-week course, one evening each week, for those impacted by the suicide of a loved one. It was not meant to be therapy but rather an opportunity to discuss feelings and emotions in a safe space. One was running in King's Lynn in the autumn and I booked myself onto it. It was a compassionate and thought-provoking course, which examined many of the emotions I'd felt in the aftermath of Em's suicide: grief, guilt, anger, blame and sadness.

I took away many lessons from the course, the most important of which was that it was OK and perfectly normal to feel any of these emotions, but that getting stuck in any one of them could lead to a dangerous downward spiral. Another key lesson was around terminology. Some people say that you will 'move on' after loss; however, that implies moving on past the event and almost putting it behind you, even forgetting it, which is impossible. How could I ever forget Em? An alternative approach is to say that you will 'move forward'. This simple adjustment enables you to take your loved one's memory with you into the future. That was definitely what I intended to do.

I am a bit of a numbers man and asked the facilitators about the statistics behind suicide. I was given a Samaritans' report from December 2018, and was told that the statistics were always a few years behind as they relied on the findings in a Coroner's Inquest. I was horrified to see that 6,213 people died by suicide in the UK and ROI in 2017.

Around this time, both Mike and I had been given dates for Beth and Em's inquests; Em's was on the Friday and Beth's the following Monday. Due to Covid, Em's inquest would be remote and I would dial in. Steve visited me once again. Sitting in the garden he explained the different verdicts the coroner might reach: 'suicide', 'open', 'accidental or misadventure' or 'narrative' (also detailed in the book *Help is at Hand*, which he gave me soon after Em's death):

- 'Suicide' is when the coroner is sure the person intended to take their life.
- 'Open' is when the cause of death cannot be confirmed and doubt remains as to how the death occurred.
- 'Accidental or misadventure' is where the person died as a result of actions by themselves or others that went wrong or had unintended consequences.

- 'Narrative' is when the coroner feels that the other conclusions are not right for these circumstances and sets out their understanding of the facts.

The coroner would make a decision based around the evidence and the recently introduced verdict of 'on the balance of probabilities', which is a lower evidence level than that used in criminal cases of 'beyond reasonable doubt'.

My brain was now in overdrive. If 6,213 people died by suicide in 2017, how many more people who took their own lives were given an 'open', 'accidental or misadventure' or 'narrative' verdict? The actual number of people who died as an act they did to themselves either deliberately or by accident must be greater. As if to illustrate that fact, the Norfolk Coroner issued a verdict of 'suicide' for Em, and the Manchester Coroner a 'narrative' verdict for Beth.

I also was determined to be open at work about what had happened. After I returned in September my first email to my colleagues was titled 'Tim's Elephant in the Room'. I asked them to not ignore what had happened to Em and our family, not to dodge or avoid me, and said that I might need their help. My colleagues were superb. One-by-one I ended up talking to everyone I hadn't spoken to while I had been away.

I did exactly the same when my new boss Rob introduced himself to me. On our first virtual meeting, I explained what had happened and how I was open to any support. He was fantastic; he told me never to feel worried about dropping everything to support my family and that he was always available for a chat. Out of the blue he asked me if I wanted to connect to another bereaved dad who was several years down the line: Richard Bland, known as Ricko.

Ricko had become friends with Rob some years earlier after Ricko had lost his son Andrew to suicide in 2013 at the age of thirty-one. Ricko is a massive aircraft enthusiast, and Rob had supported him in the production of a beautifully crafted children's book called '*BEAR FORCE*', based on AB Bear. Written with the help of a child psychotherapist, the story sees AB leave his friends in the toy shop and face the unknown. The book cleverly uses the subtext to explore the bear's possible emotions as he eventually becomes a pilot. Its purpose is to open dialogue with children about their own feelings without being asked questions head on.

A couple of days later, I spoke to Ricko. I was reaching out, trying to learn how to survive, how to get through life with the knowledge that my child did not turn to me in her moment of despair. It was incredible to hear from a dad who was much further along the suicide-bereavement path than me. He had channelled his grief in such a positive way – into a book which would help others. That chat, and subsequent ones with Ricko, were inspirational.

Mike and I also continued to talk regularly, and in December he said he had met Gregor, the son of Andy from Cumbria who was a bit of a legend in PAPYRUS for fundraising. He was going to speak to him to see if he wanted to join us on a walk . . .

I was determined to get something good out of our beautiful Em's short life. Her last selfless act of organ donation had been a first step, but I could do more. I had promised to act on her final note. I was not ashamed of Em – I never could be – and I was not willing to brush her life under the carpet. She stated that she wanted others to learn from what she'd done by spreading suicide-prevention awareness.

So that's how I ended up walking 300 miles across the country with my new friends, Andy and Mike; if our walk could save one life and stop one family enduring what our three families had been – and were still – going through then we would have made a difference. Finally, I was doing it in Em's memory so people would remember her and that her life had not been in vain – it would be a suitable legacy.

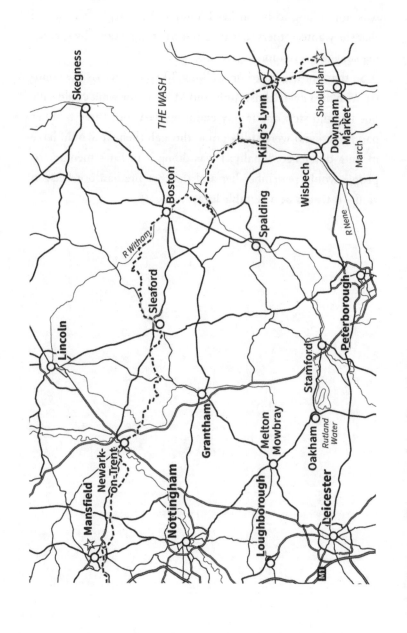

DAY 10

Mansfield to Balderton

The combination of darkness, quiet, beer and exhaustion enabled all three of us to enjoy a good night's sleep – quite amazing considering where we were. Despite deciding to sleep on the floor, in a sleeping bag on one of the mattresses, it was one of the best nights I'd had on the whole walk.

The rucksacks were soon packed and we were just about good to go, but Andy was worried about his foot. The blister had now become an open wound and a couple of his toes were swollen. He knew that by using the dressings Fiona had picked up in Buxton he would be able to walk that day, but he really wanted someone who knew what they were doing to take a proper look at it.

Since setting off nine days earlier, 3 Dads Walking had become a high-profile undertaking, so why not use our new-found fame as a platform to appeal for help? Before strapping his foot, Andy asked me to film a short video which we put out on social media. I focused on the offending blister before panning up so he could speak to the camera: 'Between us we have got five good feet . . . Is there anyone out there who could look at my foot and help me keep going?'

We were soon on our way back to Mansfield in Nigel's car, crossing the bridge over the River Trent. We'd cross back over it later in the day. It's funny how you appreciate distance differently in a car: a forty-minute journey doesn't seem that far, but when you know that you will be retracing that distance on foot it suddenly becomes quite a long way – especially with blisters.

As we clambered out of Nigel's car at the start point – the outskirts of a housing estate on the edge of Mansfield – he said he would try to find a local chiropodist or podiatrist who would be able to help. The post was already being shared on social media, so we were hopeful that something, or somebody, would turn up. The weather looked perfect for walking – a grey layer of stratus clouds protecting us from the sun and a gentle cool breeze – we were all in our shorts, with a couple of layers on under our familiar purple, teal and white Papyrus T-shirts.

Day 10's route looked straightforward, and we hoped it would offer a reasonably easy day. We would cover a few miles of bridlepaths before picking up the Robin Hood Way heading due east, then get onto the Southwell Trail, which would take us all the way to the River Trent. Once across the river we would be nearly at our destination, Balderton, a small village to the south-east of Newark-on-Trent.

Within minutes of setting off we knew that there might be an early problem. As we crossed a main road, we could see a sprawling building site a half-mile ahead, with an array of bright-yellow heavy plant machinery, orange lights blinking brightly in the early morning gloom. Clearly, the last remaining piece of green space between the edge of Mansfield and the A617 was being developed right across our footpath, but we were hopeful that our route might still be passable. There was only one way to find out . . .

Soon, however, we came across a large metal barrier blocking the route. Andy and I looked at our maps and decided our only option was to retrace our steps to the start and take an alternative path south. Such a frustrating way to begin the day – and it would delay our finish, too. Andy quietly turned around and started back from the way we had come, and I had a bit of a rant: 'How can they close a whole footpath without any redirection signs?' Mike just kept plodding on – he was good at that.

Sadly this early diversion turned out to be a bit of a bad omen for what lay ahead.

We set off again along a bridlepath on the eastern edge of Harlow Wood, which turned out to be a lovely tree-lined route, helping to take our minds off our woes. We knew that this area had all once been part of Sherwood Forest, famed for its band of merry men – we were hardly a band of merry men, but did laugh when our flags inadvertently snagged on branches, flicking into the face of whoever was following! The bridlepath became less distinct and we took care to avoid tripping over exposed root systems, occasionally getting our bare legs caught in a bramble.

We quickly forgot that we'd had to make a detour, enjoying the crunching of the leaves and twigs under our walking boots. More importantly, Mike and I knew the softer ground would be easier for Andy. After only a few hundred metres we regained our planned route at Lindhurst Farm, then headed cross-country towards Blidworth, picking up the famous Robin Hood Way, a clearly marked National Trail which would take us through the Nottinghamshire countryside.

The Robin Hood Way is an epic walk of just over 100 miles from Nottingham Castle to Edwinstone Church. It links all the places connected with Robin Hood, including Sherwood Forest, the hideout of the famous local hero and his men. We would only be following it for a few miles to Farnsfield, but it was a great reminder of the fantastic history we have in this country. These paths were there long before any of us, our parents or even our grandparents were born, and would be there long after we had disappeared. The natural world has a way of reminding us all how small we are in the grand scheme of things. Many of the trees which offered us shelter from the sun, wind and rain on our journey, the paths which we had walked, the fields we had crossed, had already seen hundreds, if not thousands, of years of use by humans – and will see hundreds more. We were just another set of human beings crossing this landscape – albeit for quite a strange purpose.

As we dropped down into Blidworth, we met a couple walking their dog. They joined us for a bit, the three of us chatting about what we were doing, where we had come from and where we were going to.

Suddenly the woman's eyes lit up as she put two and two together and exclaimed, 'It's YOU, isn't it?' She had seen us on *BBC Breakfast* and the penny had dropped.

Andy replied, laughing, 'Yes, it's us!'

She wanted to know more about why we were doing the walk, our stories and our girls. She was very excited as it turned out that she wrote the local parish newsletter, so she took our photos and said she'd feature us in the next edition.

It was strange to think that random strangers wanted our

photos, but it was amazing how far our suicide prevention message was being broadcast. Who could ever have imagined that we would be featuring in the *Blidworth Parish News* when we set out from Morland? We were being heard in the most unexpected of places.

The weather continued to be kind, overcast with a breeze – perfect for walking. We were on the broad plain leading towards the River Trent, so we had the gentlest of downhill gradients, our boots kicking up the dust as we walked through fields of stubble. I was feeling optimistic; these were great walking conditions for three tired pairs of legs.

There was a ping. We all checked our phones, and Andy exclaimed, 'My foot's going to be sorted!' It was great news. Nigel had located a podiatrist at Hyde-Barker Health, a clinic in Southwell, who could see Andy during his lunch hour. On checking our position, it looked like our arrival in Southwell would fit perfectly.

We had some spare time so recorded our daily video diary as we walked across fields of over-head-height maize. 'Here's 3 Dads Walking, well . . . 2 Dads walking, 1 Dad limping!'

We were still recording when we managed to get stuck in a hedge. This tickled us and caused much giggling as it indicated the unforeseen difficulties we encountered en route (or more specifically how we couldn't be trusted to get over a stile intact!).

At Farnsfield, we left the Robin Hood Way and took a short track to the Southwell Trail. Mike and I were trying to remember to walk at Andy's pace. Andy is a little shorter than Mike and me so he had to walk significantly more steps: if I walked 50,000 steps in a day, Mike would be at about 53,000 and

Andy at 58,000. The injured Cumbrian was already at a disadvantage before we took into account his injured foot. Over the fifteen days I reckon Andy walked over 110,000 more steps than me, poor chap.

Andy had told us how much he been looking forward to the Southwell Trail, easy walking along an old railway line that would take us directly to Southwell. But we hadn't predicted how negatively the featureless landscape would affect us, both mentally and physically. Today's route had so far taken us through fields and woods, with stunning views over gently rolling countryside. On the Southwell Trail, it felt like we were cut off from the rest of the world. All we could see were trees, trees and more trees, their branches arching over our heads and creating a green tunnel – the worst part of which was a dead-straight two miles. It was impossible to judge distance, but on we went.

It really felt interminable. We all felt as though we were getting nowhere, and Mike and I knew Andy's foot was getting worse. If we got a bit too far ahead he asked us to slow down, and he was unusually quiet. We had no one to distract us from our thoughts and low mood, which darkened with every step. Just like the time before, to the time after, losing our daughters, we had moved from a beautiful place to somewhere dark, that we couldn't see a way out of. While never pretending that our life was perfect before losing Em, it was a million times better than it was now.

It felt like I was becoming stuck in one emotion, despair. This is exactly what I had been warned about during the Anchor Project and I knew I needed to pull myself out of it, but that would be hard. The only thing to do was to keep putting one foot in front of the other, supported by my two new friends. Turning left or right was not an option, and we couldn't go back as the diversion would have been massive – and Andy was now clearly in physical pain.

At long last, when we were getting close to Southwell, we were joined by a couple of local ladies who wanted to walk with us for a while.

'We've been looking for you.'

'It's lovely to meet you!' I replied, instantly snapping out of that dreadful feeling of despair.

They were a very welcome distraction – and their arrival coincided with a glimmer of hope that the really bad part of today's journey was very nearly over. Although the couple from Blidworth had bumped into us accidentally, these ladies had sought us out and, as normal, we walked and talked, which seemed to cheer Andy up a little.

We finally reached the spot where Nigel was waiting for us with a massive and delicious lunch. Mike and I were pleased to see him because of the food; Andy was delighted to see him because he was going to drive him to the chiropodist. That section of the walk had been so hard, both physically and emotionally. Those ladies – and the prospect of Nigel and lunch! – had played a big part in us getting us to our destination. Just like our individual journeys after losing Sophie, Em and Beth, the morning's difficult passage had been supported by the kindness of total strangers, the help of an old friend, and the comradeship of each other.

We made it out to the other side.

*   *   *

While Mike and I sat happily chatting with the local ladies, boots and socks off to allow our feet to breathe, Andy arrived at the foot clinic. He was soon in the examination chair, boot and sock off, foot raised. Gareth Maguire, the podiatrist, selected an especially sharp-looking scalpel and began to cut, saying that it would be best to remove any loose skin, then dressed it to make it more comfortable. He offered to put the pieces of skin into a jar for Andy to take away with him. Funnily enough, Andy refused.

Within twenty minutes, Gareth had tidied up Andy's wound and it was beautifully dressed. Andy told us later that he felt immediate relief when putting his boot back on – the padding made a significant difference. Gareth refused to take any payment, but Andy asked how much the treatment should have cost – and paid that amount into the PAPYRUS pot that evening.

Gareth gave Andy a bag of tape, dressings and padding – enough to see him to the end of the walk.

The podiatry interlude had cost us a little time; however, it had not only improved Andy's foot but also his state of mind. He was no longer concerned about his ability to get to the end; he knew that if he looked after his foot as Gareth had shown him, everything would be fine. This was a massive turning point: at last we were confident that all three of us would be able to finish.

After lunch we were back on the old railway line again. At least we were now out of the trees, but the next section took us onto Southwell Racecourse – it was dead straight again, but this time on tarmac. The land around us was flat and we had no views, being boxed in by hedges; the straight went on for another two miles. The whole day had turned into an endurance challenge. Once again I could feel my mood darken. As we walked, the sound of our boots on the tarmac, and the rhythm of our walking sticks tapping the surface, seemed to grow louder. To top it all there was some light rain, just enough to dampen spots where we might want to sit down for a break.

The tap, tap, tapping sound was interrupted by my phone ringing and I took a call from BBC Alison. She asked if we could be back on the Red Sofa on 17 October, the Monday after we finished our walk. I was due back at work that day, so I contacted my boss to see if a later start was possible. I didn't want him to think that I was back at work and then see my face on *BBC Breakfast* – no getting away with that one!

'Absolutely no problem at all.'

A plan was coming together. Moreover, the RAF had now started to engage with my colleagues Jim and Michelle about the walk. Before starting, I'd informed my chain-of-command that I was doing a charity walk in my private time, and that there might be a little bit of media interest. Clearly, I'd underestimated the scale of the response and the RAF and broader MOD were now working on a piece to promote the 3 Dads Walking story.

Alison's phone call and our discussions about the end of the walk distracted us and boosted our spirits – we were making plans again. Things got even better when we reached the end of the racecourse path and arrived at Rolleston, a small village just west of the River Trent and Newark. We wandered into the churchyard of Holy Trinity, an ancient building which has been at the heart of the community for over a thousand years. While looking for somewhere to sit, we were approached by a local lady who was initially curious as to why three strange men were wandering around the churchyard. We explained who we were and what we were doing, putting her instantly at ease. She explained that her family had settled in the area due to her connections with the RAF.

My ears pricked up. Her dad had been a navigator on Lancaster bombers in World War II and had settled in Lincolnshire after the war. When I explained that I had been a navigator, the lady told me all about her dad, his stories and her life in Lincolnshire: it was a fascinating conversation. She said her goodbyes as we left the churchyard, still in search of somewhere to sit.

We finally found a bus shelter just round the corner. Bus shelters had become a positive thing on the walk – they offered dry seating out of the rain and wind. This was a good one, but more importantly it was where we met our saviour for the day, Lawrence – an old school friend. After leaving school thirty-three years previously, Lawrence and I had kept in touch. He had said he would join us, but I didn't know where or when, so it was great to see him striding towards us.

As we sat in the bus shelter, Lawrence took a photo of us. Of all the photos taken on the 3 Dads Walking journey, this is the one which shows us at our lowest. We were knackered, the last few hours had seemed like some form of torture, we'd had the fewest people to talk to en route and we knew we still had several miles to go before the end of the day. Creakily, using our walking poles for support, we rose slowly from the bench, shrugged our packs back into place and pushed off towards Newark. We knew we had to keep going, not only for our daughters but also for the thousands of people who had already donated to PAPYRUS for us, but we really were struggling. It was a combination of the terrain, our aching bodies after ten days of walking, and the lack of people joining us to boost our morale. It felt like we had hit 'the wall'.

'Let's go chaps.' I tried to encourage the Cumbrian and Mancunian to set off, with the excited Lawrence starting to stride off a pace or two ahead of me.

'I guess we have to?' came the weary reply from Andy, who took a painful yet determined step forward.

'Bloody hell that's stiff – I think I sat down for too long,' Mike grumbled, bringing up the rear as usual. Clearly the muscles in his legs had tightened up.

Mentally we had supported so many others and each other on the walk, and it felt now like we were all running out of steam. Despite everything, however, we knew we just had to keep going, one step at a time. We knew that our walk could make such a difference.

Thankfully, Lawrence was like a breath of fresh air. He was hugely enthusiastic about everything and had boundless energy and wanted to talk to us all. We didn't have to think about conversation – he did it all for us! It was as if Tigger had joined our group and his support was exactly what we needed – the timing could not have been better.

Walking up the B-road towards Averham, we needed to cross over a couple of times. Lawrence acted like our own personal traffic-management person, stepping out into the middle of the road and flagging down cars if they dared get near us (this trick proved a little more challenging when we crossed the busy A617!). We'd already pointed out that we'd managed to cover 200 miles without being guided across roads, but Lawrence was determined to help us.

He strode into the middle of the road and spread his arms wide, like Gandalf on the Bridge of Khazad-dûm in *The Lord of the Rings*. Oddly enough, the lady in the car coming towards him really didn't want to be flagged down by a strange man, so she didn't stop. Meanwhile, we'd taken the opportunity to scamper across behind him. Lawrence was most annoyed, but we just laughed; he'd already made such a difference to our day.

Lawrence's chatter carried us through Kelham – where we caught sight of Kelham Hall – and across the River Trent, a murky, meandering body of water. It felt like a significant moment. Rivers had governed our route choice in a few places, so to get the largest river of all out of the way seemed like quite an achievement. However, we had no time to congratulate ourselves as we still had another six miles to cover.

Our onward route took us away from the road for the next mile on the Trent Valley Way. Having soil under our feet rather than tarmac was a blessed relief. Lawrence talked enthusiastically about the role Newark had played in the English Civil War. The town was under siege from Parliamentarians several times in the mid-1640s and there is still a cannonball hole in the church spire! Furthermore, Southwell (where Andy had his foot tended) was where Charles I spent his last night as a free man before being betrayed by Scottish Commissioners before being imprisoned in Kelham Hall. Lawrence's knowledge of local history was such a welcome distraction at this stage of the day.

To Mike's great surprise, Lawrence announced that they had a mutual acquaintance. Mike's next door-but-one neighbour, Helen Allen, knew Lawrence and his wife. Beth had been babysitter to Helen's children! Within half an hour they were FaceTiming while walking through a Lincolnshire field. What a small world this really is.

We were now on the outskirts of the Newark, where we stopped to get him to take a short video of the 3 Dads striding past the '*Welcome to Newark*' sign. We began to feel like the end of the day was within reach.

Having passed eight-hundred-year-old Newark Castle we entered the rather lovely Market Square, flanked by many impressive buildings. As we were leaving a few young people stopped and talked to us. One smartly dressed young man, on his way home after a day in the office, asked: 'Where are you walking to?'

'Norfolk!' I replied.

'No way!' he said, clearly amazed that these three old blokes were walking that far.

'But we started in Cumbria ... we all lost our daughters to suicide so we are walking between our homes, from Cumbria to Manchester to Norfolk.'

His expression changed and he started to open up: 'Oh – that is so sad, so sorry. You know, there are so many mental-health issues around. So many young people are suffering and not getting the help they need.'

I chatted to him about his friends – and he knew of young people who had taken their lives. His parting words lifted us: 'Keep going – this is so needed – and so important.'

This was the motivation we needed – this conversation, and Lawrence's cheerful input, had such a positive impact on our mental state, and simply proved the power of talking can help so much. That would not be the last act of kindness shown to us that day. The young man and his friends wished us well and we went on our way, negotiating a maze of narrow streets.

Our finishing point for Day 10 was in Newark's easternmost suburb, Balderton. In fact, it was the easternmost part of the easternmost suburb ... but we had conveniently forgotten to take much note of this before we set off. In our minds, we were getting close to the finish; in reality we still had four miles to go, all on hard pavements and in failing light.

As we continued, we were stopped by a few men outside a pub having a smoke, pint of beer in one hand, cigarette in the other. Still in their work clothes, hi-vis jackets and hands dirty from a hard day's work, they were well lubricated.

'What are you guys walking for?' one of them shouted.

'We all lost our daughters to suicide and we are walking for a suicide prevention charity called PAPYRUS,' Andy replied.

'Fair dos' came the reply. When we told them more about what we were doing these generous men turned out their pockets and gave us loads of change – a real act of kindness from total strangers.

The sound of the change hitting the bottom of the bucket caused the Cumbrian to whinge 'Oh bloody hell, not more change!' once again. Mike and I couldn't help but laugh. Change in the bucket meant weight on Andy's back and he insisted on carrying the bucket – it had been his idea – but it was always a great source of hilarity when those pennies dropped in and added more weight to his load.

It was now dark and we knew we had to get these last few miles knocked off. We were walking along London Road, alongside roaring traffic, streetlights and car headlights lighting our way. The deafening noise made potentially distracting and uplifting conversations hard, so it was easy to focus on personal discomfort. My left calf had gone into some sort of painful spasm, the result of pounding on roads and hard gravel tracks. I kept walking. If Andy could walk with that foot, I couldn't give in to a little bit of calf pain.

As we entered the last mile, headtorches on, Andy called Nigel to ensure he would be waiting for us at the designated meeting place in Fernwood, only to be reminded that Nigel couldn't read maps so had no idea where the finish was – or even where he was at that moment. We managed to ascertain that he was in the vicinity, but that was all. There was only one thing for it – keep walking.

Over the bridge into Fernwood, we turned into the housing estate with 500 metres to go. Into the last 200 metres, we cut across a playing field, our headtorches piercing the dark, the light glistening off the wet grass. We passed through a small, even darker, wooded strip and onto the last 100 metres of unlit narrow lane . . . still no sign of Nigel. Frustrated, Andy phoned him and we all listened on speaker. Nigel tried to describe where he was and what he could see, but Andy's exhausted brain couldn't deal with the garbled information, and Mike and I were no help. As ever, Lawrence was eager to help. He soon identified Nigel's position and talked him towards our location. It was a huge relief to see car headlights approach, slow down and stop, and a cheery Nigel jump out.

We said our goodbyes to Lawrence on the outskirts of Newark – he'd been such a welcome companion and great source of entertainment. But we were now content to be in Nigel's car for the short journey back to Syerston and glad that the hard day's walking was over. I was really happy to return to our shed, knowing how cosy it had been the night before. It was a great place to relax, rewind and try to repair our aching bodies, and to reflect on today's battle

It had been the hardest day's walk so far. But the kindness of friends, and that of strangers, had got us through to Nigel's shed. From the two ladies who joined us on the Trail to Gareth who tended Andy's foot, and the young man and his friends in Newark to the men outside the pub, our encounters today showed there is so much kindness and love in the world, if only you are prepared to look for it and, more importantly, accept it. Today's walk reflected our individual journeys since losing Sophie, Beth and Em. We had all relied on support from family, friends and colleagues to help us navigate the complex grief that you are left in after losing a loved one to suicide; we had all sought support from total strangers and were all willing to accept it.

It was that willingness to accept help which had led Mike and I to first speak, and then later Andy to join in, as we became 3 Dads Walking. These two men had gone from being strangers to friends, who I knew would support me and my family however they could. We were bonded by common tragedy which we all understood.

It was – and is – a privilege to know them.

Money raised (excluding Gift Aid and direct donations)
   = £319,000
Day 10 distance = 24.7 miles
Total distance walked = 224.5 miles

DAY 11

Balderton to Sleaford

I think it was the loud noise that woke me – or maybe my tender calf muscle? – anyhow, as normal, I was stirring before the other two. We were now very much getting into my familiar territory – it felt like the beginning of the end was coming into view. But I was apprehensive – the trauma of yesterday was still very much on my mind.

Andy was stirring and the shed was still dark. It was raining heavily and the noise on the tin roof made me realise this might be another challenging day, but for a different reason – the first time we would have to be fully waterproofed-up from the start. There was nothing for it but to get up and make the dash across to Nigel's outside toilet in the pitch dark and torrential rain.

As we got ready, Andy used the dressings and padding Gareth had supplied to protect his foot. His laces had been slackened to make space for the extra volume, and once his boot was on, it felt surprisingly comfortable. His foot just needed to stay dry, which could be a challenge given the torrential downpour hammering on the roof.

Mike and I were both feeling the pain of walking too. My calf had seized up the day before and, although it felt better, was painful to touch. Mike's knees continued to cause him irritation, but he was our medic, carrying a copious supply of painkillers, bandages, ointments and creams. I needed something to loosen off my calf and Mike obliged, with painkillers and some cream to rub on. We hoped we could keep these minor irritations in check.

We enjoyed another splendid Nigel breakfast, packed our kitbags (including masses of Nigel-supplied snacks) and got ready to leave. I sat in the front seat to help navigate and away we went in the driving rain, the wipers working hard to keep the windscreen clear.

The conditions on the busy A1 were horrid, every vehicle throwing up a wall of spray and making the journey treacherous. I directed Nigel into the outside lane of the dual carriageway: '500 metres to go, 400 metres to go, 300 metres, 200 metres, 100 . . . Turn right *now*!'

We had made it to within a few hundred yards of where Nigel had picked us up at the end of Day 10, but he still had no concept of where he was. Suddenly he exclaimed, 'This is where you were last night!' Who knows how he gets around the country – but what a great bloke.

Lenny, one of my RAF mates, was waiting for us. He'd been in contact after Em's death and said he would join us at some point; he just happened to have picked the wettest morning we had on the entire walk! It was great to see him and after a huge hug we started catching up with life over the last few years. He didn't seem fazed by the weather. There was nothing we could do about it, so we got the rucksacks on, zipped up our jackets, pulled up our hoods and bade Nigel farewell.

Heads down in the driving rain, we marched across the flat, open fields, wet grass and mud testing the waterproof qualities of our walking boots, hoping for the weather to improve. Amazingly, after half an hour, the skies brightened with the dawn, the clouds lifted and the rain eased. When we stopped to lower our hoods, we saw a chap hurrying along the path behind us.

'Hi there,' he introduced himself, breathing fast – from his efforts to catch us, or maybe from emotion? – his face was wet, either from rain or tears. I knew instantly another dreadful, heartbreaking story was coming.

'I lost my son.' The emotion was now breaking through in his voice.

He had lost his son to suicide shortly after he had gone to university. Here was another dad who only found out that suicide is the biggest killer of young people in Britain when it was too late.

He told us his story and, as so many times before, we spoke about our daughters. During his conversation with Mike, he spoke clearly about his grief and his determination that his son should not be forgotten. He wanted his name to live on and ultimately be a positive force in preventing young suicide. He is a brave man striving to make the world a better place – we were honoured to walk with him.

After crossing the River Witham, we approached Claypole from the footpath along Well Fen Lane: the first of many fens we would cross over the next few days. A fen is a low-lying area of marshland, common in the east of Britain which, once drained, provides rich agricultural land. The fields are often large, bounded by a ditch or drain, the occasional tree or a small section of hedgerow. Although the rain had stopped, there was still moisture in the air and it felt as though the skies could open at any moment. Our band grew significantly as we were joined by Andy, Vicki, Si and others – all RAF friends. There were hugs and tears all round, as I hadn't seen many of them since losing Em.

Andy is my oldest friend. We went to school together, then joined the RAF within a couple of years of each other, and he was my best man when Sue and I married. A keen walker, he joined us for the rest of the day, while the others planned to turn back after spending a few hours with us. Andy and I had walked together when we were in our teens on several Duke of Edinburgh Award expeditions, so it was incredibly powerful to be walking with him again some forty years later. Two blokes with a life-long friendship – a constant through the ups and downs of life – that really is something to treasure.

The grey clouds appeared to be getting lighter, but they had already deposited much of their contents overnight on the fields around Claypole. As we headed along a track and then across open fields, the clay mud encased our boots – it felt like we were walking with platform soles on our boots. Fortunately, we only had to put up with this for a mile or so before reaching the road through Stubton.

Shortly after leaving the village our route took us onto a track which was much less sticky underfoot. Si was constantly going ahead of the group to record our merry band on his GoPro – he was so enthusiastic in capturing the walk. (It turned out he had a YouTube channel and would later post his edited piece to gain more support for us.)

We continued to head east, waterproofs off at last, with views ahead to the Kesteven Uplands – the last set of hills on our journey, and something of a milestone.

It was bizarre to see Mike the Mancunian and Andy the Cumbrian walking with my friends: people in my life who would normally be strangers to each other, drawn together to offer me support. I felt very privileged, and humbled to be surrounded by so much care and love. Mike remained towards the back – he'd taken up that position from Day 1 – ensuring we didn't leave anyone behind.

In our long conversations before meeting face-to-face Mike had told me about everything he had done to provide a good, happy and safe home for his family. From all the renovation work on the house, to ensuring Beth could look after herself with martial arts lessons, to the VW campervan he bought to take her to her gigs. Mike was now at his happiest talking to people. This proud firefighter was trying to rebuild his, and his family's, shattered lives. He was a good bloke, with a dry sense of humour, who bore so much pain for Beth, but also for the many bereaved parents we had met. We already had a strong relationship before we walked – a relationship with foundations in experiencing that unique grief of losing a child to suicide; of talking regularly about our emotions and feelings and, perhaps most importantly, the admission that we both felt we had failed as fathers.

But this walk had taught me so much more about him. He was a little disorganised in some respects, perhaps best illustrated by his appalling navigation around Manchester, a route he had planned in his head and not told us (so our route planner and tracker had been useless). But in other ways he had absolutely pulled it out of the bag. The reception we had in Manchester and Sale had been so emotional for Andy and me, let alone for Mike and Helen – and the number of people who met us at places with strong emotional ties to Beth was amazing. And Mike had fantastic empathy, another reason he was often at the back of the group. Someone would stop us to talk, and Mike would always be the one to listen, every time. All this talking took it out of him mentally, and he was normally the first to bed, his brain overloaded with stories and the enormity of our task.

Andy, on the other hand, the outdoor marketing man from Cumbria, would often be at the front with either him or me navigating, driving us on. I first met him on a Zoom meeting in April, less than six months before we walked.

I didn't know Andy like I knew Mike, but I did know that I could learn from Andy as he was fourteen months ahead of Mike and me on the suicide bereavement path. The first time we spoke I could instantly tell that he was a positive chap, who wanted to make a difference. When we were planning the walk it was clear that Andy had connections all over the outdoor industry and was able to gain massive support from them. He also had a marketing head on him. We all knew that the walk could attract some attention, but it was Andy – through his connection with Alison from the BBC – who really got it started.

The first time we all met was at Mike's house on a Friday night in early July – we all just hugged and then had a few beers (perhaps a few more than that) and a beautiful meal prepared by Helen. I had known at that point that the three of us could make this work. Andy was just such a funny bloke, always smiling and laughing, and massively proud of his Cumbrian roots.

When it came to walking, he had all the gadgets and clothing you could imagine. He was the fell walker, so both Mike and I had thought it would be one of us who would come down with blisters or foot problems. It came as a massive surprise when it was Andy who had the foot issues.

With Andy often leading and Mike at the rear, I played the middle man role – a negotiator. We would get a request to divert slightly off route to meet someone – Andy's instant response was no, Mike's was yes, and I would then start brokering between the pair of them. Mostly, we all ended up agreeing on the diversion once we thought about the value to someone else. We were, and are, very different characters, but we found that our individual skills, traits and strengths complemented each other – and we played to them.

So now, with Andy and me at the front, and Mike somewhere at the back chatting, we were heading towards our lunch stop at Hough-on-the-Hill (a surprise for Andy, who had no idea that Lincolnshire had any hills).

Shortly afterwards, Andy's phone rang. It was Pete Rostron, a mate of his who lived in the Vale of Belvoir, and who had been in regular contact.

'Where are you going? You're off route!'

Andy replied, 'Yes, we know, you told us to reroute. We're heading up this road after you warned us about the other busy one.'

'Ah,' said Pete, 'I'm waiting for you round the corner on your planned route.'

We were now totally confused. We'd all thought that Pete had been at home when he'd first called us. He said he'd catch us at Hough-on-the-Hill, a stunning village with charming cottages built from local limestone. Waiting for us there – somehow – was Nigel, carrying bags full of food.

We found a convenient wall outside beautiful All Saints Church, and took a seat. Pete and his dogs arrived accompanied by Gordo, another RAF mate of mine. It was great to see Gordo. We perched on the wall eating lunch and catching up on life.

With our gaiters, boots and socks off, we took time to relax, talking to everyone around us. Jim, another RAF friend and colleague, was dropped off by his daughter. We were staying at his house in Sleaford at the end of the day, so he was planning to walk with us all the way to his front door. Moreover, he knew every short cut across the rolling Lincolnshire countryside, and every metre we could crop would save Andy another painful step or two.

Andy's phone rang again. This time it was Radio Lincolnshire; they wanted to talk to us as we passed through their area. Yet another opportunity to talk about our walk and introduce more people to PAPYRUS and our message about suicide prevention.

Just before we arrived in Carlton Scroop, we joined the Viking Way, a long-distance trail from Oakham to the Humber Bridge, which we would follow for three miles or so. This was one of the most significant sections of our walk, marked by the ascent of our last hill. We entered the small village, bisected by a disused railway line which was closed during the Beeching cuts in 1965. The Viking Way ran straight through the community, taking us past the magnificent limestone twelfth-century church, St Nicholas, and then over the old railway to start the climb.

Although only just over 70 metres above sea level, Normanton Hill qualifies as a significant climb in Lincolnshire. As we ascended, my RAF mates and I enthusiastically pointed out to the rest a communications tower which looks incredibly like a rocket, creatively called 'Rocket Mast' by everyone who has been through Initial Officer Training. The tower sits around half-way up the south-west slope of the hill. As a student going through training at RAF College Cranwell, it was a well-known navigation feature and held legendary status in the minds of many in the RAF.

We reached the top of Normanton Hill with our three flags blowing in the wind. It was a massive mental achievement – all we had to do now was walk, not climb, for four more days to reach Shouldham. It would be mainly downhill until we reached the fenland around Boston.

I felt like I was nearly on home turf – I've known the area since I was twenty. A patchwork of large, open, windswept fields; beautiful honey-coloured limestone villages of pretty cottages and impressive grander houses nestled into the folds of the land, dotted with the steeples and spires of ancient churches, marking each village. It was very different from the terrain of Cumbria and the Pennines, but beautiful in its own way. From the top of the hill we had extensive views towards the fens to the east. Away to the north-east, I pointed out RAF College Cranwell and College Hall, built in the 1930s with its cupola housing the last operational aerial lighthouse in the UK.

Familiar landmarks guiding me homewards.

Our route took us gradually downhill towards the ancient Roman road of Ermine Street, which ran from London to Lincoln and then north to York. I had arranged to meet more RAF friends where the Viking Way meets Ermine Street. Here, Bryn and Rach arrived bearing hot chocolate and coffee, much to Mike's pleasure. Mike is a coffee aficionado, and wasn't happy when tea or instant coffee was on offer – 'Have you not got any proper coffee?' Andy and I regularly found ourselves apologising to kind people who offered us a warm drink which wasn't up to Mike's standards! After more hugs and tears with Bryn and Rach, years of catching up on life commenced.

While we were taking a break, an older chap approached us. Bold, chatty and a little eccentric, he introduced himself as Nigel Panting, another local, keen to walk with us (but fighting to keep his trousers up with malfunctioning red braces). Eventually, we said our goodbyes to Bryn and Rach – it had been emotional and great to see them.

Our next challenge was crossing Ermine Street, which was pretty busy – and, being straight, fast – for a B-road. Getting our tribe over safely took a fair bit of people-management, particularly since the path we were aiming for – a farm track – was 150 metres to the south on the other side.

Walking along the track, Jim asked us about our route choice. We explained how we came to choose various lines and talked about our desire to avoid roads where possible.

'Ah, that'll be why you're planning to go the long way round to Rauceby.'

This attracted our attention – was there a short way?

Jim said he often ran in this area and would usually take the road to Rauceby; he reassured us that it was very quiet and would be safe for our group. I checked the map with Andy and saw that Jim's suggestion would save close to a mile. No contest – we'd follow Jim's advice.

We were soon following a minor road with wide verges, flanked by mature trees, which went directly to the village. This was ideal.

As the group walked, Nigel showed Andy a couple of laminated A4 maps with detailed notes on the back. One was for our route out of Sleaford (including details of chiropodists, just in case), and the second showed footpath closures on the planned route out of Boston. Nigel had clearly spent much time and effort preparing these navigational masterpieces and they were invaluable to us.

Perhaps for the first time on the walk, Andy dropped back, talking to a couple about the relative merits of leather and fabric walking boots. Since we had plenty of time Andy – in lecture mode – began to discuss the development of lightweight boots in the 1980s.

'The first commercially successful fabric boots were the KSB [Karrimor Sports Boot]. In fact, I know the bloke who helped design them, Ken Ledward.'

With that Nigel piped up: 'I know Ken Ledward!'

This stopped Andy in his tracks. 'How do you know Ken?'

It turned out that Nigel had done his mountain leader training through Outward Bound, Eskdale, in the early 1980s and Ken had been his instructor/assessor. He told Andy that his other instructor was Ben Lyon, another of Andy's friends from Cumbria, who set up and runs Lyon Equipment in Tebay, one of the UK's leading distributors of outdoor equipment. Another small-world moment.

Andy spent the next hour talking to Nigel about his outdoor adventures. Nigel had travelled far and wide and shared many stories before he had to leave us to get a bus back to his car.

Just after we entered Rauceby, another village of picturesque limestone houses, more RAF colleagues came out to join us and wish us well, this time in camouflage uniform. They were led by a colleague nicknamed 'Coops' whom I'd worked with over the years. It was great to see such support and endless chatter ensued. It was just a pity (although in reality probably extremely fortunate) that the pub there, The Bustard, was closed, otherwise it would have been a long session.

Once through Rauceby, we were back onto open farmland and, better still, we were looking down onto Sleaford. The day's end was in sight – and it wasn't dark.

Before we reached the Grantham road, Jim got us all to stop and line up at a particular spot. He then took a photo, saying, 'I'll explain later . . .'

As I walked, listening to the chatter of those around me, I reflected on everyone I'd met that day. There had been hugs and tears as old friends had looked me in the eye and shared, in some small way, my pain. We'd had so much support as we walked this leg from Nottinghamshire into Lincolnshire. Many new acquaintances had personal tales to tell of loved ones and friends whom they'd either lost to suicide or who'd struggled with their mental health – and those stories were for us, privately shared, and not for these pages. But the recurring theme was the need to do more, to talk and be more open, to support those struggling and help future generations through early education. Before our walk, not one of these people had known that suicide is the biggest killer of under-thirty-fives – and now they did.

To some, I was a colleague and friend who had faced the unimaginable pain of losing a child to suicide. If it could happen to me, then it could happen to anyone. Everyone we spoke to agreed that it was all about being proactive in suicide prevention, not reactive, which is where we were at that moment. The love and support we'd seen throughout the walk were really brought home to me in the fields of Lincolnshire. Equally, the three of us had now met many of each other's families, friends and colleagues, and were all building upon that relationship which had started with the Zoom call back in April.

Jim's reroute led us onto the last bit of tarmac for the day, but we only had to walk on the hard stuff for half a mile before turning into Jim's estate and arriving at his house – it was only 5 p.m. An early finish – and in daylight! We said our goodbyes to those who'd walked with us all day and thanked them – their support had been great.

As we turned towards Jim's house a car pulled up, and a young woman and her little boy – he must have been about four – got out.

'I've been following your tracker and want to give you some money,' she said, and her little boy dropped the money into our bucket. She told us that she was a teacher at a local secondary school, where they'd just completed a suicide-prevention day and had used 3 Dads Walking as the way into the topic. We were taken aback. She'd used our stories as a simple way of introducing suicide and suicide prevention to her pupils. This was exactly the kind of outcome we'd had in mind when we'd first talked about the walk – if all schools did this, then how many young lives would be saved? She thanked us for raising awareness about suicide prevention and bade us farewell. We stood on Jim's drive feeling somewhat stunned.

Day 11 had felt considerably better than the previous two long, hard and rather uninspiring days. We were 'back to normal' when it came to the number of people who crossed our path – and that seemed to make the miles disappear more quickly. Jim's short cut was excellent, and the early finish in the daylight was wonderful.

Jim and his family, together with Martha the dog, welcomed us with open arms. Most importantly, and after Jim had provided us with a beer each, he took Mike and Andy's washing.

We all sat down to enjoy a large helping of chilli, after which Jim showed us why he'd taken the photo earlier. Every week, to highlight the changing seasons, he'd been taking the same view – and this week's image featured 3 Dads Walking!

'That was a brilliant evening – and what a lovely, lovely family,' Mike said as he climbed into the double bed which was to be his sanctuary for the next eight hours.

Today had been a great day – and finally, with Andy's foot on the mend, I knew all three of us could reach Shouldham and the end of our epic journey.

Money raised (excluding Gift Aid and direct donations)
    = £330,000
Day 11 distance = 20 miles
Total distance walked = 244.5 miles

DAY 12

Sleaford to Boston

As usual, and just out of habit, I woke first. I was ready to get going, every step bringing me closer to my shattered family who were waiting for me in Norfolk. They would still be asleep – sleep was a friend which offered temporary comfort and escape from the agony we were all living.

Andy, Mike and I had the luxury of a bit of a lie-in this morning because, for only the third time, we didn't need a lift to our start point: we would begin today's epic journey from Jim's doorstep.

Our route took us through the centre of Sleaford before branching off to pick up the Spires and Steeples Way. This would follow the River Slea east out into the Fens, which we would be walking across all the way to Shouldham.

The route had taken a bit of working out, the main issue being the myriad manmade waterways constructed to drain water from the low-lying fenland into The Wash. The majority of these run south-west to north-east, but we wanted to walk south-east . . . which meant finding bridges across the waterways . . . and there aren't that many bridges in that direction.

But we could use the natural lie of the land to our advantage. All water in this area flows towards The Wash . . . which is why we chose to follow the River Slea. Although flowing east – rather than south-east – the river eventually joins the River Witham. Follow that out to sea, and we could pick up the coast path. Simple. It wasn't a direct route, but it was a good one.

We dropped down onto the footpath running alongside the shallow, languid River Slea, where we were approached by a local man who introduced himself as Mike Lock. He had seen us on *BBC Breakfast* and he told us he'd like to walk with us. He was a keen walker, and was walking the coast of Britain stage by stage.

Mike told us he was in the Boston Masonic Lodge. They had lost one of their members to suicide. Like all suicides, the ripple effect had impacted his friends at the Lodge, who had since donated money to PAPYRUS.

Mike also told us that he had been responsible for the creation of the Spires and Steeples Way. He had been inspired to create the 25-mile route from Lincoln to Sleaford when he was an officer in Lincolnshire Council, responsible for public rights of way. He was very pleased to guide us along *his* trail, and we were delighted to have such a guide to take us on this next stretch of our adventure.

As we walked alongside the river it began to rain very hard, so we quickly donned full waterproofs. Our new friend Mike, however, produced something more idiosyncratic – a bright-orange poncho that went right down to his ankles, covering not only him but also his rucksack. It was a fantastic bit of kit, making him look like he was walking inside his own cosy tent.

Despite the heavy rain we were joined by a group of Mike's masonic friends, with their wives, all touched by their friend's suicide. The path passed through an area of woodland, and we found ourselves walking in dripping gloom. However, with the positivity of everyone around us we remained more than happy. At the end of the wood, the Spires and Steeples route went north, and our path stayed due east. All our supporters left us apart from Mike, who said that he had negotiated 'safe passage' for us over the next section. We didn't quite understand what he meant . . .

Mike pointed out the nearby ruins of Haverholme Priory and explained its links to the Finch-Hatton family, one of whom, Denys, was Karen Blixen's lover – as immortalised in the film *Out of Africa*. At the weir near the priory – and on Mike's advice – we crossed a small bridge to pick up a better path on the south side of the river.

Suddenly there was a shout: 'There's only one Timmy Owen!'

Out from a clump of trees popped an old friend of mine who'd intercepted the group using our now infamous tracker. Rich was another ex-Tornado navigator whom I'd known for thirty years or so. He'd recently left the RAF and one of his voluntary roles had been deputy head of the RAF Mental Health Network. Rich had been touched by suicide and he was a massive supporter of our endeavour. We caught up on the years that had passed since we'd seen each other.

Out of nowhere, a reporter from BBC Lincolnshire appeared, microphone in hand, to interview the three of us. As soon as that was complete, I was called by BBC Norfolk for another live interview. The interview focused on Daniel Craig's donation and when we would reach Norfolk ... Clearly things were hotting up in anticipation of our arrival.

I had planned this section of the route, and it had been checked by Andy. We knew the route followed a footpath clearly marked on the OS maps, so why did we need 'safe passage'? Mike explained that there was a short, disputed section where the landowner had unilaterally decided to block the way. This brought out my inner Basil Fawlty once more ...!

The blockage was at a farm near the River Slea. Earlier in the week, Mike had spoken to the owners and had talked to them about 3 Dads Walking, our route and our mission. They had agreed to let us through their farm, providing we had Mike as our guide.

The diversion through the farmyard was short and we were soon onto the road on the opposite side. Returning to the footpath we could see that the disputed section of path was 30 metres long, at most.

Thankfully the torrential rain started to ease and the sun was breaking through. At the bridge just past the farm, a small welcoming committee supplied us with biscuits and flasks of coffee. Off came the waterproofs again, and, after leaving mine to dry on the grass in the warm sunshine, I happily accepted a piece of delicious cake along with some warming coffee. It was a lovely place to stop, overlooking the sparkling waters of the River Slea.

While I was talking to some of our supporters, a 4x4 pulled up and the lady in the driver's seat asked what was going on. When our Mike explained, she realised who we were.

'You're the people that Mike Lock told me about! Let me give you a donation.'

We accepted the cash and she drove off . . . into the farmyard – this was the landowner who had disputed the right of way with the council. We had gained another supporter out of a potentially problematic situation. Suicide prevention was something that seemed to unite everyone.

Just as I was offered yet more cake, we were joined by another local, Sarah, who ran a hairdressing salon in New York – that is, the Lincolnshire New York. Sarah was a good friend of Sarla, our guardian angel from Day 4. Their grandparents had met each other at Melton Mowbray market decades ago, and had become good friends. This friendship had been passed down through the generations, and Sarla would be staying with Sarah's aunt, Maggie, just outside Boston on her way back to Cumbria at the end of the walk

We packed up and, after saying goodbye and thanks to Mike Lock's friends and family, continued on the southern side of the river.

Our Mike continued walking with Mike Lock, and Andy with Sarah, while I walked alone behind them, enjoying the sun. At times it was good to take some time out from the conversations and navigation, to drop back and take in the scenery, the wide-open fields, the slow-flowing river and wildlife – on this stretch herons, egrets, kestrels and buzzards – and just enjoy the steady repetition of one foot in front of another, step by step, getting ever nearer to the sea and our finish point.

Taking time out and focusing on what was around me was both calming and restorative.

For a moment, I was just a man walking.

We were still blessed with sunshine when we reached the pretty village of South Kyme. We'd arranged to use the picnic benches outside the Hume Arms in the centre of the village. When we arrived, the landlady was immediately on hand offering us tea, coffee and cake. It was another warm welcome from total strangers, and a humbling experience.

Sarah's mum and Aunty Maggie arrived, so Andy made sure he got photos taken with them to show to Sarla. We sat on the benches in the sun, took off our boots and enjoyed eating our lunch and chatting with all around us.

While we were there, I took a call from Jim. To my surprise, he and his colleagues had been working hard behind the scenes to get us a flypast of some description. It just so happened that the Red Arrows would fly over our route at 1.30 p.m. on Holland Fen, about three miles east of South Kyme, on their way south to display over Portsmouth Harbour. Jim explained that the only issue was the weather – the heavy showers that had been passing through all day might cause an issue. Flying through those at low level in a formation of nine Hawk aircraft would be too dangerous.

I explained the plan to Andy, Mike and the rest of the group and they were amazed. The only snag was that we needed to leave right at that moment to make the rendezvous.

Mike Lock and Sarah left us and, crossing the last contour line of the day, we headed out into the Fens. We set a good pace heading for our objective, knowing that we would get a great view of the famous aircraft as they headed south . . . but unfortunately for us, the weather wasn't playing ball – the clouds were building behind us. We kept our fingers crossed and carried on.

As we approached the rendezvous point the thunder clouds appeared overhead and it began to rain – and when I say rain, it was torrential. There wasn't much we could do other than put on our waterproofs and plod on.

I checked the time. This was when the Red Arrows would be taking off from RAF Scampton, and there would be no way they would be able to overfly us. As if to confirm my assessment, Jim reappeared on the opposite bank of the river and shouted the Red Arrows team's apologies across to us.

Although it was really disappointing, some things are beyond everyone's control – and the weather is definitely one of them. But we weren't here to see the RAF display team; we were here because we were 3 Dads Walking, so that's what we had to do – walk.

As the rain eased, rays of sunshine began to break through. The three of us stood together at the southern end of Holland Fen, and a bright rainbow appeared. 'Someone's shining on us,' I said.

As we finished recording another video, Bob, another of my ex-RAF colleagues, found us. Tragically, Bob had lost his seven-year-old daughter Charlie to a heart defect. He'd been in contact with me a month or so after Em had died, and we'd spoken at length about the loss of a child. His support, guidance and counsel had been invaluable to me, as was the strength of his Christian faith. He shared his story with Andy and Mike, who listened in silence.

On our walk we were constantly reminded that despite being force-fed perfect-world images and stories through the media, real people live in a world where loss and pain are common-place, although very few people talk about it. Our openness seemed to be encouraging many others to share their stories of loss and grief – we had seen first-hand how positive this was, and every time we had this kind of interaction, we were reas-sured that we were doing something that would help many people. This was exactly how Bob had helped me, and I will be forever grateful.

Coming to the end of a farm track, we knew that the next four miles would be on the flat, straight roads of the Fens. As we turned onto our first road, about 500 metres ahead we saw a bunch of people emerging from a minibus. It looked like another welcoming committee.

The minibus group was from The Pilgrim School at Amber Hill, a specialist hospital school for children with extreme anxiety that was very close to our route. This was the school's DofE group – they lined up along the edge of the road and held up their homemade banner which said '*So Massively Proud*' along with PAPYRUS, HOPELINE247 and drawings of SpongeBob SquarePants. We talked to the young people and their teachers – we were equally moved and impressed as we heard about the challenges they faced and what they'd achieved. We felt humbled that they'd taken the time to make their banner and come out to find us.

We left them clambering back into their minibus as we strode off down the flattest and straightest of roads. Not only were these roads really dull to walk on, they were painful on our feet – and dangerous because the endless straights encouraged drivers to rattle along them at high speed.

A further distraction from our walk arrived by way of an aerobatic display from a Typhoon aircraft above RAF Coningsby, which was about four miles to the north of us and the location of our accommodation that night. Between towering stratocumulus clouds, some bright white and others darker grey, there were gaps of perfect blue sky which allowed us to watch a fantastic display which seemed to go on for ages. After a couple of minutes, Mike said, 'I think I would have shat myself by now!' Andy nodded in agreement.

Turning our backs on the Typhoon, we followed the last of our straight roads towards the River Witham. Our plan was to follow this enclosed watercourse for the last few miles of the day, leaving it just before it flowed through the centre of Boston. A grassy path ran along the top of the embankment – a relief from walking on tarmac, and perfect for Andy's foot.

We soon met Avril and her dog Juno coming towards us and we walked on together to Langrick Bridge, where – following her advice – we changed our plans and crossed to the northern bank to pick up the surfaced cycle path. Here we found Sarah and her daughter, from earlier in the day, parked by the route. They kindly supplied us with coffee, chocolate bars and biscuits.

As we set off along the cycle path towards Boston, we could see why our friends had suggested this would be a better and faster way to end the day: it was a broad tarmacked path. The downside, we realised, was that it was going to be another tough finish, and I was feeling exhausted. Tired feet don't react well to tarmac. The repetitive pounding amplified our aches, and the change of finish meant we would be walking an extra mile on this surface.

We had four miles to go till Witham Way Country Park, two straights of two miles, both old railway lines along the bank of the River Witham. Mentally it was tough and it felt a bit like being back on the Southwell Trail – I could see the lights of Boston in the distance, and they seemed to be getting no closer. We plodded on . . . at least this time we had today's events and the people we had met to talk about and keep us going.

At a mile to go, it was getting dark and our headtorches went on – this was not what I had planned. Then a chap on a bike stopped us. He talked about our challenge, our grief and how that reminded him of his own loss – his mum. He talked about how much he missed her. We wanted to keep moving, but this chap was going in the opposite direction. As he spoke, he opened his rucksack and pulled out three bottles of beer. It was very generous of him and it was obvious that he wanted to talk for longer . . . but we were wiped out and all we wanted to do was get to the end of the tarmac. Eventually we made our excuses and headed for Jim as the daylight evaporated. I felt guilty that we couldn't spend more time with him, but we were so late already – and we just had to have some downtime for our own wellbeing.

Onwards we went into the gathering gloom. I spotted a shape coming towards us – another well-wisher wanting to talk? No, far better than that – it was the other Jim, that night's saviour who'd sorted out our transport, food and accommodation. I'd initially met Jim through work, but six months before our walk he and his wife Sarah had also bought our house in Shouldham... our house which we had sold simply because I could no longer bear to live there. I had found it too difficult to face those painful memories of Em's last moments every day.

Jim walked us back to his car. It was such a relief to get there at the end of another long day. Our initial plan had been to walk 20.3 miles, which we knew we'd extend by a mile or so when we'd decided to change the end point. However, it transpired that we had actually walked 24 miles ... the OS Maps app seemed to underestimate the distance.

I climbed into the passenger seat and sank into the welcoming leather; Mike and Andy relaxed in the back, all of us so relieved to have the weight off our feet. In the dark confines of the car, all three of our phones 'pinged' simultaneously. Ged had just messaged us in excitement on our PAPYRUS WhatsApp group. To our amazement, he'd been contacted by the Royal Household of the Duke and Duchess of Cambridge – HRH Prince William had been following our story and had sent us a letter of support.

KENSINGTON PALACE

Dear Andy, Tim and Mike

I heard about your 'Three Dads Walking' challenge and wanted to write to wish you every success with your endeavour to raise awareness of suicide and the invaluable work of PAPYRUS.

You have showed incredible strength and courage, not only on this walk, but in speaking openly about your experience as fathers and I very much hope it encourages other young people who may be suffering to speak out and seek help. No family should ever endure the pain you have suffered through the loss of your daughters and as a parent myself, you have my heartfelt condolences.

I imagine this letter will reach you around the midway point in your 300-mile journey, and I have no doubt that there will have been challenging times as you walk from Morland, to Greater Manchester and onto King's Lynn, but be heartened to know you are making an enormous difference to the lives of others.

This comes with my very best wishes to you all.

William

I was speechless. I was proud we had made such an impact and it was incredible to think that our walk, our stories and daughters' short lives had touched royalty. But I was sad that Em wasn't there to see the impact she was having – and I would have given *anything* not to have received that letter, and to have her back.

That night we were staying in the RAF Coningsby Station Commander's house. He was away, but had kindly offered his official residence to us. Jim had stocked it with all the essentials: beer, and a selection of cereal and milk for breakfast. On the way there, Jim offered a selection of food options and, being absolutely wiped out, we decided on a Chinese takeaway.

On arrival Jim guided us inside and showed us to our rooms. There was absolutely loads of space to spread out and unpack our bags.

Jim left us to get sorted and showered while he went to the Chinese to collect our food. By the time he was back, we had beers in hand and had been joined by Wrighty, another fine RAF chap, whom I'd served with. As we ate, Wrighty explained more about the Typhoon aircraft display we'd seen earlier – it was a 2021 Typhoon display pilot handing onto next year's display pilot, flying a rare two-seater Typhoon aircraft. Mike and Andy were suitably impressed.

We then made a group call to Ged to chat about the letter from HRH Duke of Cambridge. He explained that he'd spoken to the Royal Household and we would all be getting a copy. Ged was so excited that the work of PAPYRUS was being recognised in these circles. The profile of the charity and suicide prevention was definitely being raised. To think that HRH Prince William had taken the time to write to the three of us about Emily, Beth and Sophie was incredibly surreal.

Takeaways finished and Andy's social-media duties complete, we couldn't manage more than a couple of beers – we were whacked – so soon we were off to bed in separate rooms for the first time in several days. At least I wouldn't have to worry about trying to get to sleep before Andy's snoring started!

The next day would take us onto the sea defences east of Boston, and by the time we walked off those we would be in King's Lynn. It felt like the end was within reach. As I lay there in the dark, my tired mind reflected on our conversation with Ged. I thought about my family's journey, about my wife's despair immediately after Em's funeral and her fear that no one would remember Em in a year's time. That had not happened; I now had the future king writing to Andy, Mike and me, offering condolences and supporting our walk.

Em was definitely not forgotten – and we were being heard.

Money raised (excluding Gift Aid and direct donations)
    = £333,000
Day 12 distance = 24.1 miles
Total distance walked = 368.6 miles

DAY 13

Boston to The Wash

Despite the fact that it was still dark – and raining – when I woke up, I felt good. The impact of Prince William's letter, and the reach our story was having, along with the support from the public, felt so positive. A couple of months ago we would never have dreamt that us three blokes would be making such a difference to so many people. I felt I had a purpose, as did Mike and Andy – we were creating a collective voice.

The next two days would introduce us to a new experience: walking for 45 miles along the sea wall beside The Wash. There were several things to think about: although the walk was going to be totally flat, we'd be fully exposed to the wind. And in two places we'd have to walk miles inland alongside a river to a crossing point, only to retrace our steps on the other side – each time gaining a mere 200 metres as the crow flies! Andy was convinced we would get wind-battered and find it very hard mentally.

By the time we reached our start point the rain had eased a bit, but it was still dark. We said our goodbyes to Jim. 'See you on Saturday!' I called as we set off. The end of our walk was only three days away on the village green in Shouldham.

Dawn broke as we followed the River Slea into Boston, old merchants' and traders' buildings flanking the tidal river. Boston was once a wealthy trading port, dating back to medieval times when the town was a member of the Hanseatic League, a commercial and defensive confederation across central and northern Europe.

In the town centre our interest was drawn to a couple of things. The river was running very high as a result of the spring tides which are a constant threat on this stretch of the east coast. The water was only inches below the riverbank and defences. The second unmissable feature was Boston Stump, the impressive tower of St Botolph's Church, standing over 80 metres high and visible for miles around. It would be an ever-present landmark for the next two days as we progressed south along the sea defences.

Nigel had recommended a diversion here because of the Boston Barrier, the centrepiece of the Tidal Flood Defence Scheme. An impressive feat of engineering, it was being constructed to protect hundreds of homes and businesses from a tidal surge (a tidal surge on 5 December 2013 overcame the existing flood defences around the town).

As we walked out of the town centre and through the industrial estate on our revised route, a pick-up truck stopped by us and a chap got out. He was clearly so pleased to have found us. As he put cash into our bucket, he told us that he'd lost two friends to suicide, one of whom had been a very gregarious character, well known in the town. His suicide had been a complete shock to all his friends and family, and they were still living in the post-suicide despair we three knew so well. A story we'd been told so often – and would continue to hear many more times.

Nigel's diversion led us up a grassy slope onto the sea wall defences and the path that would take us most of the way to the finish. We would be walking on top of this feature for the next two days to King's Lynn, my local town – and where Em had once worked. For me, it was wonderful to be so close to home at last; for Mike and Andy, it was the chance to see a new part of the country and find out more about my home patch, and my life. Our spirits were high.

I'd promised the other two that the sea wall would be great to walk on: grassy, spongy, flat ... but the first half mile had been churned up by a couple of mini-diggers as they accessed their worksite and were very muddy. This worried Mike a little, as he had changed his boots for trainers to give his sore feet a little respite – and the last thing we needed at this stage was wet feet.

However, before long the route was perfect underfoot, grassy and very forgiving. We were now exposed to the elements, but the wind was coming from the west, so it was largely behind us. The sun was out and the sky was deep blue, with great visibility. It was a perfect autumnal day to be out walking.

As we strode away from Boston on the flat top of the sea wall we really could believe that we had the finish in our sights. We were now on the Macmillan Way, a long-distance path linking Boston to Abbotsbury in Dorset, and promoted as a walk to raise money for Macmillan Cancer Relief.

I was enjoying the walk. Andy's constant optimism, big smile and enthusiasm; Mike's dry sense of humour and funny quips, his compassion for others and concern about our various ailments: they were both brilliant company. Our unspoken bond had developed over the past twelve days into something really strong. We all knew what made each other tick, and how our different personalities and strengths complemented each other, which helped us overcome our individual weaknesses. We were all on exactly the same page, and stronger together.

We left the built-up area behind and entered a completely different landscape, one of birds, sea, mud, brassicas and big skies. Navigation was simple: follow the sea wall, interrupted only by odd gates and stiles. And there were plenty of cows grazing inside the meadows inside the sea wall for Mike to talk to. He loved it.

Little by little two people, spotted ahead in the far distance, grew closer. Andy recognised them as Nick and Tom from *Country Walking* magazine. Nick talked to all three of us as we walked along and Tom ran back and forth taking photos from different angles, even lying on the ground to get that perfect shot. The commitment of these camera folk is not to be doubted.

At one stage, Nick asked us to stop because he had an idea for a great photo for the magazine. He asked us to kneel on one knee, our flags fluttering in the wind above our rucksacks. The photo was brilliant and captured the spirit of the walk: our big cheesy grins and tanned faces, waterproofs on to protect us from the wind and walking poles in hand, against a backdrop of saltmarsh and wide-open skies. After twelve-and-half consecutive days of walking, testing muscles that we didn't know existed, getting up was quite a challenge. After much grunting and groaning, we made it back to standing position – each with one wet, muddy knee.

Nick and Tom walked with us for three or four miles. Nick told us that his wife worked as an administrator at The Pilgrims' School, whose DofE group we'd met the day before. She'd told him that the pupils had been really looking forward to meeting us and had returned to school very happy that they had managed to find us. This feedback was incredible, and it reinforced the value of our mission – getting young people talking about the challenges they faced and being open about suicide prevention.

At one stage I dropped back, happy to let the others walk a couple of hundred metres ahead. Once again, it gave me time to appreciate my surroundings, to feel the wind blowing against my body and tugging on my flag. The autumn sun was getting stronger as it rose and I could feel it on my face. The smell of the sea was strong – it was the first time we'd been close to salt water since setting off.

Across to my left were the saltmarshes, beyond which was The Wash. To my right were a series of old sea banks, built to protect the fertile land upon which cattle now grazed. All around were many types of birds which Andy and Mike started to name: egrets, marsh harriers, various geese and ducks, waders and even a short-eared owl. I had seen this place on many occasions from the air, but never on foot. It was strange, really, because it wasn't that far from home, and I loved this different view of a familiar landscape. Moving at a slower pace and taking time to appreciate our environment and what lives within it is incredibly calming.

Just before Nick and Tom left us, we were joined by another chap, Bryant. He told us that he had two daughters in their mid-twenties, one who suffered from anxiety and the other from depression. They'd seen 3 Dads Walking on TV and told their father that he *had* to come out and find us in order to pass on their thanks for raising awareness of mental-health issues. Bryant walked and talked with us until we were stopped by a film crew from ITV Anglia. As we were now my patch, it was my turn to be interviewed.

Since the sound guy was going to struggle in the strong wind, we all dropped down off the sea wall to find shelter. The crew and I found some protection behind a bush while Andy, Mike and Bryant sat behind a fence, sheltering the best they could. Mike and Andy took the opportunity to have a drink and a bite to eat.

We were becoming used to the demands of TV and radio, and could always work out if the interviewer was invested in our cause. It definitely felt like the ITV Anglia crew were, asking all the right questions about why we were walking and what we were hoping to achieve. Interview sorted, we climbed back onto the sea defence wall and said our goodbyes to Bryant and the TV crew.

We weren't on our own for very long. The first supporter to arrive was Sam, a runner who'd passed us and said hello as we were walking out of Boston; he was determined to catch us later in the day. He arrived bearing biscuits and bananas, which was much appreciated. Sam explained that the reason he was so keen to meet us was that he'd lost a very good friend to suicide, and he wanted to show his appreciation for what we were trying to do.

As Mike and Andy walked and talked with Sam I noticed two figures ahead. As they got closer, I recognised the beaming smile of my friend and colleague Michelle, along with her husband Robin. Michelle had been an absolute rock in the aftermath of Em's death, taking over from me when I had time off work, and prepared to step in at a moment's notice to cover anything I needed her to do when I returned. She had been an absolute star over the previous eighteen months, and it was so good that she'd come out to meet us. I had great pleasure in introducing her to Andy and Mike: they'd all heard so much about each other.

Sam turned back towards Boston, leaving the five of us walking and talking. While chatting about some of the people we'd met, I mentioned Alan Hinkes, a mate of Andy's and who'd walked with us on and off over the first two days.

'Hinkes!' exclaimed Robin. 'I know Alan Hinkes!'

Robin was the chair of the RAF Mountaineering Association and Alan, a famous mountaineer and huge aircraft enthusiast, regularly supported the Association and attended various events. Yet more unexpected and amazing connections.

Michelle had told us not to bother about lunch and that she would bring it to us. However, Robin was quick to tell us that he'd been up at 6.30 a.m. to make our sandwiches! After lunch, Robin turned back to their car, but Michelle walked with us all the way to our destination, RAF Holbeach.

Our next challenge was both a physical and mental one. Between Boston and King's Lynn several large rivers, taking millions of gallons of water from their catchment basins across the East Midlands and east of England, enter the sea – and we would somehow have to get across two of them. First came the River Welland, which meant we had to walk inland along the river for six miles to Fosdyke Bridge, then turn back along the southern bank.

Before turning inland, we videoed our daily diary, sheltering at the bottom of the sea defence bank. We talked about the people we'd met and how the sharing of their stories meant so much to us. We also talked about the beginning of the end, the 45-mile walk along the sea wall, the distance we had to walk to cross the river and the flatness that lay ahead . . .

'It's not like Cumbria,' said Andy.

We were interrupted by a WhatsApp message from PAPYRUS. Nicole Kidman – THE Nicole Kidman – had just donated £10,000. It was absolutely incredible that our story was reaching so far. She had contacted PAPYRUS with the following message:

I saw Mike, Andy and Tim's story on BBC Breakfast News and was profoundly moved by their extraordinary undertaking – what they were walking for, and why.

Covering 300 miles across the country for PAPYRUS in memory of their daughters – raising money for this vital charity, so that other families would not experience the loss and devastation of losing a child to suicide.

Three completely brilliant dads, doing a completely brilliant thing, to benefit so many. Ahead of them finishing their epic trek on Saturday, and inspired by Daniel Craig who backed them at the outset of their journey, I am matching his £10,000 to support their excellent fundraising efforts.

Given the circumstances of the past eighteen months and the impact of the pandemic, especially on the young, their work is particularly important right now.

I would like to dedicate my donation to the memory of Beth, Sophie and Emily.

Once again, we were all lost for words. I could not believe that Nicole Kidman was talking about Em, Beth and Sophie – Em would have been in hysterics.

We headed towards Fosdyke Bridge and more people came along to join us. One of these was Chandy, an ex-RAF colleague who turned up in his biker leathers bearing gifts of bags of sweets. Chandy and I caught up on life, family and colleagues. We were both on home ground; Fosdyke had been an entry point to the old air weapons range, RAF Wainfleet, which Chandy and I had both used on numerous occasions . . . only travelling a little faster in our aircraft!

Another lady, Rachel Smith, joined us. She told us that she had been widowed at thirty-one and, by way of dealing with her grief, had gone on to record podcasts featuring people she knew who were trying to cope with bereavement. She used her podcast to show others that grief was normal, that the emotions following loss were not unusual and that it was possible to create a fulfilling life after losing a loved one.

Andy recorded a short video with her. It was almost unde-cipherable due to the wind, but he managed to catch her saying that she had met 'three ordinary dads doing an extraordinary thing,' and it was 'something positive coming out of what's been a really horrible situation'.

We really were in our own little bubble while we were on the walk. We had some idea of the effect we were having because the JustGiving total kept going up, but we had no concept of how many people across the country were talking about us, our girls, PAPYRUS and suicide prevention. It wouldn't be until several weeks after we'd finished that we'd really start to appreciate the consequences of 'three chaps going for a walk'.

We'd arranged to meet Alison and Adam from the BBC at Fosdyke Bridge. They were staying in Norfolk and would film us over the next three days. Just before we got there, Adam turned up and greeted us with his normal bear-like hug. He told us that he and Alison had the camera set up on the opposite bank – they wanted a shot of us leading our group over the bridge.

Also waiting for us was an older couple who introduced themselves to me and Michelle. It turned out they were parents of another RAF colleague, Mini. Mini's parents lived locally, and this was her old stomping ground. At the planning stage I had asked Mini about the local footpaths, and she had recommended our route around The Wash. Without that valuable local knowledge I would have probably tried to take a more direct route along very straight, dangerous, minor roads that criss-cross this remote part of the country.

Once over the bridge, we were met by an excited Alison (and another big hug). She told us that BBC *Six O'Clock News* had asked for a piece on 3 Dads Walking and it would be broadcast that evening. We were stunned and without delay she interviewed us once again about our walk, our daughters and all things suicide-prevention related. I know I keep saying this, but it really was difficult to get our heads around our walk being covered on the national news. This was not what we had anticipated when we first had the idea about walking between our homes.

Pulling ourselves together, we began our return leg up the east side of the River Welland. Ahead of us lay vast saltmarshes, interspersed with deep channels cut through mud and silt, like a system of tree roots exposed to the elements. In the very far distance was the sea, a murky brown colour, like the tidal river. We were walking above reclaimed farmland, protected by the sea defences carrying our path. The wind was everywhere, swirling around us: the grasses rippled, solitary trees swayed and our flags flapped. It is a bleak, yet strangely beautiful, landscape.

We soon saw a lone figure waiting in the distance, a small woman with shoulder-length dark hair blowing in the wind. As we approached, she gave us a cheery 'Hello', but deep sadness could be seen in her eyes. She introduced herself as Tracey, a local businesswoman, who wanted to walk with us.

I took my turn in walking with her and listened to her story. Tears filled my eyes as I felt her pain. She'd lost her son Charlie to suicide in May 2020. She explained how Charlie had struggled with his mental health after suffering a series of head injuries; however, his suicide had come as a complete shock to his family.

Tracey was a lovely person – open, caring and confused as to how she had ended up in such a tragic place. Her world had been devastated just a short time after Mike and I had lost our daughters. I felt that there was nothing I could do for her apart from listen, but sometimes that's the best approach – just allowing someone to share their story and their pain.

As the sun sank behind us, our shadows lengthened across the Fens and we met the last supporters of the day, Sally Eastwood and Mark Fleming, friends of Andy's who live in the Midlands. They had taken a few days' holiday in Norfolk and had extended their last day so that they could meet us before heading home.

We walked the last mile before arriving at our end point as the sun set, passing the tower which marked the edge of the air weapons range at RAF Holbeach. We were greeted at the gates by Martin, the range manager. We said our goodbyes to Michelle, who said she would see us at the finish in a couple of days.

It had been a pleasurable day of walking. We'd covered many miles, but the terrain had been easy and gentle on our bodies and the weather had been kind. We were all smiling and in good spirits, our faces tanned from a day in the sun and wind. Andy's foot was continuing to heal, and although we all had our individual aches and pains, we knew that our bodies would hold out to the end of the walk – there were only around 35 miles left to go. Holbeach was definitely a turning point for me – and probably for Andy and Mike too. Tomorrow we would be in King's Lynn. I was so close to home and Andy and Mike were now definitely in my territory. Tomorrow they would start to unite with their families and friends who had made the long trip down to these eastern lands. Tonight would be the last night with just us three.

Before we settled into our accommodation, Mike turned on the TV in time to see the *Six O'Clock News*. While Mike couldn't watch Alison and Adam's piece on 3 Dads Walking (he hated hearing and seeing himself on TV), Andy and I watched the programme in silence. After spending the best part of thirteen hours walking and talking, seeing us, our daughters and our mission featured on the early evening news was hard to comprehend. We never imagined that Mike's idea, born out of his 2010 road atlas and our collective tragedy, could ever be this big – but it was, and it was having a powerful impact across the country.

After the news, Martin and I chatted and he presented us with six beautifully decorated cupcakes that his daughter had made for us, perfectly displayed in a gift box, together with a most unexpected donation. It was an emotional couple of minutes – we seemed to have made a real impact on him.

After Martin left, we had a quiet space just to chat and reflect on the day's walk and what we had achieved so far. We knew this was going to be the last time we would be on our own until the walk was over, and we ate and talked and, unsurprisingly, had a beer. We were in high spirits, but at the same time overwhelmed with conflicting emotions.

'What a fantastic day,' piped up Andy. 'The soft grass underfoot on the sea defences were just spot on – and perfect for my foot.'

'Incredibly powerful though,' interjected Mike. 'Tracey – just another beautiful person whose life has been devastated.'

'Just so unfair – it's everywhere,' I responded. We sat in silence for a while, quietly reflecting on the day.

The terrain had been forgiving on our tired legs and, more importantly our feet. The flat, often under-appreciated, landscape had been at its best in the warmth of the autumn sunshine and blustery wind, which had made our clothing and flags flap. It was a day which made us feel so connected with nature and the environment, and so alive.

We had been supported by friends and had met new people who all wanted to connect with us, sadly many with their own tragic tales to tell. It had been amazing that Nicole Kidman had donated to PAPYRUS, but more importantly, her words of support and the fact that she mentioned our three girls by name had been incredibly powerful. Then there were the media pieces on the BBC *Six O'Clock News*, local *ITV News*, and then *Country Walking* magazine, all of which were sending our message of suicide prevention and awareness out to new audiences.

Conflicting with our excitement and sense of achievement was the reality that so many people, good people, were losing their sons and daughters to suicide. I saw the pain in other people's faces when I met them, long before the tears started, and felt it so strongly myself. A photo of Em could knock me sideways – especially if I looked directly into her eyes, or imagined the scent of her perfume. There is just so much grief out there. Tracey's story was just one example of many, and she'd had such an impact on us. We spoke about what she and her family were going through – the devastation which suicide creates for years afterwards, which we all understood so well.

The dichotomy of our emotions was evident in every interaction we had with people – and in every conversation we had between the three of us.

As our discussions drew to a tired close, it was Mike who summed up our story and walk so far with six simple words: 'It is a story of hope.'

Money raised (excluding Gift Aid and direct donations)
  = £349,000
Day 13 distance = 20.4 miles
Total distance walked = 289 miles

DAY 14

The Wash to King's Lynn

Our alarms woke us earlier than normal after another good night's sleep. I was surprised to learn that the weapons range had been in action the previous evening – none of us had heard the aircraft flying low overhead or the explosion of their weapons as they hit the targets on the marshes. We must have been exhausted.

Today's leg was going to be the longest section of our walk and we needed to depart early. But my meticulously planned route and timings for these last two days to the finish line had been blown out of the water by a simple request from Alison, which came a couple of weeks before we started the walk: 'Tim, do you think you could arrive in Shouldham at 9.30 a.m. on Saturday as *BBC Breakfast* want live coverage of you arriving in the village?'

Simple as this request at first appeared, it really wasn't. It meant we would have to extend Day 14 and shorten the final leg. The problem was that I had planned to finish Day 14 at Admiralty Point, on the western bank of the mouth of the River Great Ouse, after walking about 23 miles. We'd then have a leisurely stroll to the finish on Day 15, following the River Nar almost all the way to Shouldham.

Instead, I would have to make Mike and Andy walk around 26 miles on Day 14. In addition, my intended route along an

overgrown footpath alongside the River Nar would be hazard-
ous in the dark, so instead we'd have to walk along a section of
the unforgiving A10 at the end of a very long day.

Our arrival in Shouldham had also been planned to coincide
with the pub opening at a good time for people to gather and
see us across the finish line. Fortunately, Nigel Walsh from the
village and Ian and Abbie from the pub weren't fazed by the
change of plan and quickly rearranged everything for our arrival
at the pub sometime after 9.30 a.m.

Since our entire association with *BBC Breakfast* had come
about because of Alison Freeman, and we had so much to thank
her for, we decided to christen Day 14 'The Freeman Leg'. It
was to be the earliest start of any day, and we planned to be
walking by 7 a.m.

Martin reappeared as we were finishing breakfast. We took
some photos with him in the pre-dawn light, packed our bags
and prepared to leave. Martin wished us well and we walked
out of the gates straight onto the sea defence wall. We were
welcomed by the most dramatic sunrise, with incredible reds,
oranges and yellows illuminating the vast landscape of marshes,
sea defences and fields, the light adding a warming glow to
everyone and everything. There to meet us were Jan and John,
friends from Shouldham – it was lovely to see their familiar
faces and broad smiles.

While Mike and I were marvelling at the view, Andy dived
into his rucksack. Ever the marketing man, he gave Jan his
phone and asked her to take a picture of the 3 Dads at the start
of our penultimate day.

'I think we've got the front cover of the book!' Andy exclaimed excitedly. The photo was amazing – the three of us silhouetted against the warm colours of the dawn over The Wash, flags clearly visible. It looked like an image from a film poster.

Jan was Richard's sister – Richard whom we'd met on Day 6 when we walked from Manchester – and she was only three when she lost her dad to suicide in 1953. She told her story of being kept in the dark about what had happened to her dad for over thirty years.

There has always been a huge stigma attached to suicide, and even more so seventy years ago when Jan lost her dad, Yorke Sails. He had fought in World War II and been wounded – but it was not the physical wounds which caused him distress. In 1953, aged thirty-eight, he took his own life, probably suffering from PTSD. Jan and Richard's mum felt no stigma, but those around her did – her first battle was to have her husband buried in a churchyard, a battle she won. There was nothing to be ashamed of in his suicide – there should instead have been total compassion for a man who'd fought for king and country, and suffered so terribly as a result. Jan and Richard strongly believe their mum, who had only recently passed away aged ninety-nine, would have wholeheartedly agreed with our sentiments. They felt she would have applauded our efforts to encourage discussion and education that would have no doubt aided her children through their young lives and would, hopefully, help very many troubled young people in the future.

The five of us were soon striding out, our walking poles propelling us on our way across the grass, wet from the early morning dew. Today's first objective was the crossing of another great river, the River Nene, on Sutton Bridge. Yet again this involved a frustrating detour: a 3¾-mile leg due south along the riverbank, then back along the opposite side, to arrive a mere 150 metres further on our way – and three hours later! This was mentally challenging but fortunately we were in good company so the miles ticked by, the sun shone, the wind had died down and conditions underfoot were near perfect, if a little damp. And behind us we could still see the Boston Stump, keeping a watchful eye on our journey.

After an hour-and-a-half's walking, we arrived at the River Nene; we could see our return path on the opposite bank. Just reeds, mud and water between our current position and where we would be in three hours' time. I could almost have jumped the river.

We headed south along the riverbank. Ahead we could see the two white lighthouses, looking like gatehouses to the water-way from a bygone time. We'd been told that the lighthouse on the far bank had been home to the great naturalist Sir Peter Scott, son of Captain Scott of the Antarctic. Sir Peter was a founding member of the World Wildlife Fund and the Wildfowl and Wetlands Trust. I could see why he chose to live there.

At the lighthouse on our side of the river, we were welcomed by another large group of well-wishers. As we stood to chat, I recognised Tracey coming towards us: she'd so enjoyed walking and talking with us the previous day she'd asked her husband to drop her off further down the path to enable her to catch up with us again.

We passed the lighthouse and continued on our way. Mike was doing what he did best – walking with stragglers or stopping to talk to someone falling behind; he'd catch up in his own time. Occasionally we'd have to wait for him, crying out 'Come on Mike!' as he approached us – but not today. The group stayed together quite well, and the long, straight walk towards the bridge, which we thought would be an endurance event, turned into a great stroll. Since the river curves slightly to the right, Sutton Bridge only came into view a few hundred metres before we reached it. The bridge is an incredible steel structure, built in 1897 to enable safe passage for ships up the River Nene to the port of Wisbech, in the landlocked county of Cambridgeshire.

We knew Alison and Adam were planning to film us crossing Sutton Bridge, but we weren't expecting so many other people to be there, applauding our arrival. I felt almost overwhelmed – all these people had come out to see *us*?

The first person I recognised was my great friend from Shouldham, Rich, who was bringing lunch (including two pork pies each). Rich and his family had been really close to Em, and he'd come with me to the Seven Bro7hers launch event in Manchester only a few weeks earlier, where he had met Mike and Andy and their families. They'd all got on like a house on fire over beers and a curry – the start of our lives and that of our respective friends entwining. Rich and his family had known Em since she was tiny. Our kids had all played together, gone to nursery and school together, and Em had gone out with Katy, Rich's daughter, to various parties and pubs. They'd been devasted by Em's decision to take her own life, and full of questions of their own. So many 'what ifs?' to which they – and I – will never know the answer.

Over the previous nineteen months, Rich had accompanied me along my journey of grief and devastation, as a friend who would simply listen. I would receive a message on my phone – '*Coffee?*' – to which I would reply '*On my way!*' and then walk to his house, to his shed where the log burner would be lit, and his coffee machine gurgling away. I'd told him about Mike and then Andy, and when I first explained the idea of a walk, he simply said, 'How do you want me to help?'

Rich had accompanied me on walks during which we recced the paths to King's Lynn (which normally involved a few sneaky pork pies to sustain us). On one practice walk, we'd walked along a footpath from Wormegay to the River Nar, the reverse of which we would walk tomorrow. The nettles had been quite bad – and by quite bad, I mean we'd walked through nettles for around a mile, both of us getting stung repeatedly through our walking trousers. Neither of us could feel our legs for a couple of days.

I had also arranged to meet Alfie Bowen at Sutton Bridge. Alfie was a young man whom Emily had befriended before she'd died – but had never met – and he had reached out to us after she died. They had got to know each other via social media, brought together by their respective talents, Alfie being an incredible wildlife photographer and Em a talented artist. But it had been Alfie's openness about his struggles with autism and fitting in with society which had drawn Em to him.

While growing up in Suffolk, Alfie had endured a horrendous time with bullying, and photography became his passion and safe space. Taking pictures of wildlife was his escape, his happy place. Alfie's story is an inspirational one of overcoming obstacles and being brilliant at what you are best at and what you love. It is about following your dreams to places you never thought you could go.

Alfie revealed that Em had encouraged him to follow his dreams and have a book of his photography published, which he'd been in the process of doing, with the support of the World Wildlife Fund, when Em took her own life. His book *Wild World – Nature Through an Autistic Eye* was published at the time of our walk in late 2021. The foreword is by Chris Packham and the book is supported by Sir Richard Branson, amongst others. Most importantly for me, Alfie dedicated the book to Em with these beautiful words:

> *Dedicated in memory of Emily Owen.*
> *A fierce supporter of my work and a special friend.*
> *It pains me that you aren't here to see the fruits*
> *of your encouragement and friendship,*
> *but wherever you are, this is for you.*

Also there to meet us at Sutton Bridge were members of the Long Sutton Men's Shed group, who'd been in contact with us. We'd been invited to visit their shed, but I'd looked at the route and realised that it would involve a six-plus-mile detour, which we simply couldn't do. I'd emailed them to decline their kind invitation but suggested they come to us – which is exactly what about ten of them did!

The Long Sutton Shed Men were an enthusiastic bunch. They'd made a sign on a piece of foil-backed insulation board that said, '*Long Sutton Men's Shed Welcomes 3 Dads Walking*'.

The Shed Man carrying this sign was determined to get it into every photo, so every time someone raised a phone or, more frustratingly for Adam, when the BBC camera pointed at us, he would push his way through the throng and photobomb every shot – he was brilliant, and made everyone laugh!

Ady and Shep, more of my RAF friends, arrived and I introduced them to Mike and Andy. They planned to walk with us for the remainder of the day. Mike was most impressed to learn that Ady had been the navigator the Battle of Britain Memorial Flight Lancaster Bomber when he'd seen it over Manchester.

Ady's daughter Katie had lost her boyfriend Dan to suicide in 2018. She sang under the name Theta and had written and performed a very powerful song, 'Stay', on the subject of suicide. Katie dealt with the immense loss by writing poetry and songs, not only to preserve her memories but also to fully reflect on just how low she felt. She said:

It was important for me to feel that darkness, as it almost seemed like I had to go through that to get to the other side. Now, more than five years on, I can say I only look back with extreme joy and gratitude that he was in my life and I feel him with me every step I take. I talk to him whenever I'm alone, I celebrate with him when I achieve something and I lean on him when I feel down. I know it's likely I'm only imagining him 'there', but it helps keep him alive within me, which is always going to be true.

We eventually sat down and, with people milling around us, started our lunchtime routine of checking our feet, eating and drinking. Andy's feet were much improved, thanks both to the medical care he'd received and the great walking conditions over the past few days. BBC Adam continued to film us and all the people who'd joined us. It felt like a travelling circus had arrived at Sutton Bridge.

Before heading over the bridge, Adam let us know that the BBC had hired a drone operator for a couple of hours. His brief was to get some eye-catching shots of 3 Dads Walking and our supporters, the first of which was to be us crossing Sutton Bridge. Time was pressing and we still had several miles to cover of the dreaded 'Freeman Leg' and, with more BBC filming to be done, we knew we had to get underway. We said thank you to the many people who had come out to give us encouragement, then headed towards the bridge.

We were under strict direction to be at the front of the pack, so we had to do a bit of cat-herding to ensure that we went first and everyone followed on behind us, a bit like we were the Pied Pipers of Hamelin. We stood waiting for the off, like runners at the start of the London Marathon . . .

Adam's phone call was the 'go' signal, and we started to head across the bridge. I could hear the hum of the drone, being flown from the far bank somewhere off to my left. This turned out to be the best drone shot of us taken that day, and it was used extensively by the BBC.

Once over the bridge, Tracey and Alfie were introduced to Alison. Alfie had agreed to be interviewed, and Tracey said that she would be happy to talk about her loss if the three of us sat next to her during the interview. All of us immediately agreed and reassured her that Alison would conduct the interview very sensitively.

The decision was made to conduct the interview at the lighthouse on the east bank of the river, where it would be a bit quieter. As we neared the lighthouse, we met Tracey's husband: another parent, full of love, who'd been sideswiped by his son's suicide – somehow Charlie had missed the support he had around him and had chosen a way that had shattered the lives of the people who loved him most.

We found Adam and Alison waiting for us in the lighthouse car park. We took the opportunity to get out of the way, find somewhere to sit, and eat and drink a bit more. While we waited, we continued chatting to Tracey and her husband; we wished there was something we could say to help them. All Mike, Andy and I could do was listen, enabling them to share their hurt and pain.

After completing the interview with Alfie, Alison and Adam set the camera up for the interview with Tracey. As always, Alison interviewed Tracey compassionately.

'As soon as I saw them I just gave them a hug,' Tracey said. 'It's like I'd always known them and they were fantastic. They were just so open, friendly, let me talk.

'It was just talking to three dads who had been through exactly the same, and they just got it straight away. They understood exactly that horrible, gut-wrenching feeling you have every morning, every time you get up, knowing they are not there.'

It was a powerful and emotional interview with a lady whose world had been shattered. Adam came out from behind his camera, his eyes full of tears. Alison looked at him and, as she started wiping her own tears away, that got me going. I think we were all crying.

Tracey told us she was heading for home and gave us all a huge hug. It was hard to watch them go, knowing the daily struggles they had to contend with.

Finally ... finally ... we set off. Leaving the lighthouse, we were onto The Peter Scott Walk which went all the way to King's Lynn – it really felt like the end was in sight! The sea wall continued to offer superb walking conditions and we had plenty of chatty companions, so time passed quickly and the progress was good.

Before turning our backs on The Wash, we recorded our video diary as we looked across the water towards Wolferton, where the Royal Train used to terminate when taking the Royal Family to the Sandringham Estate.

'Today,' said Mike, 'we've been delayed by ... erm ...'

'... Alison Freeman of the BBC who's totally delayed us by hours!' I said, completing his sentence.

We explained why we were calling this 'The Freeman Leg', then went on to say how pleased we were to have introduced Alison to some of the people who walked with us and that she'd been able to capture their stories. The more people we could show who'd gone through bereavement by suicide, the more likely it was that the broader community would begin to talk about suicide and suicide prevention. The more stories that were heard, the more conversations would start, and ultimately more lives would be saved.

We also thanked Nicole Kidman for supporting 3 Dads Walking, as we'd all been particularly moved by the fact that she'd dedicated her donation to the memory of our daughters. This summed up the story of our walk – tragedy, inspiration, love, kindness and care.

We got going again, leaving behind the tidal creeks and salt-marshes of The Wash and starting our walk along the west bank of the River Great Ouse as we headed inland for the final time. We were joined by yet more people. A man climbed up the sea wall near Admiralty Point. He was clasping three bags of food, which he kindly gave to us. He just wanted to support us and our cause.

Next came Bill and Cherry, furnishing us with pork pies from Cumbria. These pork pies were large; in fact, I would go as far as to say *massive*. My immediate thought was, '*Can I do this?*' '*Of course I can,*' my inner self replied, and within minutes nothing but crumbs remained. The food supply on the whole walk had been never-ending – it seemed that if people wanted to support us, they just brought food; which we felt duty bound to eat if we could.

Abbie from the King's Arms in Shouldham joined us shortly after – she had known Em well, and approached with a big, but sad, smile before giving me a huge hug. We started chatting about Em and about how much we both missed her. A few minutes later my eldest daughter Annie and her partner Jacob appeared with their dogs. I gave Annie a big hug and a tear came into my eye (again). I jokingly reminded her that this was all her doing – if she hadn't reached out to Mike's family via social media a month after Em had died, none of this would have happened. The impact of Em's decision on that day had such an impact on so many people's lives, and these were emotional reunions.

A lady introduced herself: she told us about her partner who, although being a well-respected professional and someone held in high regard throughout his community, was another individual who'd become overwhelmed by his own problems but couldn't reach out for help.

She also spoke about her work – teaching. She said that her pupils had seen us on TV and wanted to send their congratulations to us, and handed us a sheet of paper with messages of support written in many different languages.

She had a conversation with Mike as we walked. She had an interesting opinion that suicide should once again be made illegal. Before judging, Mike listened to her reasoning, which was basically that the act affected so many people so deeply and painfully that it should not therefore be allowed. It was a very different point of view from ours, but she saw it as one way to discourage people. Her anguish was plain to see.

The setting sun was throwing a golden light onto the brick buildings on the waterfront of the old town. Like Boston, King's Lynn had been a wealthy Hanseatic port. The iconic seventeenth-century Custom House, which used to regulate trade through the port, clearly stood out behind the medieval harbour, and the Minster rose above the ancient streets. The whole waterfront looked amazing, with a couple of working fishing boats tied up alongside. It was a welcoming sight to our weary group.

We had to cross the Great Ouse to reach today's end point and as we headed towards the old bridge, our friend Sarla appeared with a big grin and gave us all a hug. It had been great to get to know her earlier in the walk, when she had supplied us with the most amazing cakes (including my favourite, her mouth-watering tea loaf). She'd promised us another cake: but it wasn't just any cake – it was a scrumptious three-tier 3 Dads Walking cake. She'd carefully brought it all the way down from Cumbria and wanted to catch up with us before the end. Sarla's way of looking after the 3 Dads was just to feed us – marvellous!

Many of our group left us just before we crossed the river. Sarla disappeared off to her friend's house, and Andy's wife Fiona – who'd joined us a little earlier – went back to the Premier Inn where she would meet their son Gregor, who'd driven separately from university in Liverpool. Also staying in the same hotel was Alan Dunn, the Mayor of Keswick, who had been such fun to walk with on the first day. On seeing our itinerary several weeks ago he'd mentioned to Andy that he would walk the final day because 'it was the shortest'. Andy had pointed out that it was in Norfolk, some 300 miles or so away, but that hadn't deterred Alan, as he was determined to be at both start and finish – especially as the finish was at a pub.

We'd already walked 24 miles and we still had two miles to go through the urban area of South Lynn, walking alongside a busy road. There was nothing for it other than to plod on, now in the dark. Even though I knew exactly where I was, those last two miles seemed to go on for ever, especially with the tarmac pounding through our walking boots and onto our bruised and blistered feet. A small group stopped us and spoke about a charity they'd started in the aftermath of another tragic death – they were all wearing identical black T-shirts. The 8:56 Foundation had been set up after a local man, Lee Calton, took his own life in April, only six months earlier. Lee was a massive Arsenal fan and he and his friends would catch the 8.56 train from King's Lynn Station on a Saturday morning, hence the name. The 8:56 Foundation was focusing on raising awareness, reducing the stigma and increasing the profile of mental-health support available locally. We wished them well and all the best in their quest – they were fighting back, just as we were. We continued on into the fading light, desperate to reach the day's end.

Rich met us near the historic South Gate, one of the few surviving parts of the medieval town, where tolls and duties on goods going to and from the port of King's Lynn were collected. Rich was the final piece in our complex jigsaw of lifts to and from start and end points – his car awaited us half a mile or so away. With Rich alongside us we knew all our logistical planning for the entire walk had somehow worked.

We laughed ironically as we climbed our largest hill of the day, the bridge over the King's Lynn-to-London rail line, before walking the last few hundred metres to the Tesco car park – what an iconic place to finish. As we arrived, Shep pulled three cans of beer from his rucksack and we gratefully drank them. We said our goodbyes to our group and clambered into Rich's car for the short journey to Shouldham.

We dropped Mike off at 'The Chalk and Cheese', which describes itself as a B&B *'with an eclectic mix of curios'*. Mike's wife Helen had made the booking for herself, Mike and Monty the dog, but when Bridget and Andrew, who run the place, found out that it was Mike from the 3 Dads, they refused to take any money. The kindness of people we came across on the walk and in our personal journeys was constantly overwhelming.

Rich drove the short journey to our house and dropped Andy and me off. As we unloaded our kit it was strange to look through the window to see Keith and Alison from the Seven Bro7hers Brewery standing in our kitchen. It was a reminder of the convoluted trajectory our lives had taken to bring so many people who, only a few months ago, were unknown to each other, on a journey that would finish the following day in this Norfolk village. 'Very odd,' as Andy would say.

It wasn't long before Mike, Helen and Monty arrived – Fiona and Gregor were staying in King's Lynn with the folk who had travelled down from Cumbria, so Andy was with us on his own. This was only the second time all our families had met, but it was comforting to see how that bond, born out of devastation, allowed all of us to talk openly and supportively. We sat down and enjoyed our last supper of the walk, along with a few beers.

We had walked from Cumbria to Norfolk, three middle-aged – some might say old – blokes who had only met face-to-face four months earlier. We had been strangers, but our shared experiences, both in suicide bereavement and over the past fourteen days, had made us the greatest of friends. Physically the walk had been an achievement, but more importantly, it had been a healing process. We told our families stories about meeting so many other people bereaved by suicide, many of them parents like us, all with their individual tragic stories – but with a common ending. We spoke about the suicide survivors we had met, with hugely powerful stories of how they were now living, really living, with careers, families and a future – these people had proved to us that there is hope, that people could come from the darkest of places and live well.

But most of all we laughed, enjoying each other's company over a delicious meal before heading for bed and our last night's sleep on our 300+ mile walk. Emotionally and physically, we were wiped out.

Money raised (excluding Gift Aid and direct donations)
  = £337,000
Day 14 distance = 26.4 miles
Total distance walked = 315.4 miles

DAY 15

King's Lynn to Shouldham

Tim's story

It was strange to wake up in my own bed and be showering at home. It was strange not to be packing up my kit and thinking about how it would get to the next overnight stop. It was strange only to be preparing for a nine-mile walk and not a 20-plus mile walk. It was strange only to half-fill my drinking water bladder. It was strange only to have a few snacks in my rucksack. It was strange to bump into Andy on our landing. It was strange to think that everything we had been planning was nearly at an end. In fact, the whole thing felt strange.

It was early morning, earlier than usual. My alarm had woken me at 4.45, although I was already dozing and half-awake in anticipation of how the day would unfold. We needed to be out of the house by 5.35 a.m. and take the short journey to King's Lynn before starting our walk back to Shouldham so that *BBC Breakfast* could film us live – that was strange too.

Rich and I had previously timed out these last nine miles and drawn up a 'Last Leg Timing Sheet'. I had built in flexibility if we needed to change the deadline that Alison had given us. With *BBC Breakfast* viewing figures peaking at 9.30 a.m., the pressure was on.

Rich arrived, having picked up Mike, and we drove up the A134 and A10 to King's Lynn. It was a route I had driven to the hospital when Em was born. It was a route I had driven nineteen years later, following an ambulance when Em attempted suicide. It was a route I'd driven five days later to be with her and hold her in the hospital when her life support was turned off. It was the route I had driven to her twenty-five-minute funeral service at the crematorium. It was not a route I relished: I felt physically sick as I sat in Rich's car, the headlights piercing the darkness ahead. It was a route that had been part of my and my family's life, and it was now the route we were taking to the start of the last day of our walk.

I must have been quiet.

'You alright?' came a question in a Mancunian accent from the front of the car. I explained the significance of the route and my thoughts – flashbacks, I guess.

'Bloody hell, Tim – just reminders everywhere' came the reply from the Cumbrian sitting next to me – they both knew exactly what I was going through as they had had the same type of reminders, triggers, as they had walked across their home territory.

As we approached King's Lynn, Andy's phone rang and it was Alan, Mayor of Keswick – or, rather, 'the lost Mayor of Keswick'. Not used to the lowlands of Norfolk, he had no idea where he was. It was clear to me from his description of his surroundings that he was near the South Gate, so Rich told him to stay still and he'd collect him after dropping us off at Tesco.

Illuminated by the car park floodlights, there were loads of people waiting to meet us: three of my old colleagues from the

RAF – Bamber, Matt and Tim – as well as Matt's wife Nat, who'd been such a help in the immediate aftermath of Em's death. She'd helped us out with all sorts of shopping and been a tremendous source of support.

My younger sister Torz and her husband, another Matt, together with Em's cousins Freya, Ben and Ollie, had driven up from Devon. The pandemic and the distance meant that I hadn't seen Matt and the cousins since Em had died, and our reunion was understandably emotional. We all hugged – they had lost an older cousin which they had to deal with, isolated from the rest of the family. This ripple effects of Em's death had been felt across the country.

There was also David. He was the NHS transplant nurse who'd supported me and my family in the three days leading up to Em's death in the local hospital.

David had since been in regular contact with me. He was the one who'd told me about the Order of St John Award for Organ Donation, which Em would be awarded … she would have laughed at that. When he found out about the 3 Dads, he'd been determined to show his support so meeting him meant so much to me – that important final part of Em's life had not been forgotten.

Once Rich had arrived back with Mayor Alan, we had a complete group, and with a 'Let's go then, chaps!' from me to the other two dads, we were off. Our last day had begun.

We quickly made our way around the Hardwick roundabout; one good thing about being out so early on a Saturday morning was that the roads were quiet. It was strange to see my new friends, a Mancunian and Cumbrian, walking on my home turf, talking happily to my friends and family. Darkness slowly lifted as the sun began to rise, hidden behind a layer of grey cloud.

We walked past West Winch and Setchey (known as 'Setch' locally) and picked up the picturesque Nar Valley Way. This linear walk runs from King's Lynn through Narborough, Castle Acre and Litcham to Gressenhall, just north of Dereham, so around half the county of Norfolk. The River Nar is a rare chalk stream and a Site of Special Scientific Interest. It was a river I'd regularly enjoyed walking along, trying to spot trout in its clear waters.

Daylight started to break as we came onto the Way and I took the opportunity to called Nigel, my old friend, chair of the parish council and organiser extraordinaire. When the BBC had told us they would be filming live at the finish, I had gone to see Nigel to say that the event could be bigger than I'd ever imagined, and he had suggested a meeting in the pub.

Ian and Abbie had already offered to open the pub and provide breakfast for our arrival, together with an evening party. But with the BBC interest, the event was going to be larger than we'd planned. Nigel had tasked the Shouldham Entertainment Committee to make the arrangements, and they'd tackled the task with the sort of enthusiasm and dedication that makes Shouldham a special place to live. Nigel wanted an update to ensure we were on time, as he had been in touch with BBC's Alison to orchestrate our arrival onto the village green. I promised to stay in touch to give him regular updates as to our position.

I checked my watch – 7.10 a.m. – time to move. We continued alongside the River Nar, before crossing a small bridge and turning south towards Wormegay. This footpath was the one Rich and I had christened 'Nettle Alley', but I needn't have worried: just in time, the parish council had carried out their annual cut of the footpath.

As we walked, I could see the ground rising in the distance towards Shouldham Warren. We were still walking on flat, drained land, but ahead lay chalk downland. I made a comment to Andy about 'hills', and he just laughed.

'They are not hills!' he bantered back.

They were to me.

As we walked along Nettle Alley, I was interviewed by BBC Norfolk Radio, who'd been following our story all the way. I was out front, still walking, navigating and being interviewed when a figure dressed in bright waterproofs approached from a distance. It was Dickie, another of my ex-RAF mates. Who knows what the radio audience thought as they heard him enthusiastically bouncing towards me, shouting, 'Timmy!' He told us that he had coffee and treats waiting for us in his car, a mile or so further on.

As we entered the small village of Wormegay, passing the earthworks of the old motte and bailey castle, several villagers came out of their homes and clapped us as we passed. This was really weird – it was a route I knew really well and had walked incognito several times – but now I was being applauded for doing pretty much the same thing.

Dickie ran ahead to his car and opened the boot to reveal his generous offering of flasks of coffee and edible goodies. The amount of sustenance could have fed us all several times over, but we really couldn't hang around for long as we were on a tight schedule. I felt so guilty for not finishing off all of Dickie's offerings . . . but the BBC was waiting.

We continued on up gravelled Church Lane towards the remote thirteenth-century church of St Michael, All Angels and Holy Cross, before starting a slow descent from 'the hill' – just 40 feet above sea level – across Petticoat Drain and then the new bridge at Black Drain and into Shouldham Warren.

The Warren, a tall pine forest on sandy soil, dates back at least four hundred years and is now used commercially for timber, but it also provides a superb place for many outdoor activities. It was once a huge rabbit warren, producing meat and fur for trade. It's my local stomping ground, a place where I walk dogs, where I run and cycle, where the kids played and made dens. I was now home. I could feel the emotions rising inside, but I focused on the landscape, the trees, the hedgerows – anything to try to contain my emotions and keep my thoughts to myself. I knew that if I let myself start crying, I wouldn't be able to stop.

We were on the ancient byway, which once connected Wormegay to Shouldham, climbing gently up the tree-lined avenue, passing the swing which locals had improvised by throwing a length of rope over the branch of a tree. We quickly reached the summit – a mountainous 72 feet above sea level – and it really was all downhill from there.

More people joined us in the car park at the edge of the Warren. We continued along the straight road to the edge of Shouldham and the playing fields, the happy chitchat around us getting louder as we approached our finish point. The excited chatter was at odds with my rising emotions and thoughts of Em. Once again I tried to contain them – but this time it didn't work.

I had tears coming into my eyes when I saw the playing field which held so many happy memories, where I'd stood on the side lines and watched Em play many a game of football from the age of five to eleven. This was the place where Em and I had camped, had barbecues and cooked breakfast. This was the place where Em had loved watching the pig-racing at the village fête. In the snow over the cold winters of 2009 and 2010, this was the place Em had joined in massive snowball fights, her fingers red with cold, and yet still she wanted me to pull her around on a sledge. At the far end of the playing field were the swings and the slides, upon which she had played endlessly from before she could walk, when she used to loved being swung and squealed in delight as I pushed her higher and higher. This was a place where she met friends. Memories from a simpler time. This was Em's place.

As the playing field came into full view, we saw a huge crowd comprising many members of the football club: the committee, managers, the players and their friends and families. There were two lines of players in their sky blue and navy football kits, marking our way as a guard of honour. We walked between them, everyone clapping and cheering; it was incredibly emotional for me.

I fixed my eyes on Nigel, organiser of all the arrangements in Shouldham. His big smile beamed across at me: it was great to see him and know that everything was in order. I said a very quick hello and we had a chat about what was happening, a brief and welcome distraction before I made my excuses – I had a couple of people I needed to meet.

Phil Harriss, another villager, had been in contact with me over the past week. Friends of his, Keith and Carole, had just lost their son Ryan to suicide. Ryan had only been twenty-four years old, had just obtained a first-class degree and started work in a Covid testing laboratory during the pandemic. He'd been struggling with mental health and work issues, which led to him taking his life around the time we started walking. Keith and Carole were spending time in Phil's cottage in Shouldham to grieve and find solace, and Phil suggested we meet on the last day of the walk and just chat. And that is exactly what we did.

In the midst of the crowd of clapping, cheering and happy people, I met Keith and Carole, greeting these strangers with a big hug, all of us in tears. Only Mike and Andy realised who I was chatting to, and why. It brought home to me the real reason the three of us were doing the walk.

Just over two weeks ago, probably when I was on the train, travelling north to the start line – perhaps when we were getting the message about Daniel Craig's donation – Keith and Carole wouldn't have had a clue that they were about to join our club, our dreadful club, the club no one aspires to be in. Suicide is horrible – it shatters so many lives, and here were two beautiful people who were destroyed and trying to navigate a way through the aftermath.

For once it was the other two dads saying, 'Come on Tim!', which tore me away from Keith and Carole. We needed to get going to meet the BBC. Keith and Carole wanted to join our final few hundred metres of the walk.

A police car was on the lane waiting to escort us. I couldn't see if it was the same police officers who had been so supportive in the aftermath of Em's death – it was only a small local team so they were probably involved in some way. It was great that Nigel had secured their support.

Nigel gave us the green light to move. The police car, blue lights flashing, drove ahead of us at walking speed, and behind us loads of people – around a hundred, if not more – followed us along New Road to the village hall for another short wait on Nigel's command. Here we were joined by Geoff Taylor, a Highland Piper whom I'd met in the pub before the walk. Andy had been carefully carrying photos of Sophie, Beth and Emily, and he took them out of his rucksack and gave the photos to me and Mike. The girls would be there with us as we crossed the finish.

The village green was just around the corner. I knew my emotions would be all over the place and I tried to keep my focus on things – trees, the tarmac, the barn to my left, the old school to my right – anything to keep my emotions under control.

Andy looked at me, 'How you doing?' Mike looked at me.

I sighed and responded by raising my eyebrows. I dared not speak in case it started an unstoppable flow of tears.

Like the playing field, the green is bursting with memories of Em. In the far corner is her old primary school, St Martin's. The King's Arms, which was just about to welcome us, is where she worked on and off over the last four years of her life. It is where she was loved by her colleagues and how she knew so many of the locals. The village green is where she spent a many happy village fête, playing games to win sweets and being challenged to bouts on the greasy pole, often ending up lying in a pool of cold water in hysterics, having been knocked down by a wet pillow. Finally, it was on the route of her last journey to the crematorium, where tens of people had stood and wept as we drove by on that dreadful day.

'Go!' Nigel called . . . and we went. The waiting was over and I could now focus on the last few steps. This was it.

The village green was a mass of people applauding, waving PAPYRUS flags and cheering. Two lines of Union Jack bunting channelled us into an arch marking the finish line, draped in PAPYRUS bunting. There were PAPYRUS-branded flags and sun shelters in the colours of our T-shirts. Shouldham Entertainment Committee had done a fine job.

We had the photos of Beth, Sophie and Em in our right hands and our distinctive walking poles in our left. So many people were there that my senses were blown – and then I spotted Evie. The previous night we'd chatted, and she was undecided about whether she wanted to walk with us across the finish line. She clearly had made her decision and was wearing a purple PAPYRUS T-shirt to match mine.

She came towards me and slipped her left arm inside my right, the one holding the photo of Em. I quietly said, 'Love you,' and she replied immediately, 'Love you.' I squeezed her arm to reassure her.

We walked towards the finish line, proudly holding the photos of the girls and with Evie tucked into my right arm, her fingers now tightening. I could see Ged from PAPYRUS already talking to Alison, while Adam had his familiar camera on his shoulder, filming for *BBC Breakfast*. I could see loads of people – too many to mention individually – including my family, friends, neighbours and villagers, Em's friends, my colleagues, Mike and Andy's families and friends, plus staff from PAPYRUS. Many of these people had walked with us, brought us food and accommodated us, and it was humbling that they also wanted to be part of the end of our story. People from across the country had come to our village in Norfolk, as had the nation's press.

Monty the dog raced across the finish line to greet Mike – and then we were across.

We were immediately intercepted by Alison, Ged and Adam, with Adam directing his camera at us and Alison holding out her microphone. As Alison chatted to us, she pointed to the photos of our daughters. I instantly forgot about the millions of people watching us live on *BBC Breakfast* and just focused on talking to her.

'Hello Andy, how are you doing?' asked Alison

'Oh alright, it was a very pleasant stroll in,' replied Andy, a little lost for words.

Alison pointed the microphone at me. 'It was a lovely reception from everyone here and we had loads of people walking with us from King's Lynn this morning, and it is very emotional. We just met a couple who lost their son three weeks ago and it brings the reality home,' I replied, referring to Keith and Carol, and continued, 'We're doing this for a reason: to raise awareness that people need support out there.'

'What were you thinking as you walked up there – I noticed you have your girls with you?' Alison asked, referring to the photos of the girls.

'We're thinking about our girls, Sophie, Emily and Beth, but we are thinking about everyone else's kids as well,' replied Mike.

Andy continued the conversation. 'There have been so many people we have talked to who have lost their children, and not just recently . . . so this thing carries on for decades – you don't lose it. We have always got a hole in our lives that are our girls, but it's been fantastic to actually share some time with a lot of people . . . and help people along the way.'

'It makes it seem all worthwhile, doesn't it? What set off as something small has grown and grown – and it just shows that it touches everyone, in every walk of life – it touches people,' Mike added.

In amongst all the celebrations around us, this interview really brought home our reasons for doing the walk, and how many people across the country needed support.

I took up the story: 'When we lost Em I remember feeling totally alone. But every family we met had felt the same; just individual voices whose story could be easily overlooked. But in meeting these people we realised that we have a collective voice. If all of those hundreds of bereaved people we've met during the walk could speak collectively, then their voices would be powerful. Together, we could get the message across that many young suicides are preventable.'

Andy, Mike and Ged all spoke, with Ged calling us 'life-savers'. We didn't consider that when we set off, but we did now know that by talking about suicide and suicide prevention openly, carefully and compassionately, we had started conversations which had allowed others to open up. If people could share their stories and struggles, and most importantly, seek help, then lives could be saved.

There is so much amazing human kindness out there – but it was hidden until we uncovered it. We'd stayed with strangers who'd fed us, washed our clothes, allowed us to stay in their homes, and run us and our kit around. People who would not normally stop and talk had engaged us, then emptied their pockets when they'd heard our stories. They had walked and cried with us. If only those who are struggling could see what kindness there is out there – there is hope.

Alison then put her hand to her earpiece – donations had surpassed £400,000 on our JustGiving fund as the broadcast had been delivered to homes across the UK. It was unbelievable – there was no doubt that the BBC coverage had been instrumental in driving the numbers up.

I moved onto interviews with ITV Anglia and the *Eastern Daily Press*. There were photos with the mayors of King's Lynn and Keswick, and hugs from everyone. Sarla had arrived with her three-tiered cake, the girls' names iced onto the layers.

Evie had been amazed that she'd been on TV and really wanted to see the footage. Alison and Adam took her into their BBC vehicle, which was parked in a special reserved slot on the village green, arranged of course by the brilliant Nigel. I loved seeing Evie sitting by Adam, enthralled by the footage he had taken.

Landlord Ian came and found us, and together with friends and family we were piped into the welcoming pub, where bacon sandwiches and beer awaited us. We had a couple of beers in the cosy pub, the open fire heating up the crowded bar, before the three of us went our separate ways. We knew that our lives would never be the same – too much had happened, too many conversations had been had – so our 'normal' would be a 'new normal'. This walk had changed us: we had moved forward with our grief, and collectively, we would continue. This walk may have been over – but our journey definitely was not.

Evie, Sue and I walked the few hundred yards back home. I couldn't help feeling subdued that the walk was over. My mum and dad, together with my sisters Kate and Torz and their families, all came round for a cup of tea and a chat, and also to see Molly, our four-month-old golden retriever puppy, who was the centre of attention.

It was the first time my sisters had seen our new house – we'd moved in six months earlier. I couldn't face living in our old self-built 'forever' family home – the memories were just too painful. In fact, it was the first time our families had all been together since Em's death. It felt empty without Em – she was always the life and soul of the party at family gatherings.

After a couple of hours, everyone left to return to their accommodation, apart from Torz and her family who set off back for Devon. It allowed me and my family to have a chilled-out afternoon before returning to the pub for 6 p.m. I was happy to be home – where I belonged.

That evening it was an emotional walk back to the pub, the pub where Em had worked until the pandemic hit, the pub where Em's wake would have been held in normal times. Instead, it had all been over so quickly, with us back home by 10.30 in the morning. No wake with family and friends, no celebration of Em's short life, no time to do those usual rituals when losing a loved one. Like so many families across the UK and the world, the Covid pandemic and subsequent restrictions had taken their cruel toll. But tonight, Em's family, friends and the village had another chance to gather and remember her.

The pub was heaving, absolutely rammed, and the busiest it had been from before the pandemic. It was Ian's birthday a few days later and he normally had a party with a band. He'd combined that with an arrival party for the 3 Dads, fundraising for PAPYRUS by donating the profits from two barrels of beer, one purchased from and one donated by the Seven Bro7hers. One half of the pub was full of our supporters and the other of Ian's friends, plus more supporters and villagers. Outside, under a covered area, more of my friends gathered, including the group of chaps I drink with every Thursday.

Rich, Dale, Nigel, Brad, Wally, Dan, Paul and Keith – the 'Thursday Night Men', as we're known – come together every week to talk rubbish and sometimes play cards. But behind that façade we are just a group of middle-aged men who've all faced a variety of life's challenges. A bit like the 3 Dads Walking, we give each other peer support, often masked by banter and dark humour. With the exception of Dan (who was away and had kindly given his house to Andy), the others were all there to support me and enjoy a pint or two. They'd all been an incredibly important source of support over the past eighteen months.

Our total funds raised on JustGiving at the end of the day was around £520,000, not including Gift Aid and donations given directly to PAPYRUS. Hazel Russell, Head of Fundraising, who'd been there at the finish line and was now on her way back north to count up once again, confirmed the following day that the total was an unbelievable £709,137. Considering we had collectively set out to make a modest £9,000 we were all so pleased – in fact we were ecstatic. We knew that the money would make such a difference to PAPYRUS and was a huge injection of unexpected cash to this small charity.

In that packed, noisy Norfolk pub, full of people from across the country with their different accents, I sat back with my pint and reflected. It was odd to see Mike and Andy, their families and friends, engaged with my family and friends in my local. I would have preferred it if the three of us never had cause to meet, but at the same time glad we'd met through our surviving kids joining us up in the most devastating of circumstances. There was nothing the three of us could ever do to get Em, Beth and Sophie back, but we felt we had made a difference, both to our own lives and, more importantly, to others.

We now had such a strong bond. I knew that we would remain friends – I had no idea quite how that would work, especially given the physical distance between the three of us – but we all knew that there was more to do. We had been empowered by the reaction to our walk, perhaps most significantly by the many suicide-bereaved people we had met: there was an absolute need to continue to shout loudly on their behalf. The three of us now had a collective voice and we needed to find a way we could use that voice to make a difference to society and to our young people, ultimately saving young lives. We needed to keep those conversations going in households across the UK – mums and dads had told us that they were now able to have those conversations because of what we had done.

To do this we all knew we needed each other, we needed our friendship. The three of us, together as 3 Dads Walking, had become greater than the sum of our equal parts, and our suicide-prevention message had become such a powerful thing it would be negligent of us not to continue on in some way. To do that I needed Andy and Mike and they needed me – we were bonded.

People were talking about suicide prevention, and an incredible sum of money had been raised to help PAPYRUS save more lives. Most importantly, the kindness and humanity that had been shown by so many people since Em's death to my family and to the three of us on the walk was all around us here in the pub where Em had worked. If only the three girls could have seen how much they were loved, how many people their deaths had touched, and what us 3 Dads had done in their honour, I am sure they would have realised that they'd made the wrong decision. Nothing can, or will, take away that feeling that their deaths, like so many others, have been such a tragic waste of precious and talented lives.

I hope our story will make sure others avoid the path we have had to tread. I hope I have honoured Em's final wishes: '*Don't be ashamed of what I have done . . . if others learn from what has happened . . .*'

For those who know the pain of suicide, know that there is a way forward. For those who have thoughts of suicide, know there is help. You are never alone. There is always hope.

Andy's story

Upon arrival at the holding point, we stood around chatting to various members of our group, the babble of voices a backdrop to our anticipation at the prospect of completing our 300+- mile walk.

Feeling the mounting excitement, I reminded myself of why we were here – the suicides of three young women. I stepped back to draw breath and think about the strange and circuitous journey I'd come along following Sophie's death. It's not hard to recall the sheer horror and pain of the first few hours and days following the loss of your child; it's always there – usually pushed to one side or buried under the new memories created – but it's always there.

I looked around at our supporters and wished we'd had no reason to come together. Watching Tim and Mike talk to the group, I'd have given anything never to have had the need to meet these men whom I'd grown to love. If we could only turn back time . . . This was one of the reoccurring thoughts of all of us bereaved by suicide, thoughts that could crush your soul. What if . . . If only . . .

Somehow we have to find a way of living, of moving forward. Whether we like it or not, life does indeed go on. We might want to hold the clocks or ignore the outside world, but there lies danger. The vortex of grief that these questions generate sucks the life out of those left behind. We'd met many bereaved people who were struggling to move forward, but we'd also seen that starting to talk about grief and your emotions allowed a little relief. Bottling everything up, not sharing and trying to sort everything alone was destructive. However difficult it seems, we need to talk, to be more open about our feelings. It's the only way we can allow others to help . . . and believe me, we all need help.

My reverie was broken when Tim looked at his watch and announced it was time to get going again. We followed the River Nar for a short way before turning south towards Wormegay and Shouldham beyond.

As we entered Shouldham Warren, we filmed our last (and possibly shortest) video diary – a brief piece reminding people that this was our last day and we only had one-and-a-half miles to go . . .

After fourteen days of walking across the ever-changing terrain of the English countryside, through all kinds of weather, sometimes just the three of us and frequently with a large group, always thinking about Sophie, Emily and Beth, it was with mixed feelings that we began to walk through Tim's local woods.

The whole experience had been tremendously uplifting and life-enhancing – being open about our loss had encouraged so many other people to talk about their experiences and emotions. Being allowed to listen to these people's stories had been a real privilege . . . and now it was all about to come to an end.

We were joined by more people as we came out of the Warren woods and began to make our way into the village. We walked onto the playing field to meet dozens of people waiting for us, including the junior football team who gave us a guard of honour salute as we walked through them.

All of this felt particularly bittersweet – with the end of the walk almost in sight, the morning up to that point had felt almost celebratory. But here was a stark reminder of what had prompted us to get off our backsides in the first place, a reminder of all those suicide-bereaved parents we'd met as we walked, a reminder of our daughters and the pain and anguish we also carried within us.

We'd met so many inspirational people during our time away from home, many of whom wanted to make a difference for other families. We'd heard, so many times, 'If this helps save just one life then it's all been worthwhile.' That was exactly how we felt – one life was worth all the effort we'd put into walking across the country. The response we'd received as we walked showed us that we *had* made a difference to many people; some had reached out to PAPYRUS for help, others had used our high profile to begin open and safe conversations with their children about their worries.

After talking to the recently bereaved family for a few minutes, Tim hugged them. It was time for us to move on. *BBC Breakfast* was waiting.

We said hello to Nigel, a retired RAF Warrant Officer who thrived off organising stuff, who'd got the village sorted. When Alison and Adam arrived they found that Nigel had created a media cordon, the centre of which was reserved for the BBC. Later, Alison told us she'd been amazed, saying, 'Every village needs a Nigel.'

Nigel was on the phone to Alison and he told us to hang on until he got the go ahead from her. We stood at the end of the playing field and had a chance to say a few words to the people that surrounded us – the whole thing felt completely surreal.

After a couple of minutes, Nigel allowed us to move on, escorted by a police car. We made our last 'hold' at the village hall, where we were joined by a Highland Piper, Geoff Taylor, and old friend of Nigel's, who fell in behind us with countless numbers following him.

Before we moved off, we each took out a photo of our daughters, the ones we'd held in front of us for the photo taken as we walked out of my house fifteen mornings earlier. We would hold images of our girls to our chests as we walked the final 200 metres to the finish.

Nigel was still on the phone to Alison; the clock was ticking and he finally released us . . .

As we rounded the corner we were confronted by the village green full of people, hundreds of folk waving PAPYRUS flags and applauding us in. The village entertainment committee had laid out a wide finishing corridor defined by PAPYRUS-branded bunting with an arch at the end.

As we walked into the corridor, we began to pick out many faces we knew; some people had travelled miles to be there to welcome us. Evie, Tim's daughter, ran out to meet her dad, linking arms with him and walking towards the finish line with us. Ahead of us in the finishing area was Ged from PAPYRUS, along with Alison and Adam doing their live feed for *BBC Breakfast*.

As we approached the finish arch, Helen let Monty off his

lead. He made a beeline for Mike, obviously excited to see him again. The arch had a 'tape' to mark the finish, actually PAPYRUS bunting being held by Fiona and Gregor. The crowd continue to cheer and applaud as we crossed the line. This was it. Walk done . . .

We were immediately interviewed by *BBC Breakfast* and we talked about the celebrity support we'd had and how their involvement had helped raise the profile of our walk; we also spoke about the individuals who had dropped money into our collection bucket.

Ged said, 'You are life-savers – you have changed the land-scape and shattered so much stigma in the last few weeks. People are now able to share their stories that will prevent other future deaths.'

It was all a bit overwhelming; it made everything seem so worthwhile.

We talked about the awesome kindness that we received the whole way across the country, where we stayed, those who fed us, the bag carriers, the people we didn't know who offered support along the way. It reinforced our faith in human kindness.

Before wrapping up, Alison asked if we had any advice for any worried parents so we were able to stress the importance of talking and open and supportive conversations. We spoke about HOPELINE247 and the professionals who manned it and reflected that if our girls had been aware of the help that was available then they might still be with us.

We hadn't known what to expect with our interview with

Alison, but one thing that took us completely by surprise was just how long it lasted. Being live on *BBC Breakfast* we thought the coverage may have lasted a minute or two, but the whole piece lasted just short of twenty minutes.

Strangely enough, throughout the whole interview, I never had any sense of this being a finish; yes, we had completed our walk, but we crossed the line with an awareness that we had unfinished business. The question was, what were we going to do next?

We had begun to contemplate what we could do with our collective voice – we knew we had (accidentally) created a platform and people seemed to be willing to listen to us. Over the next few days, we would have numerous conversations that would help us plan our next steps – but that wasn't for our final day.

Once the interview was finished, we fell into the mêlée: hugs from family and friends, conversations going on in every direction and various members of the media asking for comment. There was another crew from ITV Anglia who wanted to speak to Tim, and then a reporter from the *Eastern Daily Press*, as well as other media – it all became a bit of a blur.

We were asked for photos with the two mayors: Alan Dunn, Mayor of Keswick in his T-shirt and shorts, and the Mayor of King's Lynn in fur-trimmed robe and tricorn hat. We also got ushered to the PAPYRUS gazebo where Sarla was waiting for us with the amazing cake she had brought down from Cumbria.

After more talking, it was finally time to go to the pub. Our walk to the King's Arms featured the piper leading us across the village green to the pub's door, where we were greeted by Ian, the landlord. The pub was full of our supporters – there were so many people to talk to – but this time, we had a pint in our hands. After two or three beers, and a bacon, mushroom and sausage sandwich, it was time to escape, shower, sleep and change.

Once in the house, I dumped my kit and got into the deep bath for a long soak (longer than intended as I fell asleep) – then it was into bed for a couple of hours' sleep before going back to the pub.

After waking up mid-afternoon in a strange house I tried to rationalise the walk, what had happened earlier in the day and think about the evening ahead. The 3 Dads had been in each other's company every day for the last fifteen days, and during that time we'd shared the most intense emotional experiences and had had challenging conversations with dozens of people every day. All that had suddenly stopped. What had we achieved? Had we achieved anything at all? Would anything we had done make a difference? How long before 3 Dads Walking would be forgotten?

This was the first time since the start of the walk that I got dressed in anything other than a white PAPYRUS T-shirt. Going downstairs, I got more hugs from Fiona and Gregor before heading back to the pub.

At the back door, I was introduced to a Shouldham local – another Andy Airey! What an odd way to start the evening. Shouldham Andy was originally from Bolton but had lived in the south for quite some time – it was good to know that the Aireys can survive in southern climes!

The pub was alive with people. One half was taken up with

our supporters, an incessant whirl of people to talk to, a fantastic pizza to eat and beer (from Seven Bro7hers Brewery) to drink. It was wonderful to be surrounded by so many people who we loved and had been instrumental in making the 3 Dads' walk happen.

Fiona said a few words about George, explaining that Sophie's mum couldn't join us because she was undergoing chemo, and made an announcement about the 'Doors of the Camino' poster that George had recently reprinted. George had created a beautiful poster featuring photos of doors and shuttered windows that she had taken while walking the Camino de Santiago – she'd walked 500 miles in memory of our daughter in the summer of 2021, and sales of her self-published poster helped raise funds for PAPYRUS.

This prompted Gregor to ring George. Once off the call – although really pleased that he'd spoken to her – he was very upset that she couldn't be with us. More tears were shed thinking about George suffering her third course of chemo, stuck back in Kendal when she would have loved to have been at the end-of-walk celebration.

Before too much drink was taken, Fiona and Sarla got we 3 Dads to cut the cake, giving us the chance to say a few words of thanks to everyone. Fiona and Sarla offered the cake around the pub, asking for donations as they went – and raising almost £400!

The rest of the night was filled with chat, introductions, laughter and a few tears. Before everything got too messy, I suggested that we should leave in order to catch *Match of the Day* (it seemed like a good excuse!). After saying our goodbyes, we left the pub and headed for the house and one final drink before collapsing into bed.

It was the end of a long and emotional day – and a long and emotional walk.

Mike's story

Walking out of the King's Arms towards the B&B with Helen and Monty, my head was full of all the voices and faces of the last fifteen days. It was difficult to make sense of any of it, but most of all the fact that Beth had taken her own life. My little girl was dead and that was the reason 3 Dads Walking was happening. That was why I had walked more than 300 miles with Tim and Andy. These other dads had lost their beloved daughters, Emily and Sophie, to suicide and were prepared to stand shoulder to shoulder in a fight to save young lives. It had been quite extraordinary.

Our accommodation was a small chalet set in the garden of a larger building known as The Chalk and Cheese, a quirky little B&B. I treated myself to a long bath, shortly followed by an afternoon nap. What a novelty after two weeks of walking.

I was determined to beat the rush to the pub's pizza van and, along with Helen and Monty, we were first back to the King's Arms. People soon started to wander back in, the call of Seven Bro7hers beer and an excuse to party was proving too much.

The evening was something of a blur. Mythical locals that Tim had described during our long grief-ridden phone calls came to life. Familiar people and family mingled with new friends, all brought together by tragedy. I remember being with

Helen, Charley and Gaz, Alison and Keith (Seven Bro7hers), my sister Lindsey (who'd travelled more than four hundred miles from Blairgowrie in Scotland), Horse, Suze and Tegan, and John Sulek and his wife Bernie.

Fiona Airey's speech was so emotional. She talked about Andy's ex-wife and mother of Sophie. You could sense how close they were and how they had united in grief. It was so sad George could not be there due to the debilitating effect of chemotherapy.

I was the last Dad in the pub, sitting with John and Bernie Sulek drinking bourbon. I have no idea what time I left, but the band was still in full swing and the people of Shouldham were still partying hard.

Money raised (excluding Gift Aid and direct donations)
   = £520,000
Day 15 distance = 9.1 miles
Total distance walked = 324.5 miles

3 Dads Walking: The Aftermath

Andy

Waking in another strange bed had become the norm but this morning, for the first time in a couple of weeks, I was with Fiona. Other than a slightly thick head, I was feeling exhilarated; still not sure as to what we had achieved, but realising that we had made quite a difference to the awareness of suicide prevention across the country.

Everything that had happened the previous evening, and over the fortnight before, felt completely surreal. It was difficult to comprehend the chain of events that led us to be in a stranger's bed in Norfolk after being apart for fifteen days. We knew that as we picked up the pieces following Sophie's suicide our lives would never be the same again, but it was almost impossible to understand that the trajectory we'd been catapulted onto in January 2019 would bring us to this place two-and-half years later. Just bizarre.

Equally bizarre was the change in plan regarding getting home; Fiona had driven from Cumbria and we had planned to head directly home from Shouldham. Things had changed. *BBC Breakfast* asked us to appear on the Red Sofa (in Salford) again the following morning; this wasn't too bad for Mike and me, but more of a challenge for Tim, who was due back at work (and Salford is a bugger to get to from Norfolk).

With help from *BBC Breakfast*, we came up with a solution. Tim would come to Salford with Fiona and me. We'd stay overnight near Media City, so could be on the Red Sofa bright and early the following day. Fi and I would then continue our journey home and the BBC would arrange for Tim to be driven back to Norfolk.

We collected Tim at midday and set off on the first stage of our journey north. The first 70 miles took us back across Lincolnshire and Nottinghamshire to Newark, in many places close to the route we had walked a few days before. We arrived in Salford in the late afternoon and had a pleasant and relaxing evening before getting an early night.

Eleven days after last being in Quay House, we were back again, in our T-shirts and walking kit. Fiona came with us; we signed in and waited for Mike, who turned up a few minutes later. Once reunited we were escorted upstairs to *BBC Breakfast*, where the backroom staff greeted us as though we were longlost friends.

We joined Dan Walker and Sally Nugent on the Red Sofa, and yet again were given the opportunity to talk in detail about our girls and our walk. Unexpectedly we were then asked to make a quick appearance on Radio 5 Live, with Colin Murray. Colin was only able to ask a couple of questions before the show ended – as we left, he said he's invite us onto his late-night show so he could talk to us properly (we did indeed appear on his show, but unfortunately he was ill so he missed us again).

Hugs all round, we went our separate ways: Mike on his short journey back to Sale, Tim all the way across the country to Norfolk and Fi and I back to the car for a couple of hours' drive back to Cumbria. The end of 3 Dads Walking . . .

Our journey back home to Morland wasn't direct. I had promised to speak to Fiona Marley-Paterson, the regional ITV Border reporter, so we arranged to meet on the Tebay-to-Appleby road as it crests Orton Scar, about seven miles from Morland.

We met her in the car park high on the limestone escarpment overlooking the upper Lune Valley and walked along a nearby footpath to escape from any traffic noise. ITV Fiona asked me about the walk and the people we met along the way. I was given the opportunity to talk about the conversations we'd had, focusing on 'why are we not talking about this?' Akkie, the cameraman, asked us to go down the path and walk towards him so that he could get some film of us walking and talking as set-up shots for the piece.

Fiona later told me that many people had reacted to these set-up shots very powerfully. We hadn't realised at the time but Fi is around the same age Sophie would be had she still been alive, so many people seeing the pictures of me – a dad, walking with a young woman who could have been his daughter – had been moved to tears by the images alone, never mind the subject we had discussed.

From there it was a short drive to Morland . . . then . . . home at last. I crossed the threshold seventeen days after I'd walked out of our front door with Mike and Tim. Our worlds had changed again – only this time for the better. We had met some wonderful, inspirational people along our route, we'd learned more than we could have imagined about suicide prevention and the positive power of being open about emotions, and we had developed a collective voice for parents bereaved by suicide. We had been given encouragement from every quarter to keep talking, to keep being open about suicide and to keep asking the question about why we, as a society, weren't talking about it.

Over the next couple of days, as well as washing and sorting my kit, I had several conversations with Mike and Tim. We reflected on our time away and talked about what we could do next.

I'm an enthusiastic letter writer, particularly to my MP, so I suggested that we should write to the government to ask why suicide prevention wasn't part of the school curriculum. Over a series of emails, we crafted the letter which we posted to 10 Downing Street on 27 October. We also copied in the Department for Education and Gillian Keegan, Minister of State (for Care and Mental Health).

Letter sent, we waited. I can't say our lives returned to anything like 'normal'. We had approaches from media on a daily basis, we received invitations to talk to all and sundry at myriad events, and we tried to catch up with friends and family we'd not seen for weeks.

A few weeks later, we received a reply – Gillian Keegan would like to meet us. Unfortunately, due to diary commitments at both ends, we wouldn't be able to have a meeting until the New Year. It was a shame we couldn't see her earlier, but getting to talk to a senior member of the government was a great step forward.

The second response to our letter arrived in early December, from the Department for Education. It laid out the changes that had been made in education, particularly around promoting positive mental health; however, one sentence reignited our indignant anger: 'The statutory guidance on Relationship, Sex, Economic and Health education sets out that, when teaching the new subjects, schools should be aware that children and young people may raise topics about self-harm and suicide.'

It was the phrase 'children and young people **may** [my emphasis] raise topics about self-harm and suicide' that got us riled. 'MAY'? This seemed to imply that schools don't need to talk about suicide; in fact, it looked like they were being discouraged from talking about it. This is completely bonkers! If suicide is the biggest killer of young people in the country, we shouldn't be hiding it away – we should be telling every young person about it so they can be aware of the risk, understand that there is help out there and know who to go to when help is required. NOT to talk about suicide cannot be a sensible choice of (non) action. This just wasn't right.

We were correct in feeling we had unfinished business. By accident we had created a platform, and our message about the need to talk about suicide and suicide prevention was being heard. Now we had written confirmation from the government that they were discouraging schools from talking about the biggest risk in our young people's lives.

We realised we weren't finished. We had to get out and shout about suicide prevention again. We had to get the government to listen to our concerns and those of many other suicide-bereaved parents we'd spoken to along the way. Our voices had to be heard. All we needed to do was decide what we were going to do next . . .

Epilogue

Onwards

We can still feel every footfall,
Every blister, every stride.
We'll remember boisterous weather.
Every vista, deep and wide.
But our journey ends with friendships
With so many questions raised.
We've been walking,
We've been talking
Of the ones we couldn't save.

As you took us through your stories
We were humbled and aware
Of how hard it is to face up
To the sorrow we all share.
They're still members of our families.
We still say their names with pride.
We've been walking,
We've been talking,
And they've never left our sides.
Helen Taylor

Epilogue

Onwards

Acknowledgements

Our families, who gave us unwavering support throughout. We could not have done this without them.

Our friends who offered encouragement and advice (along with the odd bed).

Everyone who stepped forward to feed and water us along the route and those who gave logistical support which ensured all our kit made it from Cumbria to Norfolk.

A special thanks to the people who welcomed us into their homes or helped arrange accommodation:

George – Kendal
Lynn – Cumbria
Teena and Malcom – Wennington
Jon – Dunsop Bridge
Charley and Gaz – Poynton
David – Buxton
George and Libby – Matlock
Nigel – Newark
Jim – Sleaford

Jim – Lincolnshire
Helen – Boston
Martin and John – The Wash
Rich – Norfolk

We would also like to thank Helen Taylor for the Epilogue, and for the poem 'Our Girls': a beautiful piece of writing that landed unexpectedly in the 3 Dads Walking inbox. It stopped us in our tracks and reduced us to tears – the link between walking and talking is key to understanding the safe space we accidentally created around us.

Organisations which helped us:

Ordnance Survey – Maps and support with digital route planning
Mammut UK – Clothing and equipment
Leki – Trekking poles
The Creative Branch – Our website
Open Tracking – The tracker
Sidas UK – Insoles and socks
Comfyballs UK – Underpants
Platypus – Hydration bladders
Traybakes – Traybakes
iP Design and Print – Business cards and banners
Bowland Pennine Mountain Rescue Team
Seven Bro7hers Brewery
Manchester Airport Fire and Rescue Service
The Inn At Whitewell

Acknowledgements

Quarlton Fold Farm
Toby Inn, Edgworth
Buxton Crescent Hotel
RAF Coningsby
The King's Arms, Shouldham
The Chalk and Cheese, Shouldham
Shouldham Entertainment Committee (Nigel and the team)
Love to Frame (Russ and Andrea)
Hope Valley Records

Further Resources

Young Suicide – The Facts

- Suicide is the main cause of death in young people under the age of 35 in the UK.
- In 2020, 1,726 young people under the age of 35 took their own lives.
- Over three quarters of these young people were boys or young men.
- On average, more than five young people take their lives each day.
- Over 200 teenagers are lost to suicide each year.
- Research shows that, with appropriate early intervention and support, suicide by young people can be prevented.

Suicide Prevention

PAPYRUS Prevention of Young Suicide
The UK charity dedicated to the prevention of young suicide and the promotion of positive mental health and emotional wellbeing in young people. They believe that no young person should have to struggle with thoughts of suicide alone.

PAPYRUS HOPELINE247 is a confidential support and advice service for:

- Children and young people under the age of 35 who are experiencing thoughts of suicide.
- Anyone concerned that a young person could be thinking about suicide.

Open 24 hours a day, every day of the year
Call   0800 068 4141
Text   07860 039 967
Email pat@papyrus-uk.org
www.papyrus-uk.org

Samaritans
Available night and day for anyone struggling to cope. They make sure people have somewhere to turn for support when they need it most.
Open 24 hours a day, every day of the year
Call   116 123
Email jo@samaritans.org
www.samaritans.org

MIND
The charity that advocates making mental-health issues a priority. They offer help whenever needed through information, advice and local services.
Call   0300 123 3393
Email info@mind.org.uk
www.mind.org.uk

Baton of Hope
A countrywide suicide-awareness and prevention initiative aimed at smashing the stigma surrounding suicide.
www.batonofhope.org

Andy's Man Club
A men's suicide prevention charity offering free-to-attend peer-to-peer support groups across the UK and online.
Email info@andysmanclub.co.uk
www.andysmanclub.co.uk

Suicide Prevention UK (SPUK)
A compassionate and understanding lifeline for those grappling with their mental wellbeing or thoughts of suicide.
Helpline 0800 686 5652

Every Life Matters
Cumbria-based suicide-prevention and bereavement-support charity.
Call   07908 537541
Email info@yourcompany.com
www.every-life-matters.org.uk

If U Care Share
County Durham-based suicide-prevention and bereavement-support charity.
Call   0191 387 5661
www.ifucareshare.co.uk

Headlight Project
North-East-based suicide-prevention charity.
www.headlightproject.org

The Martin Gallier Project
North-West-based suicide-prevention charity.
Call   0151 644 0294
www.themartingallierproject.org

Boys in Mind, Girls Mind Too
Somerset-based suicide-prevention and mental-health-support charity.
www.boysinmind.co.uk

Suicide Bereavement Support

Bags for Strife
A charity set up by people who have lost loved ones to suicide. They have all experienced blame, anger, guilt and sadness. Now they want to share what helped them to help those whose journey is just beginning.
Email   info@bagsforstrife.co.uk
www.bagsforstrife.co.uk

The Compassionate Friends
The Compassionate Friends support people when a child of any age dies through any cause. They have local support groups and online message boards with special sections for childless parents and those bereaved by suicide.

Open every day 10am–4pm and 7–10pm
Helpline 0345 123 2304
www.tcf.org.uk

Cruse Bereavement Care
Cruse supports people after the death of someone close. Their trained volunteers offer confidential face-to-face, telephone, email and website support, with both national and local services. They also have services specifically for children and young people.
Open Monday and Friday 9.30am–5pm; Tuesday, Wednesday and Thursday 9.30am–8pm
Helpline 0844 477 9400
Email helpline@cruse.org.uk
www.cruse.org.uk

Survivors of Bereavement by Suicide (SOBS)
SOBS offer support for those bereaved by suicide through a helpline answered by trained volunteers who have been bereaved by suicide, and a network of local groups.
Open every day 9am–9pm
Helpline 0300 111 5065
Email sobs.support@hotmail.com
www.uk-sobs.org.uk

Child Bereavement UK
Support and advice for bereaved families.
Open Monday to Friday 9am to 5pm
Helpline 0800 0288840

Winston's Wish
Practical support for bereaved children, young people and their families.
Open Monday to Friday 9am to 5pm
Helpline 08088 020 021

Mental Health Support

MIND
The charity that advocates to make mental-health issues a priority. They offer help whenever needed through information, advice and local services.
Call   0300 123 3393
Email info@mind.org.uk
www.mind.org.uk

CALM (Campaign Against Living Miserably)
Standing together, united against suicide: CALM provokes conversations, runs lifesaving services and brings people together to reject living miserably and get help when they need it.
Call   0800 58 58 58
www.thecalmzone.net

8:56 Foundation
Norfolk-based mental health charity.
www.856foundation.org.uk

Young Minds

National charity supporting children's and young people's mental health.

www.youngminds.org.uk

Students Against Depression

A website offering advice, information, guidance and resources to those affected by low mood, depression and suicidal thinking.

www.studentsagainstdepression.org

YANA

An East Anglian based charity providing mental health support for the agriculture and rural community

Call 0300 323 0400

helpline@yanahelp.org

www.yanahelp.org

If you would like to donate to PAPYRUS in support of 3 Dads Walking please go to: www.3dadswalking.uk